God in the City

God in the City

ESSAYS AND REFLECTIONS FROM
THE ARCHBISHOP'S
URBAN THEOLOGY GROUP

EDITED BY
PETER SEDGWICK

MOWBRAY

Mowbray
A Cassell imprint
Wellington House
125 Strand
London
WC2R 0BB

215 Park Avenue South
New York
NY 10003

© The Archbishop's Urban Theology Group 1995

All rights reserved. No part of this publication may be
reproduced or transmitted in any form or by any means,
electronic or mechanical including photocopying,
recording, or any information storage or retrieval
system, without prior permission in writing from
the publishers.

First published 1995

British Library Cataloguing-in-Publication Data
A catalogue record for this book is available from the
British Library.

ISBN 0–264–67397–2

Typeset in London by York House Typographic Limited
Printed and bound in Great Britain by Biddles Ltd, Guildford and King's Lynn

Contents

Foreword

Theology in the most deprived areas of our cities has to be a living reality which encounters the harshest suffering and forms some of the deepest maturity in the Christian life. Living the Christian faith in the midst of poverty and desolation is a profoundly disturbing experience. The daily encounter with pain and despair tests even the strongest Christian commitment. Yet in these areas there are also to be found some of the most vibrant, hopeful and dynamic expressions of Christian love in the contemporary church.

Ten years ago, the report *Faith in the City* caught the attention of the nation. Since then much work has been done by the churches in urban priority areas, in collaboration with the government and voluntary agencies. In spite of growing poverty, there are many signs of new Christian communities and of forms of partnership between the churches and secular agencies coming to fruition.

These essays celebrate the resilience and compassion shown by those who live there and speak powerfully of the presence of God in the City. They have been written by a group whom I commissioned to work together on the gospel in urban life. The group has met for four years, and represents in its membership the diverse nature of contemporary English Christianity. It unites the academic study of theology with the lived experience of urban faith. What has bound it together is the pursuit of a vision for the truth of the gospel in our harshest social conditions. It speaks of the group's shared discovery of a wisdom which transcends poverty, while being deeply immersed in that reality. The essays offered here are a witness to the joyful liberation which the gospel can bring to even the most dehumanizing context. I hope they inspire others to explore their own theology of salvation for urban life.

✝ George Cantuar

ARCHBISHOP OF CANTERBURY

Acknowledgements

Our thanks are due to Archbishops Robert Runcie and George Carey. They have supported us since the inception of the group in 1990, and made possible three residential meetings each year since January 1991. In particular, the Urban Priority Areas office in Church House has been of invaluable assistance, both through its officers (Pat Dearnley, Alan Davis and Gill Moody) and its secretary, Sylvia Clayton, who spent much time transcribing texts and receiving correspondence. We should also like to thank the clergy and people of the parishes where we held our meetings: in Leeds (St Margaret's, Cardigan Road, South Headingley), East London (All Saints, Poplar), Nottingham (Holy Trinity, Lenton), Wolverhampton (Holy Trinity, Heath Town and the Hope Community) and Sheffield (St Thomas', Brightside). Finally we learnt much both from all those who responded to our circulation of the first drafts of these essays, and from those who came to talk with us as a group: Peter Selby, Elaine Applebee and Ken Leech.

Particular acknowledgements to:

The Hope Community, Heath Town, Wolverhampton, for the poem on pp. 65–6;

Carmen Brearley, for the poem on p. 69;

B. Feldman & Co. Ltd, London WC2H 0EA, and Redwood Music Ltd (Carlin), Iron Bridge House, 3 Bridge Approach, Chalk Farm, London NW11 8BD, for the extract on p. 72 from 'I'm Forever Blowing Bubbles', words and music by Jaan Kenbrovin, James Kendis, John Kellette, James Brockman and Nat Vincent, © 1919 by Remick Music Corp., USA. All rights reserved.

'Blowing bubbles: Poplar' was originally published as *God in the Inner City* and 'Here's hoping: the Hope Community, Wolverhampton' as *Here's Hoping* (both as New City Specials; Sheffield: Urban Theology Unit).

The Contributors

The Archbishop of Canterbury's Urban Theology Group 1991–95

DAVID FORD is Regius Professor of Divinity in the University of Cambridge. He spent fifteen years living in inner-city Birmingham and teaching in the University of Birmingham and in the Centre for Black and White Christian Partnership.

LAURIE GREEN was born and bred in the East End of London and has lived and worked all his life in the inner cities of London, Birmingham and New York. He is now Anglican Bishop of Bradwell in south Essex.

SUSAN HOPE is vicar of Brightside and Wincobank, Sheffield, and has lived and worked in the area for nine years: her parish has a grant from the Church Urban Fund to re-order the church building as a centre for the community.

RUTH McCURRY is a publisher, but for over twenty years was a teacher in UPA schools. She was a member of the Archbishop's Commission for Urban Priority Areas, and is a Trustee of the Church Urban Fund.

AL McFADYEN is lecturer in theology and religious studies in the University of Leeds; he lives and worships in a socially and racially mixed parish in Leeds which incorporates a UPA.

GILL MOODY is the Church of England's Bishops' Officer for Urban Priority Areas. Having lived in inner-city Vauxhall for nearly eight years, she recently moved to Market Harborough with her husband Chris and two children Tom and Sam.

MICHAEL NORTHCOTT is a lecturer in Christian ethics and practical theology in the University of Edinburgh; and a non-stipendiary priest in the Scottish Episcopal church of St James', Leith, in the dockland area of Edinburgh.

PETER SEDGWICK was Vice-Principal of Westcott House, and convenes the group. He has lectured at the Universities of Hull and Birmingham, as well as working for nine years in UPAs as parish priest and theological consultant.

NOVETTE THOMPSON is a Methodist minister in Neasden, NW London. A black British woman from Birmingham, she has worked in this, her first appointment, for three years.

MARGARET WALSH is a Sister of the Infant Jesus and founder member of the Hope Community. She has lived and worked in Heath Town, an inner area of Wolverhampton, for the past ten years.

TOM BUTLER, Bishop of Leicester, also attended some of the meetings of the group as a link with the House of Bishops from 1992 onwards.

ALAN DAVIS was a member of the group as Archbishop's Officer for Urban Priority Areas until September 1992.

Introduction: mapping an urban theology

PETER SEDGWICK

Urban life: 1895–1995

If one looks at studies of urban parishes exactly a century ago, what strikes one is the close fit between church life and the surrounding society. Social life was organized into clubs and groups, hierarchical, male dominated: so were parishes. There was a clear understanding of the nature of authority, and social life as well as parish life reflected that too. Revelation was also seen in such authoritative, unambiguous terms: there was a fit between what was being revealed (God's nature, will for humanity and means of salvation) and what was communicating that (the sacraments, Scripture, priesthood or ministry). There was no 'collapse of the house of authority', as it has been called.

This meant that parishes of whatever denomination acted in ways through which the surrounding culture could be carried on from generation to generation. With the hindsight of a century, perhaps the most important social ministry was not soup-kitchens, housing, or even links with the political parties: it was simply this socializing function, whereby to be (say) a Roman Catholic in Newcastle in 1892 was to grow up in a perfectly clear and certain world in terms of both the nature of God, the morality of the church and church organizations *and* the nature of society, the relationships of men and women or adults and children, the nature of work (paid or unpaid), and political participation as well. This world lasted certainly until 1914, and in some areas until the 1930s. One study of working-class women in a South York-shire pit village in the twentieth century shows clearly such a reality. This certainty of relationship stares one in the face, even if many of these women were not church-goers, except for baptisms, weddings and funerals. But where regular church-going was concerned, there was clarity about relationships both to God and to each other. Different denominations expressed the theology in different ways, but the same authority patterns were found in each theology.[1]

The twentieth century has seen a loosening of certainties and relationship, both in theology and culture – whether church culture or society. Much has been written on this, especially on the 1960s and Vatican II. But (again with hindsight) in the 1990s a different perspective might be offered. The phrase 'post-industrial society' or 'information society' is often vacuous, but it does have a glimmer of truth. Manual jobs began to disappear from urban areas, and were neither replaced nor compensated for by a matching decline of urban population, from the 1960s onwards. Cities shrank, but jobs shrank much faster – not only in cities, but in areas like the East Durham coalfield, made up of small urban communities.

As the jobs went, so the culture not merely changed, but began to break up. Not merely was it ceasing to be authoritative, authoritarian and either to be accepted or rejected (I am ignoring all the rebellious struggles of the 1950s onwards), it was ceasing to exist at all. For the first time, whole groups of people were irrelevant economically, and increasingly culturally impoverished.

Such areas had always been poor. It was a cliché of J. B. Priestley's that there was more wealth on one deck of the *Mauretania* than in all the urban reality of Tyneside which built her, and mined the coal which powered her. Exploitation was not new, although it lessened after 1945. But those who lived there took pride in what they contributed to society, economically and socially, even if society did not reward them fairly for that contribution. So the ambiguous relationship of working-class culture to the wider society was a feature of the twentieth century. Close-knit, culturally homogeneous, they could look down on the effete middle classes (who could not mine coal, unload a ship, make steel) while retaining a certain deference.

That ambiguous relationship is found in scores of histories of church life this century, especially in more recent ones. Industrial Mission began when Bishop Hunter realized just how alienated working-class life was from the churches. Although Hunter had a long record in the 1930s of being an archdeacon who was heavily involved in work with the unemployed, his move to Sheffield (where he was bishop) led the communist shop stewards of one steel plant to refuse to meet him in 1941. 'What use is he to anyone?' Hunter reacted in the same way as the French worker priests did: workers must be met on their own terms, which included the reality of class and class conflict.[2] It is also found in the recognition by Michael Ramsey of the self-contained nature of mining life when he was Bishop of Durham: very different from a predecessor, Hensley Henson, where striking miners tried to overturn his car in the 1930s.

All this is now history. There are areas which retain much of their past culture, such as London's East End, or Co. Durham; and there are new cultures which have arrived, especially black culture. Football and rock music are also powerful. I do not want to paint too bleak a picture. But the overall reality is so different from 1892, or even 1942, that one must continually be reminded of this fact. These areas produce almost nothing of value: it is not their fault, exactly the opposite, but it hurts the pride of these areas terribly.[3]

Poverty and unemployment

The debate about the effects of poverty and unemployment has been bitter. On the one hand there is the view taken in this article. A reduction in the number of simple manual jobs on offer; poor education and training provision in declining urban areas; the lack of facilities such as nursery facilities for single mothers all lead to an intense difficulty in being able to engage in paid work for many people in inner, urban areas. The alternative view holds that an 'underclass' is defined by a culture that devalues work and social responsibility. People lose the will to work because of the attitudes they hold and the culture they belong to. Several Cabinet members of the present government have held this view.

This article (and indeed all the contributors to this book) would deny the reality of moral decline in urban areas. Instead an ecological model is preferred. Urban areas in recent decades have seen the flight of those with skills in factory work to the suburbs, and a concentration of people with limited educational resources takes its place; often this is due to inadequate funds for schools or training. The area enters a sharp decline, and those unable to participate in the labour market grow. The term 'underclass' is not especially helpful, but the non-working are not just the same as the poor (though the two groups may overlap). Non-working refers to those who wish to work but for whom the opportunity to achieve paid work is an illusion. Growing unemployment creates growing poverty, which in turn denies people the ability to participate at a basic level in the common culture. The old working-class culture, strongly based on paid employment, begins to break up.[4]

The issue then is what happens to a particular group when it ceases to be economically valuable to the rest of society: not exploited, but irrelevant. What purpose is there for those growing up as the children of the long-term unemployed, who will be unemployed themselves? Of course, one answer is to say that it does not have to be like that: you can protest, join the fight for justice etc. All that is important. But if that struggle is not to be on behalf of others, but with others, what sort of culture now exists which can sustain that sort of protest? The answer is one in which authority, responsibility and relationships are breaking down more and more. Economically the decline of urban areas pulls the culture down with it.

This is not a judgement on individuals: it is instead a comment on what has been called the negation of humanity, or the loss of culture. Nor (very firmly) is this a glorification of suburbia, comfortable Britain, and those whose lives are economically useful. There is much that these areas have to learn from urban areas, as Austin Smith has rightly said again and again. Nor, finally, is it a denial that there are seeds of hope; churches and other community groups show that there is much to give thanks for in urban areas. However, what I am arguing is that the social reality of urban Britain is very sick indeed. If you compare those who were poor a century ago, and the percentage and location of those poor today, there is a striking continuity. But that misses the whole point. Culturally those areas were rich a century ago, and economically they supported the comfortable lives of late Victorian men and women. Now these areas are culturally in a state of shock, and economically they are written off. That is enormous discontinuity. This is not (to repeat) a judgement on the culture of such areas. It is simply to argue that there is a manifest feeling of crisis, and of loss of identity, in the culture of inner, urban areas.

Salvation in urban theology

So, finally, we move to the tasks of an urban theology: what might be called theology after working-class culture. What are the tasks for such a theology today, and what priorities should be mapped out for the urban theologian? The answer for me is focused on culture, and the argument is straightforward. There are four stages to the argument.

(1) The central reality of urban life (including such areas as East Durham) is that it is overwhelming the people. Equally central is that people (especially children) cannot cope with being over-whelmed. Being overwhelmed causes stress. Of itself, stress can be sometimes a good thing, although it is also part of an individualist culture where particular people are pushed into accomplishment. Stress, for example, can be shown in performing music, or sport: pushing oneself to the limit and beyond. But stress also has severe consequences. Where stress itself cannot be coped with (never mind the being overwhelmed which causes stress), the results are horrific: isolation, depression, violence, apathy, cynicism. That is a

fair statement of how much urban life is experienced by its victims. A vicious cycle develops of stress leading to isolation, leading to more stress, and so on. Explosions of violence, joy-riding, imprisonment, vandalism, racial prejudice are the familiar consequences.

(2) The answer is found in giving people the ability to cope, and the sense that they have this ability (which can then be communicated, often non-verbally, to others). That leads into a series of issues for the urban theologian, and indeed for anyone else: the issues which sustain the whole nature of this book.

   (a) Validation of people in their actions and beliefs, by listening to and supporting who they are (such as the chapter on Joseph).

   (b) Creating an atmosphere of security, with consistency, limits and reliability. Care and attention are then experienced as love. Much urban experience is neither caring nor attentive: sadly, that is true sometimes even of those who work professionally in such areas. But some chapters show the reality of such love, such as that on sanctuary.

   (c) The nature of honesty and openness, with information about what is going on, even if it is bleak and not good news (such as the chapter on crime).

(3) The overwhelming nature of urban life, its outworking in stress, and the failure to deal with stress is theologically part of the nature of sin. So too is the non-validation of people, the lack of security, or openness. Sin flourishes when the good is corrupted: and the working-class culture of 1895 (though very poor, authoritarian and sexist) appears to an outsider like myself as good, a century later. It was of course not all good – it had many faults. But compared with 1995, it had much to offer. Sin, then, is dishonest, non-attentive behaviour which destroys those already vulnerable.

(4) Salvation can then be defined here as love building the city: by enabling those who live there to take responsibility and be creative; by participating in the energy of God; by developing a freedom which is part of creativity and co-operation. But salvation is not (quite) the same as redemption, although the point is a fine one. Redeeming, or buying back, those trapped in sin entails all the actions expressed in (2) (a)–(c) above – validation, security, honesty, etc. – and relating them to the story of God as expressed through the story of Jesus. Salvation, or making whole, is developing redemption into the new embodiment of authority in small institutions, which can be persuasive as they appeal to a vision of what-might-be.

Implications for urban theology

There has been a revolution in urban ministry since 1895, and urban
theology must change as well. Alongside the continued questioning of
the economic order, and the political control over people's lives (which
I certainly accept), I would like to suggest a different way for urban
theology. The central three categories are those of sin, redemption, and
salvation (or sanctification). The task would be focused on the reality of
daily life in urban areas, and therefore a cultural reading of those three
ideological categories is central. However, they must be related back to
the relationality and creativity of God, as Trinity.

This introduction sets out the context of the rest of the book. Running
through nearly all of the chapters is the theme of the enormous change
in the culture of inner, urban areas: what is virtually a collapse. The fear
which this creates is seen in the chapter 'Crime', and the despair is
found in the chapter 'Enterprise and estrangement'. Alongside this
there are new, vibrant cultures, such as black culture, and the enduring
theme of sexuality ('The body'). The victims are frequently the children.
This cultural change affects deeply the urban-church relationship,
which has been such a feature of twentieth-century church life. Those
who live in this collapse live in the midst of sin and great sickness, yet
they exist affirming the ordinary decencies of life ('Here's coping'), and
showing signs of hope ('Sanctuary'). Above all worship and spirituality
give a firm, tough answer to the starkness of despair, interpenetrating
the compassion shown so often. It is a matter of prayer and righteous
action. As Bonhoeffer said fifty years ago, religious language may
become alien in our society, but these two realities remain.

So beyond sociological analysis, and complementing the social and
economic response to the overwhelming sense of chaos, urban theology
must speak of affirming people where they are. What is needed is
security and an ability not only to cope but to create a new way of life.
Lack of hope or security is related theologically to the category of sin;
redemption is about validation and affirmation; salvation is the creation
of new forms of social life which give meaning to people's lives. Urban
theology needs to be small-scale and particular. It should listen to the
stories of where people are, how the destructiveness can be turned
around, and what a new way of life would be. This is a much smaller-
scale theology than *Faith in the City*, but its cultural-psychological
realism appeals greatly. Things are getting worse, not better: we may as
well practise some honesty. Realism need not mean pessimism.

Above all, this urban theology points to the necessity of praise and
transformation. In the 'sense of place' which is so dominant in urban life

there can also be a sense of belonging, of community and of dignity. Here the affirmation of people and the creation of new patterns of urban life get taken up in the transforming love of God. The central reality of prayer turns realism away from pessimism. It points to the presence of God in the city. In the sickness, the despair and yet the hope, God can be found. The very small-scale nature of our examples and stories witnesses to this presence. It is a claim made with a full recognition of the frequent denial of any God at all: and it is in that tension that these chapters are written, out of the experience of the contributors. Urban theology is written after the collapse of the old, working-class culture, but the search for a wisdom based on the Spirit remains in the midst of the stress and pain of urban life. So the Spirit of God and the spirit of the city are seen in one vision: fragmented, broken but intensely real.

The outline of this book

This collection of essays begins with an awareness of how important the report *Faith in the City* was in the revival of urban theology. It was not the only reason why urban theology became a central issue in the life of the church, but it did create a great momentum behind it. There was, of course, urban theology in many areas before this report, and in different denominations. Nevertheless, the report changed the life of the churches across Britain, whatever denomination they were. So Ruth McCurry, a member of the original commission which wrote the report, and a trustee of the Church Urban Fund, which funded many projects which flowed from it, reflects on what it achieved. Gill Moody, the Bishops' Officer for Urban Priority Areas, puts urban ministry in its context now. What does *Faith in the City* as a report mean today? Finally, in the opening section, an academic theologian, David Ford, discusses with Laurie Green, Bishop and former parish priest in urban priority areas, what theology means in such areas. It is distilling out of daily experience that which speaks of God. This is also our own story, which describes the joyful and painful struggles we had as a group, from 1991 to 1995.

How do people cope with and celebrate their experience in urban life? The second section of the book turns to stories as a way of illuminating the urban reality which is at the heart of this book. Margaret Walsh tells three stories of people she has known (the names are of course fictitious) and of the community she helped to found ten years ago in Wolverhampton. Laurie Green writes about the area of East London where he grew up as a boy and came back to as parish priest. This section speaks powerfully of what urban life is all about: it is raw, challenging and very moving.

Urban theology, I have argued, is not only about stories. It is also about sin, redemption and salvation. The third section outlines what this means for a detailed analysis of urban life. Our essays here are not comprehensive: how could they be? What they describe is first how congregations praise God dynamically in the inner city, and so 'praise open' their future. David Ford and Al McFadyen ask why worship matters to Christian ministry, and why it is not an escape from the world. If worship is dynamic, so is the expression of people's bodies in the city, with all the earthiness of sex and the pain of crippled lives on the street. What, Laurie Green asks, does it mean to say that Christianity is about God becoming human in this context? Sexuality and Christian faith are deeply intertwined. The argument moves on to incarnation and the 'sense of place'. Jesus revealed God's incarnation in Galilee, where there was a culture under severe stress. Urban decay and poverty show how urban culture is stressful for its inhabitants, yet there can be a deep sense of place, and of belonging: so there can be redemption (affirming people's lives in spite of it all) and salvation (acts of community groups, and the celebration of new life in worship and secular culture). Michael Northcott goes on to look at those who most need help, those who are the children in urban areas. He gives a graphic account of how children do not cope through delinquency, and yet (as so often in this book) finds examples of love and hope in projects which work with, and alongside, children. Novette Thompson, a black Methodist minister, also speaks of the failure of British education for black children, yet she calls for community regeneration through spiritual regeneration. Here is a new community struggling to be born. Peter Sedgwick and Al McFadyen in different, but related, chapters highlight the reality of being alienated from the community, and the growth in crime which appears out of control. Both these chapters address political issues. Al McFadyen criticizes John Major, while Peter Sedgwick sees the danger of imposing work in return for benefits. If these are critical essays, Sue Hope, a parish priest in Sheffield, speaks of how people can find sanctuary and hope in the life of the parish church through belonging in many ways to the Christian community. So can there be real transformation in all this confusion of joy and pain, excitement and suffering? David Ford believes that there is a deep issue here of how people are made, and identities formed. Transformation is highly personal, and dignity is always possible through the love of God.

This love, this divine energy, means that the Church must not be afraid. In a final chapter Peter Sedgwick asks if it is really possible to celebrate the bewildering variety of human life in the city. This book has argued passionately that it is still possible, and that this celebration must go on in many different contexts. The book ends with an affirmation of urban theology as it is practised in daily life, as the city changes into new patterns very far from the reality of our Victorian ancestors, but still vibrant, still dynamic, still full of the promise of God's love and mercy.

What we offer here is a response to the culture of urban areas, especially inner city and outer estate areas. We are not primarily practising social analysis, but that is what we presuppose. We are not primarily calling for change in government policy, although we presuppose that as well. We are above all else affirming those who live in our cities, and finding God in daily life. It is a theology which is intensely personal, small scale and concrete. Realism is the central tenor of this book – this is how it seems to us – as is honesty. Yet realism includes the reality of transformation and hope, and the presence of God in the city, as people struggle with freedom and love. We recognize the pain of life without paid employment for many people, but we believe that community and personal life can be changed. That is what this book witnesses to, and why we believe the Christian community still has a place in urban areas.

Notes

1 Reg Davies, 'Working-class women in Denaby Main, South Yorkshire 1914–1984' (University of Hull MA thesis, 1992); Anthony Archer, *The Two Catholic Churches* (SCM Press, 1987) (on Newcastle upon Tyne before 1964); Hugh McLeod, *Religion and the People of Western Europe 1789–1970* (Oxford University Press, 1981); W. S. F. Pickering, *A Social History of the Diocese of Newcastle 1882–1982* (Oriel, 1981).

2 L. Erlander, *Faith in the World of Work* (Uppsala, 1991); G. Hewitt (ed.), *Strategist for the Spirit: Leslie Hunter, Bishop of Sheffield* (Becket, 1985).

3 The most compelling study is written by a journalist who returned to Britain from the United States: Robert Chesshyre, *The Return of a Native Reporter* (Penguin, 1987).

4 For the debate, see the following:
Charles Murray (ed.), *The Emerging British Underclass* (IEA, 1990); David Smith (ed.), *Understanding the Underclass* (PSI, 1992); F. Field, *Losing Out* (Blackwell, 1990); P. Willmott, *Urban Trends* (PSI, 1992); W. J. Wilson, *The Truly Disadvantaged* (University of Chicago, 1990).

Part One

Faith in the City 1985–95

Ten years on

RUTH McCURRY

The *Faith in the City* report (1985) was part of a process of bringing faith
to bear on the world, a process which involves seeing what the situation
is, judging it and taking action. To give examples from the preface to the
report: 'We decided at the outset that we must spend some time in the
UPAs [Urban Priority Areas] *to see for ourselves* the human reality
behind the official statistics ... we saw ... and we listened ... We have
to report that we have been deeply disturbed by what we have seen and
heard.' The preface goes on to look at ways of judging what has been
seen: 'Clearly these are symptoms of ... One way of seeking to understand these phenomena is ... Another possible analysis (which we shall
make some use of ourselves) is ... None of these methods of analysis is
fully adequate; all are simple aids to understanding ... ' This leads to
the strong statement of judgement: 'It is our considered view that the
nation is confronted by a *grave and fundamental injustice* in the UPAs.'

And the action? Recommendations for action are found throughout
the report, and the final words of the preface summarize them:

> We call on Christians throughout this country to listen to the voices of
> our neighbours who live in the UPAs, to receive the distinctive
> contribution that they (not least the black people among them) can
> make to our common life, and to set an example to the nation by
> making our support of and solidarity with them a high priority in our
> policies, our actions and our prayers.

The process which led to the publication of the report was itself an
example of seeing, judging and acting. The Commission as a whole
visited almost all the government-designated Urban Partnership
Authorities (as they were then called), Liverpool, Manchester, Tyneside, the West Midlands and the London UPA Boroughs of Islington,
Hackney and Tower Hamlets (the Stepney Episcopal Area). Seeing and
hearing took place throughout packed weekends in these places, and in
between smaller visits were made by smaller groups to 'pockets of

3

deprivation', and a mountain of evidence was received and read in addition to extensive background reading of what had been written in the field.

The eighteen members of the Commission, with their four resource people, brought in a wide range of UPA experience, as well as academic and professional experience. Some had lived all or much of their lives in UPAs and hardly needed to visit them; but they took part in the visits so as to be part of a collective 'seeing'. Others had written books on education, on equality, on employment, on politics or theology; or were involved with institutions working in the urban field. Many members had some direct personal experience of being marginalized or rejected by society or by the Church, whether as black people, gay people or women, while others were typical pillars of society. These were the people whose task it was to judge what they saw and to act by publishing a report which would recommend action and lead to action.

The ten years which followed the publication of *Faith in the City* have seen a great deal of action, not all of it recommended in the report. One might look first at the actual recommendations of the report: 38 of these were for action by the Church and from my limited knowledge I would say that the results would be these:

1. Action carried out in full: 15
2. Carried out in some places, not in others, or partly carried out: 10
3. Not carried out at all, so far as I know: 9
4. I do not know but suspect something may have been done some-where: 4

Of the 23 recommendations to government and nation:

1. Carried out: 1
2. Partially carried out: 1
3. Programmes, policies recommended to be extended or improved but actually abolished altogether: 9
4. Not carried out: 12

The spectacular lack of relationship between the recommendations to the government and nation, and what actually happened in the past ten years, needs some explanation. The pace of change in society has been rapid: hardly was *Faith in the City* published than its recommendations in fields such as housing, education, social services, welfare benefits, health were out of date. During these ten years we have had a govern-ment which called itself radical: it set out to change society and fast; and the institutions of human society can be destroyed much faster than they can be built.

An example of this can be seen in education. Between 1944 and 1980 slow but steady progress was made in the attempt to offer suitable and equal secondary education for all; at first a selective system was tried but its disadvantages gradually became apparent: children could not be labelled and assigned to their future positions at the age of eleven; 'parity of esteem' could not be achieved as between grammar schools which selected the highest scoring students and which received larger budgets per student, and secondary modern schools which received the pupils the grammar schools had not selected, together with smaller amounts of money with which to educate them. The comprehensive alternative was not easy, and it took many years for teachers to learn to do it well. This was the moment when *Faith in the City* was being written. But further progress was not to be. Selection and unequal funding have been reintroduced as 'reforms': the very things which had been proved not to work.

The figures make it quite clear that now the rich are richer and the poor are poorer, and that quite a large number of our population, including even students, are living at a level where they cannot afford to eat, to dress and to keep warm. They resort to begging, prostitution and crime.

With hindsight it is often said that ten years ago, or in fact twelve or thirteen years ago when we were working on *Faith in the City*, we should have taken more seriously the writings of the New Right; we should have understood how receiving benefit or living in a council house undermines people's sense of responsibility and so on. This point is well made, if the alternatives proposed are earning one's living and buying one's house; it is less convincing if the alternatives for many are homelessness and hunger. I do not myself buy the New Right's answers, but I agree that we should examine their questions seriously and that the Commission did not do so. There were in fact people involved in the Commission who knew very well what Novak and others were saying. But at that time it was difficult to believe that a serious government would actually act on what they were saying. What we have to learn, ten years on from *Faith in the City*, is that we do now have to take them seriously and answer them point by point; and even more important, find a vision which can combine a spur to responsibility with a curbing of capitalist excesses which trap people into bad situations for the profit of a few, and a welfare system which rescues those for whom things have gone wrong.

Having given the above figures as a rough sketch of the outcome of *Faith in the City* I should say that, within the Church, its findings and recommendations have rightly been treated as *not* the last word on the subject, nor have they been venerated as the laws of the Medes and

Persians; the See, Judge, Act process is an ongoing cycle, not a once-for-all doctrinal statement. Once this cycle is set up all three of its components continue to work. Those who have once seen go on seeing, judging and acting; those who take action find that the action itself throws up new experiences, draws new people into the groups of 'seers' and enables new seeing to happen. And new experience, new seeing, requires new judging and new, or adjusted, action.

Seeing

A great deal of further study and discussion has happened in the ten years: individual cities and UPAs have produced their own reports, such as *Faith in the City of Birmingham*. So has the Church of Scotland. One report, in the Stepney area, preceded the Archbishop's Commission on UPAs; another, *Economic Justice for All*, the Pastoral Letter on the economy by the United States Catholic Bishops, was being written at exactly the same time. There has been a further official report *Living Faith in the City*.

Judgement

Under the heading of 'Judgement' and 'Action' a great deal of work has been done by the Archbishop's Officer for UPAs in conjunction with the Boards of the Church in reviewing the work of these boards and evaluating progress in the light of *Faith in the City* and *Living Faith in the City*.

This book is a part of the continued work of judgement which has followed the publication of the report. The papers produced by the Archbishop's Urban Theology Group have concerned themselves with the major issues faced by the people and the churches of the Urban Priority Areas; but this is very different from an official report: it is a search, an attempt to discern the work of God in the urban context. This requires a new seeing, and several of the papers here are descriptive, in perhaps a bolder or more light-hearted style than that of the official report; sometimes we seem to be describing our friends, with love and concern; sometimes we are quoting them. Our judgement is not of them: though we judge many of them to be urban saints. Our judgement is directed to the situation in which they live: and we have tried to be more theologically daring in seeking out what is God's work and what is the devil's. What is the connection between praise and sin and transformation? If there is no connection between worship and changing life for the better, then why should the Church have anything to offer? But we have to see the connections, and the working out of forces for good and evil in the real lives of the urban scene. The process we have followed is described in the third chapter.

Action

Action has been happening everywhere, but one major example is the work of the Church Urban Fund. Its setting up was a recommendation of the report, and has been a major action; and the giving, mainly by church members, of £22 million has also been a major action. But this is not the main point about action: the purpose of the Fund is to overcome financial problems which *prevent* local action in the UPAs. People in UPAs have been taking action to achieve justice, or to make life liveable, in their own area for many years – since long before *Faith in the City*. I myself was involved in the setting up of a playgroup in Armley, Leeds, where there was nothing at all for under-fives; later with the setting up and running of a Women's Aid Refuge in Tower Hamlets, with Tower Hamlets Law Centre, a youth club and a training workshop as well as with setting up and running Step by Step, the East London Lay Training Course which enables people who feel themselves powerless to find their voice and their strength in the local church.

In doing all of these things I was working with other local people, most of whom, unlike me, had been born and brought up in the area and intended to lead the rest of their lives there. But the efforts of these people to better themselves and their neighbours are so often thwarted by lack of money – to repair the church hall for the playgroup, to get a building for the refuge or workshop, to employ a professional to work alongside them on a project of their own devising. This is where the Fund enters the action – it does not initiate or carry out the action; it helps to remove the financial barriers which make local action so difficult.

But local action there is: a mighty army of witnesses shows that Christian faith can issue forth in action for the good of everyone; that Christians can act with people of other faiths and none, and yet at the same time find strength and inspiration in their faith to do this; that new life can spring up in the most unlikely places, and as a result of the most unlikely actions. This has much to teach the Church itself, and feeds back into the local UPA churches which in many places are finding themselves renewed as new people are drawn into their life by seeing the Christian faith in action, and as the existing church people see a new point.

So the Church in UPAs has changed; and the wider Church has changed by becoming more aware and more concerned. The Archbishops' Commission on Rural Areas contributed to this process and increased the movement of church people towards being aware of their context – the parish in which their churches are set. The use of audits has helped clergy and church members to be more aware of the people and conditions around, and has drawn them into responsibility and action.

I believe too that the idea of justice has been moving more to the fore in church people's thinking, not just as an idea but as something to be acted upon, and that this added to the courage shown by the Synod in embarking on the greatest step of justice and renewal in recent church life, the ordination of women. Some new wine has been making its way through the veins of the old Church and giving it the courage to face the onslaughts of the press and the reproaches of those who do not want change. And 1,400 new women priests in place of up to 200 departing men has rewarded this courage, and started another process as important as that started by *Faith in the City*. I hope the Church will open up in the same generous way to black people and all those prevented by poverty or other disadvantage from taking their full place in the Church and in society as a whole.

Life in the city

GILL MOODY

It was winter and we were sitting down to our evening meal in the
Vicarage when the phone rang. It was one of the Youth Club helpers;
someone had set fire to the rubbish outside the church and they had
evacuated the premises. Chris went over and I followed on with our
children. By this time two fire engines had arrived and a further two
could be heard in the distance. The fire was quickly put out and the
members of the Youth Club were chatting and laughing as they
watched. A teenager blamed one of our local drinkers; the alcoholic
blamed the teenager. Later that evening, Chris went to the off-licence
down the road run by a Bangladeshi family. The father was very upset;
he had seen the church burning and he had seen the Youth Club
laughing as it burned. In his grief at the sacrilege, he spoke clearly for
the first time about the abuse he received from some members of the
Youth Club; about how some of the young people regularly taunt and
steal from the local alcoholics.

This story illustrates how difficult it is sometimes to categorize reality of
life in Urban Priority Areas. This incident touches on inter-faith issues,
on criminality, on poverty and on self-destructive behaviour. The Theology Group agreed there would be value in looking in a fresh way at
some topics and themes which had particularly affected members of the
group. These themes drove our discussions and allowed us to combine
experience and theological reflection in a dynamic way.

This sidelong look at life in UPAs is rather like looking in a mirror.
Many who have been involved with these concerns for any length of
time will be aware of undergoing a conversion: a conversion which
overturns the way they think about issues; which makes them see
things differently.

Rocks and castles

Faith in the City is still quoted. It has given rise to initiatives marked by vision and imagination, many of which are formulated in response to shadows, perceptions, on reactions, on experiences which have both harrowed and empowered. Statistical evaluations of living conditions in UPAs, on the other hand, have been the rock on which these initiatives have developed and which have given authority to the voice of those fired with the vision.

Statistics can be used to demonstrate relative need. Since *Faith in the City*, Census figures have been used to formulate a parochial index of deprivation to ensure that priority is given to the most deprived parishes. Dioceses have been encouraged to find ways of weighting their quota systems to ensure that people are paying what they can afford. High population figures in inner-city areas should be taken into account when deploying stipendiary clergy, and figures are supplied to dioceses to enable them to measure their deployment records.

So if knowledge and information are foundations, how can impressions and perceptions be turned into useful building blocks for building-up the Church?

Giving substance to shadows

Many people's perceptions of life in UPAs are still determined by some powerful stereotypes. Before moving on to outline the substantive achievements of the past ten years it is important to challenge these stereotypes. In truth

- There is no such thing as a 'genuine UPA person';
- Those who live in UPAs are as capable as anyone else of mature and thoughtful relationships;
- Those who live in UPAs are as intelligent or otherwise as those living elsewhere;
- People who live in UPAs are, by nature, no more criminal or violent than others;
- People in UPAs are often insightful by virtue of their struggle.

It is the horrific deprivation endured by many living in UPAs which is the problem; not the people themselves. It is the blocks which are placed in their way and the barriers erected which contain them that create the fear at the root of many of the myths. (The chapters 'Enterprise and estrangement' and 'Crime and violence' explore these ideas in much greater depth.)

The greatest achievement since *Faith in the City* is the recognition of potential; the recognition of growing confidence. This book makes clear that Urban Priority Areas should not be regarded as a poor relation of the more affluent Church; but as a rich resource of faith, talent and confidence.

Confidence in proclaiming faith

Sister Margaret's interviews with two residents of the estate where the Hope Community live in Wolverhampton demonstrate vivid integration of personal faith with daily existence, expressed in terms which are both direct and profound. But who asks? Is the Church so tied up with social programmes, that it forgets the most important reason for its existence, to nurture faith in community? Who asks, in your church, how you talk to God? Who asks where God is in your life? Or even if you believe in God at all? Some UPA clergy report a conversion in preaching style, especially in areas with large numbers of black and Asian residents. I remember myself, doing a short spell of supply teaching in a school in Camberwell. I had been trained to understand that if you wanted to get children interested in RE, you would need somehow to start with a hook: by appealing directly to some aspect of their teenage secular experience. In Camberwell, my classes could not understand why I did not start from the Bible. Some of my most difficult pupils made it very clear to me that they wanted direct biblical teaching. Being explicit about faith, relating it to everyday life is essentially an act of confidence and one which is there for the asking. But, who asked?

Tied in with this is the ability to speak out in a prophetic way about issues of justice. As with the prophets in the Old Testament, there is an immediacy about this drive to speak out which arises out of a personal sense of God's intimate involvement in the suffering of the human race. It is closely involved with the drive to transformation explored later in this book. UPAs, themselves, present challenges to unjust systems whether in the Church, the local authority or the British National Party.

Following the publication of *Faith in the City*, the swift establishment of the Church Urban Fund enabled relatively easy access for congregations to large sums of money. Some would claim that there were basic questions which should have been addressed, prior to this happening. What, for instance, are the theological principles which might steer congregations as they turn faith into action? On the other hand, the

Church Urban funded projects have provided a wealth of resource material to feed these discussions.

Confidence as partners

It has gradually dawned on many urban congregations that they have a crucial role to play in forging alliances and partnerships to address the needs of the local community. The chapter 'Sanctuary' demonstrates a crucial role for churches as safe spaces, places of holiness. Churches can be the places where groups in conflict can come together, on neutral territory. One senior police officer, when pressed to say what was distinctive about the churches' role in partnership, pointed out 'People trust you; they respect your faith, they don't think you will cheat. Basically, you have integrity.'

At their most basic level these partnerships may be with those of other denominations, where there is a value in using the gospel as a common base for vision in the area. What is the point of setting up a youth club, for instance, if the Baptists down the road already have one, which could do with a bit of support? Working together on community projects has for many churches, of all denominations, produced a common ground for putting aside differences. It has stimulated vital discussions about common faith and rooted ecumenism in the created order in a practical way.

Increasingly, in some areas, partnerships have been formed with those of other faiths to the same ends. The Inner Cities Religious Council, which is chaired by a junior minister from the Department of the Environment, is beginning to bear fruit. The past two secretaries have been seconded to the Department from the Church of England, with some financial support from other faith groups. The Council holds regular meetings with ministers and officials to discuss policy issues and has for many faith leaders provided access to Whitehall in a way which would have been unthinkable ten years ago. On another level, the Council holds a series of regional conferences, which when working at their best, serve to stimulate practical inter-faith action and discussion. Above all, it is becoming usual to talk, not about what the Church is doing in response to urban deprivation, but what the faiths are doing.

Partnerships with secular bodies are sometimes more difficult to pin down. These are happening at many levels, ranging from the Urban Forum, organized by the National Council for Voluntary Organizations, to partnerships formed at diocesan level with local authorities. The Kirklees partnership is one such example, where the Wakefield diocese has been instrumental in forging an alliance with financial and other resources committed on each side. Many churches are closely involved in regeneration initiatives such as City Challenge, some playing a conciliatory role between warring partners, others bringing to the partnership a detailed knowledge of the targeted areas and communities.

More significantly, local congregations are developing their own local partnerships, with mental health organizations, the police or local tenants associations, for instance; providing premises for neighbourhood forums. The arena can be rough and where resources are involved it can easily make it a bit of a market place. The local church activist who has discovered entrepreneurial skills has to be particularly careful not to lose sight of his Church's greatest gift: *We are trusted; our faith is valued; we have integrity.* If we have got it, let us not lose it.

Confidence in organization

In their article 'New role for the Church in urban policy' (*Crucible*, July–September 1994), Paul Hackwood and Phil Shiner called for urban policies which support and resource people-led regeneration schemes. Its basic premise was that people know best what is needed in their area and that, given appropriate resources and training, they would be capable of making a significant difference. Small schemes can have far-reaching effects in economic, social and environmental regeneration. A large number of people who have grown up in areas of extreme deprivation are likely to be more able to plan effectively, better strategists and more capable of managing resources. If you have lived as a single parent and had to struggle to manage on a low income, if you have had to juggle child care and employment, cope with having to make a damp flat into an attractive home for bringing up children, why should the many skills you have developed not be used constructively on a wider scale?

The Church of England has been struggling to enable people from UPAs to gain access to its systems and to its range of ministries. There is a temptation to rest hopes on schemes like Local Ordained Ministry to provide the solution for people living in UPAs who have acknowledged leadership roles in their local areas. Does this mean that they are unable to exercise leadership in other contexts? Is it their lack of confidence or the wider Church's unwillingness to accept what they have to offer? Does the Church feel sympathy for people from UPAs while they remain in their context, but feel uncomfortable when they move away? There may be other good ecclesiological reasons for schemes like Local Ordained Ministry, but does it really have special benefits for those living in UPAs?

Confident, lively worship

In the Liturgical Commissions publication *Patterns for Worship* and in other recent publications, attention has been given to the need to relate worship and liturgy to local culture. Where differences in culture are apparent, as is true in many inner-city areas, it has been much easier to explore this creatively.

Black Anglicans have a great deal to teach predominantly white congregations about prayerful and enthusiastic styles of worship. The common assumption that black people have a lot to offer to the Church because *they have a good sense of rhythm* is patronizing and diverts attention away from the main issue. Where black people are fully involved in the life of a congregation, that church is more able to pose itself critical questions about how it responds to the gifts among its worshippers. It is able to forge a life for itself which is sensitive to people's culture.

Confident in giving

It appears from the statistics prepared by the Church of England Central Board of Finance, that giving levels in UPAs are often as high, if not higher than those in non-UPAs. Much more work should be done to determine why this should be so. However, many Boards of Finance recognize that UPA congregations are often giving at sacrificial level. Some people are putting £5.00 in the collection plate each week when they have less than £100 with which to feed and clothe two children and pay bills. What do wealthier congregations have to complain about? Why should we all be seeking lower levels of personal taxation? People who are struggling financially deserve a bit of credit, and a bit of support.

Confident mature Christians with a corporate faith

Ruth McCurry has said in her chapter that one of the most important developments since the publication of *Faith in the City* is the significance now attributed to the working out of faith in relation to context. If UPA congregations have indeed developed in confidence, now is the time for a more systematic exploration of what these churches have to offer the wider Church. It is no longer the case that the wealthy Church should care for the poor deprived UPAs. Forced by financial crisis, it is facing the anxieties, the upheaval, the struggle, the call to sacrificial generosity

that those living in UPAs have been facing for decades. It cannot afford
not to listen to UPAs. Above all there is *life* in UPAs, despite the intense
destructive forces of poverty and community neglect. It is life at its most
pressing, at its most varied, immediate and rich.

I have come that you shall have life and have it abundantly.

Distilling the wisdom

━━━━━━

DAVID F. FORD AND LAURIE GREEN

Why do we need an urban theology?

A Church of England report called *Faith in the City* hit the headlines in 1985.[1] After two years of visits and listening and rooms full of evidence the Archbishop's Commission, in that report, addressed the questions of Britain's Urban Priority Areas. They focused upon questions of belief and belonging; of justice in education, health, welfare, order and law, housing; and much more. They called upon the Church to become local, outward-looking and participative. It caught the imagination of the country and was acclaimed by some eminent urban theologians as the most important Anglican publication of the century.[2]

Reaction to the report suggested that the agenda was rightly defined, and the factual evidence of deprivation and inequality was never questioned by its critics. But in one area alone the report was felt by many to be profoundly deficient, the area of *theology*. There was plenty about faith *and* the city, but was there enough concern about the *connection between* faith and the city? There was, throughout the report, a conviction that the poor should have Christian 'care and compassion' shown to them '*both* by personal ministry to individuals *and* by social comment and action'.[3] But the Commissioners looked to others to provide a theology for all this experience, noting that

> Our task as a Church is by no means only to show concern for the
> victims of oppressive social conditions; it is also to find ways of
> discerning and receiving the gifts of those who have worked out a
> genuine Christian discipleship under circumstances of 'multiple
> deprivation'. The failure of the Church today is not just a failure to
> respond to need; it is – perhaps still more – a failure to attend to the
> voices, the experience and the spiritual riches of the 'poor' in its midst.[4]

The report gave to the Church a vision of getting the poor out of poverty and quite rightly so, for enforced poverty is obscene, but it did

16

not go on from there to investigate what vision lies beyond freedom from poverty. That requires a further project, for freedom from is not necessarily freedom for.

Faith in the City established once and for all that Urban Priority Areas (UPAs) raise deep questions for the whole of our society and also for theology. It painted a picture of a part of our society where the context is so challenging that it is still difficult to convince many British people that the inner cities are as deprived as they in fact are because it is all so far removed from their experience of their own part of Britain. It is a context which is striking in its particularity. But particularity is an essential aspect of the Christian revelation, for within the theological world the most profound example of particularity is without doubt the incarnation of our Lord Jesus Christ as a male, Jewish human being in first-century Palestine. God chooses to express Godself within that context and yet reflection on that particular experience of God in the world has resonated time and again with what human beings have experienced elsewhere in their particular circumstance. But sometimes we find that the circumstances are so very distinctive that what emanates from the experience of God and gospel in one context within which God's revelation takes place is quite different and seemingly contrasting with the experience of the gospel in a different context. This is to be expected in such a particular, contextual and incarnated revelation.

We distil from our limited experience and thought the theology that we have written here. It stands witness to what for us God is about in the city. Our theology always has this single aim of witnessing to God. We hope that this witness can resonate with what God has been about elsewhere. Christian theology engages with questions of meaning, truth and practice in relation to God and the gospel. Those of us who inhabit the urban context are gripped by the urban situation and likewise gripped by the gospel. The 'grip' of the urban situation and the 'grip' of the gospel cry out for a wisdom that engages the reality of both, and this community wisdom helps to shape and in turn is shaped by Christian theology. The Christian community acting together can carry diverse experiences in its wisdom, and can take from this great treasure house of experience and wisdom such treasures as will help it in each new context within which it operates. This distilled Christian wisdom, experienced and carried within the Christian community, is the 'tradition' of the Church, born of its experience of doing theology in various contexts.

Not surprisingly however, those who live in the depths of the UPAs sometimes find it difficult to distil the wisdom from their experience.

The experience presses too harshly, oppressively and incessantly. The following comments from inner city practitioners are perhaps typical.

> Living and ministering among a people who are so alienated from Church, society and indeed from themselves, I have become aware of the need for different approaches and new theologies if we are to bridge some of the great divides between those on the margins and those in the mainstream. As a 'practitioner', I am often at a loss to know where we are going with our 'local liturgies' or indeed with our sharing of scriptures, or to understand the root causes of injustice or the 'system', so that we can do our bit to help create a new social order based on the values of the Kingdom of God. We try to make answer for the hope that is in us but as we become more deeply involved, I find it more and more challenging to put words on the 'Hope'.

> Thinking is often done on your feet in the Inner City. There seems little time for such pursuits as reflective reading or study of the issues when one is actively involved at pavement level. I suppose it is a question of priorities but I cannot resist the call of the door-bell or of the people who live on the pavements and balconies of life.

> We are the privileged ones who experience the gospel as it is lived in the UPAs and of course we know the great need there is for an Urban Theology especially among a people for whom the official Church is often irrelevant. But even trying to describe my experiences is so difficult.

For all its difficulties, there are countless examples in Britain of those who are nevertheless engaged in the doing of urban theology, that is, a theology made in the particular context of the urban experience. Much of it is fragmentary, much is unpublished, indeed unwritten. But there is a charge upon the wider Church to find and focus this theology and to engage in a productive dialogue with it.

The establishment of an urban theology group

In March 1990 the ACUPA Officer, Pat Dearnley, felt that one of his last initiatives before retiring from office should be to bring together a group of academic theologians and local-level UPA practitioners to work at the question of urban theology. At the same time, the progress report entitled *Living Faith in the City*[5] suggested quite independently that a group should be set up which would meet over a long period of time to engage with the challenge issued in the original *Faith in the City* report, that there should be a concerted effort to seek out and understand urban theology or urban theologies.

So Pat Dearnley talked with Peter Sedgwick who was then Advisor on Industrial Issues to the Archbishop of York. Peter had worked in parishes in East London and Co. Durham before moving to teach theology at Hull University. He was given the task of choosing a good mixture of people and acting as their convener. David Ford had spent fifteen years as a layman in St Luke's Bristol Street, Birmingham, before going on to become Regius Professor of Divinity in Cambridge. He had been deeply involved with the follow-up to *Faith in the City* and so was a natural group member. About that time, Laurie Green moved from the Aston Training Scheme, back to his roots in Poplar in the East End of London, so it seemed a natural move to include him as well. He had lived all his life in the Urban Priority Areas of London, New York and Birmingham and had a particular interest in the nature of theology. Laurie brought with him Sr Margaret Walsh who had been reflecting on her work in the Hope Community in a deprived area of Wolverhampton. She was a Roman Catholic Sister of the Infant Jesus and knew first hand of some of the toughest housing estates of the Midlands. A strong evangelical perspective was brought to the group by Sue Hope, a vicar in Brightside, Sheffield. Her parish had received a Church Urban Fund grant which had enabled the church building to be reordered as a centre for the community. The Methodist experience was provided by Novette Thompson. Novette was a Methodist minister in North London who had been born in Birmingham of African-Caribbean origin. She had been involved in the interdenominational community group Claiming The Inheritance. Al McFadyen and Michael Northcott were both professional theologians. Al was an active Anglican layperson who had been involved in youth work in Leeds, Birmingham and Bristol and was teaching at the University of Leeds. Michael taught ethics and sociology at Edinburgh, having worked in urban ministry in North East England, Manchester, Kuala Lumpur and Leith. The team was completed by Ruth McCurry who had spent many years in Armley, Leeds and the East End of London as a teacher. She had helped set up influential Christian lay training courses and was now working as a Christian publisher. Her contribution was to prove essential, especially in that she had served on the original 'Faith in the City' Commission.

The group met together in 1990, with Alan Davis, who succeeded Pat Dearnley, acting as secretary. By September of the same year there was an agreement with Archbishop George Carey that there should be a link with the House of Bishops so as to be able to oil the wheels and create good communication and to this end, Tom Butler, Bishop of Leicester, looked in on the group from time to time. When Gill Moody took over as ACUPA Officer to the group, there was clearly the open possibility in place for further creative cross-fertilization.

So the group was formed comprising a broad representation of the concerned academic and the embattled practitioner. Gender, age, denomination and ethnicity were reasonably well spread through the group, so all in all, the group felt reasonably well-prepared to respond to the challenge together. But were they?

Problems and tensions

However, it seemed that there was an inevitable tension deliberately written into the group from the outset. To begin with there was suspicion between those working in an academic milieu and those operating within a more practical context. Those tensions eventually proved one way in which a disciplined theological engagement with urban realities was to be mediated, but this dynamic certainly was not there at the outset. It was necessary for the group members to live with one another's differences, and to work with these. Such divisions were far greater than simply being academic or practical in an approach to theology. Members' recollections of the early meetings focus the tensions well:

> I wondered whether it would ever be possible to create trust between urban practitioners and academic theologians. At conferences and gatherings I had only felt antagonism and defensive attitudes from both camps. It would clearly take time and hard work to move beyond that into a working relationship that could spawn something worthwhile.

> Sitting with these academics I felt very privileged to be with such experienced and wise theologians who also happened to be such nice people! However, I often felt completely lost and unable to grasp the abstractions. In the light of that it was difficult to hear the academics say they felt inadequate in our presence.

But the tensions were not merely between academics and practitioners. On the broader canvas we have to remember that there are very different ways of looking at Britain's urban reality. Some will look from the perspective of those who are employed to talk to bishops about UPAs but don't actually live there themselves; others are from the 'detached' world of the sociologist who sees long-term processes and developments emerging across society. There is the perspective of the intense particularity of the person living and ministering in urban areas. Such divergencies mean that even the diversities of church tradition, theology, personal beliefs and academic learning, become contextualized in different ways. The differences in theology are certainly not reducible to social contexts but they are expressed differently in each context and may even be said to be experienced altogether differently. Those who actually experience the Urban Priority Area first hand will be forced to witness to a different system of meanings and values; indeed they will experience God differently, and a particularly urban theology will follow.

So perhaps the real tensions in any group or any endeavour attempting to search for authentic urban theologies, are not so much between academic and non-academic, nor between liberal and conservative, or whatever else. Instead, they spring from the experience which urban reality brings to bear on people. Academics may well share intense particularity with local practitioners. Others will look for trends; yet others will seek to speak 'to the Church'. And, in truth, each of these positions runs through every one of us, or at least through most of us. But which ones will predominate and be valued as most 'authentic' by the truly urban theologian?

The offering of honesty and acceptance

Despite early tensions and misunderstandings, a strong belief in the group on the part of its participants kept it going. It became clear to all as time progressed that a collaborative project of this kind could only be successful if real trust and knowledge of each other could be accomplished.

It was to take over two years, almost to March 1993, before the group settled to a way of working, and a trust in one another had fully developed. Holding their meetings in Leeds, Wolverhampton and Nottingham proved useful but the steady base of Poplar was most enriching and easy. There grew up a sense of exhilaration as members were able to share what gripped them intensely and others resonated with theology improvised out of an unpredictable interplay of Bible, experiences, urban sociology, political analysis and involvement, historical perspective, prayer, worship and personal story.

But this productive dynamic was only arrived at after crises within the group had helped us to acknowledge our shared inadequacy in the face of the tough urban realities with which we were dealing. This acceptance was likened by some members of the group to what the inner-city theologian and Passionist Father, Austin Smith, refers to when he argues that it is only when we are truly confronted by the passion of the inner city, when we stay with our inadequacy over against the way we experience transcendence in urban life, that we will ever taste the nearness of the crucified God within it.[6] The group felt itself to be no longer looking for an answer before being truly confronted with the depth of the problem. No longer was it acceptable to use theology as an escape from, or a control upon, the realities of the urban or to impose upon the urban scene the trite descriptions and set-piece theological answers, but a fully urban theology was now the quest.

The outcome: two publications

The brief given to the group by the Archbishop had been to meet together for a concerted period and to publish whatever proved likely to be helpful material for the furtherance of a British urban theology. We were aware of the extent and vigour of the urban theologies which are already evident on the British scene and therefore to encourage the writing up and publication of some of these treasures seemed to the group to be well worthwhile. This aspect of our work will issue, we hope, in the publication of a 'reader' in urban theology to be published soon.

But there was also work in which we ourselves had to engage, work which has found expression in this present book. To this end we set about focusing on a number of issues which we believed to be crucial to UPA experience. From those we chose just a few which we felt capable of addressing and after group discussion on each topic, a group member was asked to write a paper on that issue. That draft was then scrutinized and discussed again and then sent out to friends in the field, who wrote vigorous responses. The chapters of this book are the result.

It may be thought strange that we chose eventually to adopt a method which was bound to issue in a great diversity of content and style rather than a systematic, linear or sequential piece of work which may have looked more academically authoritative. This has been a deliberate act because only such a diverse collection would be congruent with our sense of the realities with which we are seeking to deal. The book therefore includes contextual stories, social analysis, stories from particular communities, pieces focused on significant issues and verbatim reports of interviews. It is not sequentially written but is a thoughtful testimony to the fragmentary nature of urban life and experience. And yet we plead with the reader not to consider the chapters separately, for despite initial appearance our intention is that the essays should be taken together so as to give a kaleidoscopic effect and an awareness of provisionality and vulnerability, consonant with the UPA experience. To create this patchwork effect we have not tried to cover all aspects of the urban scene but rather we hope that urban readers will, as they read, add other patches imaginatively to the work from their own experience.

We could of course have sought to contrive a systematic theology rather than content ourselves with this moving kaleidoscope, but even though two of our number are by profession systematic theologians, we believe that this would have been untrue to what we observe as God's self-revelation in the inner city UPAs. Systematic theology is only one genre of theology amongst others and there is no reason to suggest that if a theology is not systematic that it is therefore in some sense inferior. The gospels of the New Testament are themselves examples of a patchwork or pericopal genre of theological discourse but they are certainly not inferior because of that. Similarly, the diversity of our contributions in this book is born of the fact that they recognize the diversity of the group itself and the fragmentary nature of the situation of the UPA in which the incarnate God is broken among us. So we present very different types of discourse in these pages.

Yet this is not to say that the reader will not have opportunity to note that there are certain nodal points which recur from one chapter to another and which are linked and hinged together not so much by a systematic framework which we have contrived to lay upon the evidence but by a range of unsystematic connections, such as common elements and feelings within stories and situations and the recognition of anchor points such as worship and prayer within the Christian community itself. The reader will also want to know that we have been strictly disciplined in our writing by a number of constraints. The first constraint has been, as we have already observed, the very untidy reality of the UPA scene to which we have had to remain faithful. The careful theological conversations of the group have been the second constraint, but the third indicates that these constraints have also been liberating factors, for above all the group's life has been underpinned by a framework of shared worship and common prayer.

The nature of the resultant theology

If Christian theology is about following through questions of meaning, truth and practice in relation to God and the gospel, then it is obvious that most theology is not academic. It is done by millions of people who try to think, and explore basic matters such as: Is God real? How do we come to terms with death? What is worth living for? Can there be justice here? Who was and is Jesus? What is the right ethics for my work? What is it right to hope for?

Academic theology pursues such questions with the help of various disciplines such as biblical interpretation, history, philosophy, ethics, psychology, sociology, systematic theology, and so on. Within each of those there are various methods and schools of thought. It is easy to see how it can be highly specialized and feel remote from ordinary living, but it need not be. The challenge is to make connections and take on responsibilities. Urban theology of the sort we have been doing tries, on its academic side, to make connections between some of those disciplines and Urban Priority Areas. It also sees that the academic is responsible not just for excellence in those disciplines but also towards religious communities and towards society as a whole.

That is easy to say but what those wider responsibilities mean in practice is engagement with particular situations and relationships. The results are usually rather messy, leaving plenty of loose ends and gaps. There is no way to integrate everything smoothly. But that goes for the reality too – intractable, fragmented and contradictory, just as we have observed. It calls for a variety of approaches, with none of them the 'master'. That allows for a variety of ways into this theology, and different sorts of relevance. So we do not expect that everyone will connect with every chapter of this book, and part of the point is to provoke reflection upon the reader's own urban experience. We have already found that happening amongst the dozens of people who responded to earlier drafts of each piece, and to them we are immensely grateful. In this regard we were fascinated at the number of times comments were diametrically opposed one to another, as if to prove our contention that urban theology simply has to be provisional, diverse and fragmentary if it is to do justice to the UPA experience.

In the end, we come back to the picture of a distilling process. It has been four years mixing together. Drop by drop we have been bottling the juices that have come through the heat and pressures of the group and our urban situations. What we hope is that some readers at least will find something to savour, that they can blend it with what they have distilled themselves, and that the resulting liquor will energize them in their life and thought.

Notes

1 *Faith in the City: The Report of the Archbishop of Canterbury's Commission on Urban Priority Areas* (ACUPA) (Church House Publishing, 1985).
2 Cf. Revd Dr John J. Vincent, unpublished paper 'Wanted – an urban theology' (1993), p. 1.
3 *Faith in the City*, para. 3.29.
4 Ibid.
5 *Living Faith in the City: A Progress Report by the Archbishop of Canterbury's Advisory Group on Urban Priority Areas* (The Central Board of Finance of the Church of England, 1990), para. 2.21, p. 16.
6 Cf. Austin Smith, *Passion for the Inner City* (Sheed and Ward, 1983).

Part Two

Stories

Here's coping: Janice

MARGARET WALSH

JANICE: I had quite a happy childhood. We never really wanted for anything. My Mom went without. She'd have holes in her shoes! I remember her coming to get us from school in the winter. She'd be frozen solid, and she'd still come out with her head scarf on. My Dad was away a lot but that was better for us because he was so strict. We had plenty to eat. There was always fruit on the table. If I buy fruit now, the children are so excited that it is gone in one day! The only meat we ever have is chicken. I used to pinch beef from the supermarket. I'd have palpitations by the time I got to the till – I'd die if they caught me! I don't do it anymore. It isn't worth it. I didn't think of it as stealing because they are rotten with money anyway. They overcharge you on this, that and the other. I wouldn't steal from a person!

School was all right, once we got to Scotland, 'cos we got settled, but up till then, every time you made friends you had to move and start again; my Dad was in the army. I used to 'skive' sometimes, but I think everybody does that. I remember having a pair of stiletto-heeled shoes. I had to wear these Hush Puppies but I used to leave them at my friend's on the way to school and would swap them for the stilettos. After about six months, my Dad said 'Oh, those Hush Puppies have lasted you well. I think I'll buy you another pair.' We used to fold our skirts up as well, so we had mini-skirts on!

MARGARET WALSH: What's life like now? What's a good day for you?

J Just everything running smoothly. I take the kids to school, do a bit of work, and then I usually go up NewStart [a drop-in centre for those recovering from mental illness]. That stops me getting bored. I don't like to be on my own. I like the company, even though it's a bit crazy in there sometimes. When the kids come back from school, I go home, cook their tea. Sometimes I take my washing round my friend's, 'cos I haven't got a washing machine. I pay her and peg it out. I'm usually

27

ironing at night after the kids have gone to bed. That's it. When
NewStart is closed I usually go to Lynette's and sit with her for a bit,
'cos the kids can play out. She likes the company. But I can't stay
round there long 'cos the kids have to go to bed.

M W   What would you do if you had the opportunity?

J   I like looking after kids best because that wouldn't be like working to
me. That would be easy wouldn't it? I had a part-time job, child-
minding. When I started, the cook went sick and I ended up doing her
job as well as child-minding. I used to have to make hundreds of
sandwiches – loads and loads of sandwiches! I didn't enjoy the
cooking. It was a set menu and I'd never made pizza before in my life;
they ate it though! I like cooking curries and spicy things.

M W   So what makes you feel good and worthwhile?

J   The kids I think. I do get fed up, and sometimes I've thought 'It's not
worth living anymore!' but if I'm not around, then they haven't got
anybody have they? I wouldn't be just hurting myself, I'd be hurting
them as well. So, I think that's what keeps me going, knowing I've got
no choice. I've got to keep on going.

M W   How do you survive when you feel so down? I know that you just
said that the children keep you going, is there anything else?

J   God keeps me going as well, 'cos I think he must have a plan for me.
All the things that have happened to me in my life can't have been
just because of me. There must be some reason why. I don't know
what it is.

M W   What stands out in your mind when you remember the things
that have happened to you?

J   Horrible relationships, like with Andrew's dad. That was awful, that
was. Just eleven years of beatings all the time. 'Copping' it for
nothing really – just because he was jealous and he imagined things
that weren't happening. Then, I met Hardip. He is Indian and there's
this culture thing that's hard to take. He says it's not there, but it is!

M W   So, they are the two big relationships in your life?

J   I had boyfriends when I was younger, but nothing serious. I got
married when I was sixteen and I shouldn't have done. I don't know
... I must have been mad. I thought it was a clever thing to do! It
wasn't clever!

M W   How long had you known him before you decided to marry
him?

J   Not very long – about six weeks. But I'd already got Lydia from a
relationship – not a proper relationship. I must have thought that I'd
get left behind if I didn't get married to the first person who came
along. But ... he wouldn't go to work! He wouldn't be told what to do

by anybody! He couldn't hold down a job, so I used to go into the fields every day, fruit-picking – to survive really.

Lydia used to come to the fields with me, and Andrew stayed with his dad. Then there was Charlotte and then there were more, and they just kept coming! It's like, I've had kids all my life! I started when I was fifteen. I have had eleven and I've lost three. One of them I had bloody kicked out of me by my husband!

I went in hospital afterwards for a scrape, 'cos they had to take what was left away and he was knocking off my friend! Straight away, after I came out, he was beating me again.

M W   So, in what way did he 'kick the baby out of you'?

J   He gave me a good hiding, like, and I lost the baby. He threatened me in the hospital. They had to send for a security guard. He was going to beat me in my bed!

M W   Do you know why he was going to do that?

J   No! He used to keep saying I was a whore and a prostitute. I kept trying to get rid of him but I couldn't, 'cos I had this 'bent' social worker that tried it on with me, and because I didn't, he went on his side, and so every time I tried to get anywhere, he was in the way.

I even went to a refuge once and the social worker phoned them up and told them to throw me out! He even stood there when my husband was hitting my head against the back door! Oh! He was something else, he was.

M W   So, how did you get away from your husband?

J   Well, he kept overdosing, and he'd take his wallet with him to hospital, so I'd have no money. The last time he did it, I asked the ambulance man to let me take my housekeeping money. So I hid it somewhere. The next morning, I couldn't find it anywhere, I was going demented, and then Gareth [son] said he'd found this bottle of whisky in the garage. I bloody drunk half of it didn't I? So I had alcohol poisoning and the ambulance came.

Well, that was just what the social worker was looking for, wasn't it? He took the kids off me. The two of them.

M W   The other three had been taken before?

J   Yes, they'd gone. I couldn't handle Andrew, he was too much. He was cracking me up and he was affecting the other kids too, so he had to go. Charlotte kept stealing. She was only nine then! So she had to go. Then I only had Gareth and Catherine. When they took Gareth he was fighting them off – 'cos my friend told me. 'You're not taking me from my Mom!' he was shouting.

It was awful when I came back from hospital. No kids around, just their toys. So I thought 'Well, I ain't staying here no more. I've got nothing to stop for.' I left a note and told Robert I was going to be a prostitute. And I did. I came to Wolverhampton on the train, and I'd got nowhere to go, no money, nothing. And this black man picked me up at the station and he said I could stop at his flat, and it started from there. And that's how I met Hardip, 'cos he used to go around with them.

M W   Do you ever see Gareth or your other children?

J   Andrew [son] phoned me the other night and said he was bringing Gareth up to see me. I want to see him but I know that'll put even more pressure on Hardip, 'cos he can't stand my other kids.

M W   When did you last see Gareth?

J   When he was six.

M W   And what age is he now?

J   Well, he's been in the army – for six weeks! – and then came out. It was too much for him. But he looks like me, out of all of them. He's lovely! Like Bijay [son] really. Very loyal. I was drinking when he was young. His dad would come in and say 'Where's your Mom hid the cider?' 'cos I used to put it in the washing machine! I hid it all over the house! He'd say 'She hasn't got any.' I was seeing someone else, it was a policeman as well! We used to go swimming every Monday, and I'd take Gareth with me, and he'd never say a word to his dad. Never.

And Catherine – she's beautiful she is, with blonde, really blonde hair and it's long – her Grandad raped her, and he raped Charlotte. That's another thing I couldn't get over! I was sixteen when I first went to live at Robert's house, and his dad came into my room one morning and he took all his clothes off and tried to get in bed with me. I was screaming 'Leave me alone.' He did, but he put £5 on the bed.

I went straight down to the shop where my husband was working and I said 'Look! I've got something to tell you. You ain't going to like it, but I've got to tell you.' And I told him. That's why I couldn't understand why, when it happened to Catherine, he wouldn't believe it. But all the evidence is there. He's been convicted for it. They even had a case conference a few months ago, and they wanted to know if I thought Catherine was at risk.

M W   So how old is Catherine?

J   Fourteen. And she's living with her dad, right opposite where her Grandad lives! And he's still got access to her! There's nothing I can do. I could kill him, I could! I could just get a gun and shoot him! To think that he's done that! He couldn't get me so he's had my daughters. It's awful! Terrible!

M W   So you haven't seen Catherine for a long time?

J   He wouldn't let me see her!

M W Where's Charlotte now?

J Oh God! She's just a wreck. Ecstasy, any drugs she can lay her hands on. Living with all these Pakistanis. I don't know if she's trying to copy me in that or what. She's so pretty, such a pretty girl and she's wasted her life.

M W And now you've got three children with Hardip?

J Yes ... and ... he wants another one! I can't believe it. I can't see how he can want another child, when we're arguing all the time. It's no good on the ones that are here, never mind having another one.

M W So, when you say, because of all the things that happened in your life there must be a God in it somewhere, in what way do you see God in those events, those relationships?

J Well, I had those kids from the first relationship, but their Dad was just trouble. He's gone for good now. He's disappeared! I can breathe a bit better. I'm calmer in myself.

I think that God knew it wasn't my fault I'd lost those kids, so he gave me a second chance to have these three. It's almost as if he's said 'Well, here's three – even if the man might not be around that much. These are for you to look after.' So I think that's why they're special. They've been given to me specially, so I've got to look after them, even if I fall by the wayside – which I do, sometimes.

M W In what way do you fall by the wayside?

J Drinkwise. I made a mistake last week. I don't usually touch alcohol in the daytime 'cos I know that I'll carry on all day. I did and there was a blazing row and then you [Hope Community] came down and Andrew [son] was there and the police came ... and he wouldn't go. I had to get the police to make him go, and they handcuffed him, didn't they, and took him. The next day I felt awful but I just got better.

I would like to go to the pub once in a while, but there's nobody to baby-sit the kids. If I do have a drink, I have it in the house when everything's finished and the kids are sleeping, and then I'll have maybe two or three cans.

M W How important is the cannabis to you?

J Oh, it's very important, that is. Yep! I usually have a couple of them before I go to bed, and then I eat – 'cos otherwise I haven't got any appetite. That's the only time I eat. I'll go and eat anything then. I mixed up that stewed steak you gave me with baked beans the other night – and curry powder – it was really nice!

M W So, when you look back, what kind of friends do you tend to make? What kind of people are you relaxed with? What attracts you to people?

J   People who look after their kids all right. I had one friend – she moved to Wales about three years ago, and we got on really great. She used to think the same as me, so we didn't have to say anything. We'd just look at each other and we knew what the other one was thinking. And she was exactly the same with her kids as I was with mine. I mean, if they were squabbling, you wouldn't interfere, not unless they were battering each other to death! We just got on great. But, I get on better with men, I don't know why. I think it's because they don't talk about people like women do. They're straight. You can say what you want.

M W   And the close men friends you've had … you've already mentioned Robert and now Hardip; what were they like as partners?

J   Er, I don't know about Robert, but I know that Hardip loves me. He rants and he raves and even when he leaves, I know he's always going to come back. It's like we're bad for each other but there must be something good about us, else we wouldn't still be together. I don't know what it is. We're arguing all the time. He's got his ideas and I've got mine – and they clash!

   A lot of men don't know how to treat women. They just have kids by them and they are never at home and that's no life! I think a couple should share. That's where the problems have been between me and Hardip. He thinks that a woman is supposed to look after the kids, keep the house clean and tidy and wait on the man hand and foot and for the man to go out whenever he wants to. We argue a lot about money or the lack of it! All these things he wants, and I can't even get a washing machine. He's on about buying a car, and I'm thinking 'Look at how many years I've been waiting for a washing machine!' To me, the washing machine should come first, 'cos he's the one moaning when his clothes aren't washed on time, ready for him to wear.

M W   And what about food? I know you're often stuck for food.

J   Last Friday, I got all psyched-up, ready to go and get all the shopping, and he came in saying that his money hadn't gone through in the bank. He hadn't got a penny and we'd got no electric or anything. That's when I came over to you for food. I'm all right now 'cos I got paid today, but all this weekend's been really bad. Mind you, somebody helped me to get the electric on. I was going frantic and he fiddled with something so that I got my emergency back.

M W   How do you and the children cope when there is no food in the house and when there's no electric?

J   Usually I manage to get them food. They don't like it much when the ice-cream van comes and they can't have any. I borrowed some money yesterday and I kept 75p for ice-cream. So, Ranjet [son] got his lolly and Abbie [daughter] got her ice-cream. It's when they have school trips and things like it that it's really bad. No way can I afford those. When it was just Bijay going, I could manage. But now there's three of 'em. It isn't just the trips but having enough to make their packed lunch and giving them something to spend.

M W Would you say that is the case with a lot of the Mums?

J Yeah ... must be. I think that's why a lot of them do the other things that they have to.

M W Like?

J You know!

M W Go on ... tell me.

J Prostituting themselves.

M W In order to make ends meet?

J To feed the kids really, yeah ... that's what I mean. I've done it. That's how I got the money I had this weekend anyway. It's horrible. Bijay doesn't like it but he knows. Some time ago, I managed to save enough to get him a Sega. Well, I got it out of the catalogue, so I could pay it off weekly. This one night I was all dressed up to go out and get some money, and he said to me 'You ain't going!' and I said 'But I ain't got any money!' 'Sell my Sega then. Sell my Sega!' You should have seen his little face! So, I just couldn't go that night! He knows what I am doing and he is only nine.

    I don't think I will go on the streets anymore. It is too frightening. If I got killed there wouldn't be anyone to look after the kids would there? In the early days, I had to drink half a bottle of sherry before I had the nerve to go out. I was so frightened! It really is a horrible thing to have to do. It hurts you and makes you feel dirty. Well, it makes me feel dirty – not that I am doing anything dirty. It just makes me feel like that. But I can shrug it off when I can see the kids eating, and then I think it's worth it. I don't know ... when Ranjet goes to school, maybe I can make more out of it then. I can't do a lot now 'cos the kids are there.

M W So, have your partners been happy for you to be in prostitution?

J Hardip doesn't really like it, but it's just a way of life isn't it? But most of them do it. 'Whatsit' up the road does it. You know her! She has four boys. She looks lovelier in the contact book than she does normally. But look at her kids! They're dressed beautiful, got everything, all the high name trainers, leather waistcoats and everything. That makes me feel 'You could do that', but I don't think I'd like to put my picture in a book, 'cos my kids found one of them on the pub car park, and they brought it to me and said 'Look! Steven's Mom's in this book! And there's so-and-so, and there's so-and-so.' If I put my picture in, then the kids would suffer, wouldn't they? Then again, I don't know if they would, round here … there's so many mothers what have to do it.

M W   It's a dangerous way of life?

J   Yeah. I was taken to this house the other day. I was stupid! They were alcoholics. This one began to pull my clothes off, while I was standing there! He looked mad. I started shouting 'Look! You told me that there was these two men that would pay. I'm not going with them, but I'm not going away without any money either.' And he says 'Well, I'll give you five for the one and five for the other', and he just brought me back. When I told Hardip he was cross. I said 'I got ten pounds and I didn't have to do anything.' And then when I told him what happened, he said 'You stupid woman! They could have done anything they wanted to you, and there wouldn't have been a lot you could have done about it and look what damage it would have done to you mentally.'

I know I am safe so long as Hardip can be there and can make sure there is no messing about. That they don't try to kiss me or mess about, that they just do what they have to and go. It's the pulling around that I never liked. I hate that. You know when some men try to touch you places, I can't stand that! That drives me mad! Or they try to kiss me, and that's horrible too.

If I didn't have kids I'd just kill myself, really. Loads of times I felt like it. I mean, I've got my sleeping tablets … Like last night I was praying 'Oh, God! Just take me!' but, if I did that then what would happen to them? So I'm just surviving for them. Sometimes I think … they could have better, that they deserve better than me. And Bijay! Oh, God! He said to me yesterday 'Bloody pissed again! You're always bloody drunk!'

M W   That upsets you?

J   Yes, and he says 'You're always crying!' I do cry a lot. I haven't got anyone I could turn to.

M W   What would give you a real break now?

J   A holiday … but not on my own with the kids. We went a few years ago and I was really scared to be in this big house. It was a nice place – by the sea – but the silence really frightened me and there was this picture on the wall … some really weird looking saint! I was scared to walk past it! I felt that he was watching us all the time. I'd never go like that again. I became so nervous that I even got diarrhoea!

M W   You'd have to have someone with you?

J   Yes.

M W   And yet you're not scared in Heath Town?

J   No, I suppose I've got used to it.

M W So, when things get really desperate, who do you depend on?

J   Nobody ... Just myself. I miss my Grandad a lot, I know if he was still around I wouldn't be in this position, 'cos he was the only one who never used to put me down. Everyone else did, even my Mom. If I did something wrong, she would broadcast it. Grandad was always defending me. Out of all the grandchildren, I was his favourite ... I don't know why. He died when I was about nineteen. Grandad only went to church to reserve his plot in the graveyard! He knew he hadn't long to live. When he was dying, I will always remember him saying 'Get me a cross. They won't let me in! Get me a cross.' And I got this saint's thing, to make people better, and he said 'Take it away from me, take it away! I want a cross.' And I stuck it under his mattress, hoping that it would help. I even dream about him!

He loved his cider as well! I think that's what started me on the drink. My Gran used to go mad at him, 'Been to the pub again!' He'd get this little wine glass and he'd put a little bit of cider in it for me. I think that's what gave me the taste for it. It killed him. It gave him cancer, and it was all in his stomach and his bowels. He hated my first husband, 'cos he used to beat me, and Grandad couldn't stand that. He was lovely! I'm going to cry in a minute!

M W What are your hopes for the children?

J   I don't know. I often wonder what Bijay's going to turn out like. I mean, the police raided Jason's, next door, last week. I saw the three cars pull up and I was hysterical. I just said to the kids 'Get in! Quick!', 'cos I could tell what was going to happen. They already had the battering rams to break down the door! I mean, Bijay's seen so much! We lived in Hawthorne House [tall block on the estate] and when it was raided, he used to carry £2–300 up the stairs, for me to look after, for the different drug dealers. And he knew what he was doing. It's a shame! He hasn't had any childhood really.

Then the police got Simon last week didn't they! And broke his arm! I'm glad I was out. Put his arm right behind his back and snapped it! And if Bijay was ever there, when they raided ... I mean they ain't got no feelings for some half-caste kid! They just treat them like trash. A friend took him once, up to the Traveller's [pub], and they come to arrest someone, and when he brought Bijay back, he was shaking from head to toe. He was really in a state, 'cos he said he'd jumped on the table and they'd got the dogs, and the dogs were barking. He was terrified!

I think that if Bijay had the chance he could be a professional footballer. This bloke from a football club spotted him playing about with the other kids and said that he has real talent. He took our address but he hasn't got in touch. If he becomes a footballer and has money, then maybe he will look after me.

M W   So you worry about the bad experiences he's had . . . that this will affect him later on?

J   Yeah. I mean when they grow up here, they're either pimps or drug dealers, aren't they? They want all the nice gear, all the latest clothes and that's the only way they can get it. I said to him the other day 'If you deal in drugs, you can't live here 'cos I couldn't take the police coming in here and smashing everything up.' And he says 'I will live here!' . . . But he hates prostitution, really hates it.

M W   Bijay has a lovely nature. I'm sure that he'll be all right. And you show him a lot of love, don't you?

J   I try to . . . he won't have it any more. Like when I took him down the Play Scheme the first day. I gave the other two a kiss but he wouldn't have one. I suppose he thought he'd look like a sissy if I kissed him in front of anybody.

Abbie won't let me cuddle her. She goes to Conny [aunt] for her cuddle. I went into bed with her this morning, and I said 'You're lovely-jubbly, give us a cuddle!' and she says 'Go away! I don't like you!'

M W   Why do you think she said that?

J   I don't think she likes what I'm doing . . . She's been after these denim shorts for ages, and she wants some lace leggings, but I said no. I can't stand to see little girls like her in shoes with heels on, or anything like that. They grow up quick enough, and if they look too alluring they might attract the wrong attention. I'd like her to be a nun!!

M W   Why's that?

J   So nobody would hurt her.

M W   I still can't get at the secret of how you keep going. I know you've said you keep going for your kids and I know you've attempted suicide a number of times, haven't you?

J   Some years ago, but not now.

M W   Because of the kids?

J   Yes. I had them, I've got to look after them.

M W   So, when the kids are grown up and left home, what then?

J   I don't know . . . I just don't know! Hardip sometimes says 'I don't know what you are going to do when they have grown up and have gone!' I wouldn't like to be on my own. I would like to think that when they grow up and have children, that they will bring them to me and so I will always have children around me.

M W   Janice, tell me again about the God that you mentioned the other day . . . the God who helps you.

J   I don't know what to say. He is just there. That's all.

M W   In what sense is he there?

J   He's got to be there or else nothing wouldn't make any sense.

M W   When did you become aware that there is a God?

J   When I was very young. I used to read the Bible when I was in bed and my Mom used to teach the children Bible stories. My Dad was in the army and there were no churches at the camp, so she took the kids for religious instruction. No one told her to do it.

M W   Do you do the same for your own children?

J   Yeah. I talk about him. Bijay gets quite interested. The other day Abbie asked me why a man over at NewStart always looks up and raises his hands to the sky. I told her that he thinks he can see God. And she asked: 'Well can he?' I said: 'Well, maybe he can. Every time he gets a cigarette he thanks God for it and when he gets a cup of tea, he also raises it up to God, to thank him for it.' And Abbie just accepted that.

M W   What is your favourite Bible story?

J   When the disciples told the children to leave Jesus alone and he said: 'Suffer the little children, let them come to me.' I like that bit best because I can picture him with all these children around him. I also like the Good Samaritan. I think that is important because neighbours should really look out for each other but they don't.

M W   Does the story of the Good Samaritan encourage you to behave differently?

J   Yeah. I think it is important. But there are some people that you just can't help. Like somebody who comes here and is a drug addict. There is nothing I can do for her. When she came last Sunday, I was busy, doing all my washing by hand. I thought 'Oh no!' because she pulls me down with her. I said: 'You can stop for a little while, for I am busy' and then she asked if she could make a cup of tea but I had only three tea bags to last me till Monday. She went off in a huff.

When I met her in NewStart the next day she said 'I'll never ask you for help again!' That really hurt me, because I am always helping people at all hours of the night and day. I have sat there trying to encourage them and to listen to their problems, but this one, I can't help her because she hasn't got any beliefs. She doesn't even care about herself.

M W   Do you talk about God to people?

J   Sometimes. I try to encourage people by telling them to live. I have seen so many friends commit suicide. When David killed himself, I only then realized that the church won't give them a funeral, will they? He was taken straight to the Crem. You were there, weren't you? They said that the church wouldn't bury him. I couldn't believe that anyone could be that cruel. I may have got the wrong end of the stick. However a person dies, they deserve to be sent off properly.

M W   Do you talk to God?

J   Yeah . . . and I shout at him, an' all. I get mad when I see the kids in Rwanda and that, just dying! It's not their fault. I was arguing with my Mom on the phone last night. She was saying that it is men that have done that. God has set down the rules and they have not obeyed them. I was saying to her 'How does a Father that loves, allow that? I couldn't stand back and watch my kids suffering! I would just have to do something.' Sometimes, I wonder if God is really there and if he is, why does he wait so long before he does something about it?

M W   When you meet in death, what do you expect God to say?

J   I don't think he will condemn me for all the things I have done, 'cause I think he knows what my heart is like. Looking back, I think I have done well for my children. I know that they haven't all turned out as they should have done, but they could be worse . . . they could be murderers!

   I don't often go to church . . . I don't think I am good enough. I like the children to go, though! I would like to go to confession but I could never talk to a priest . . . a man . . . about things I get up to . . . It's much easier to talk to a woman.

M W   If you could imagine life differently how would it be?

J   I would like to be a New Age Traveller. If I had a van, I'd take off, I would. I'd take the kids. When they go to school, they learn nothing and when they leave they can't get jobs anyway, so I think that they would learn more going around the countryside.

M W   Does God help you to make decisions?

J   Oh yes!

M W   How does God do this?

J   I just know what's right and what's wrong. Maybe it's the way I was brought up by my Mom. We have similar ideas, although she doesn't approve of my drinking and she thinks that if you smoke cannabis you will go on to heroin, which isn't true because I haven't gone on to anything else. I couldn't afford it anyway!

M W   You have mentioned Jesus and the Father. Would you like to say anything more about who God is?

J   I don't even know if he is a person. I remember years ago, when I asked someone why you can't see God and they said to me that that is because he is so powerful. He made the sun and you can't really look at the sun because it would blind you! I imagine that whatever he looks like, we wouldn't be able to look at him. If we can't look at the sun and he has made that, then we can't really look at him. I don't know whether he is a man or a force or what.

M W   You seem to relate to God as a male. Is there any female in the
God you pray to?

J   Only when Mary comes into it. She was Jesus' mother so he must
have liked women to pick her out. She is gentle, beautiful really. I've
got a lot of pictures of her in the house and prayers and statues.

M W   How do you show your love for God?

J   I believe that God loves me but he must get angry as well, like any
father would . . . or mother! You still love your children but this does
not mean to say that you approve of what they are doing! You always
stick by them, don't you? I know that God will never get too angry
with me . . . that he will always stick by me. Sometimes, I wonder why
I am suffering so much – especially when I see other people who are
really evil and they seem to have everything. I think that maybe it is
because they have never suffered that they don't understand what it
is like to go without.

M W   Tell me something more about how you meet God . . . how you
serve him.

J   I meet God in people and I serve him in people. Some think I am a
nutter! They think I am mad because I am soft. Like, if the ice-cream
van comes and if there's kids playing with my kids, even if it is the
last pound I've got, I'll buy ice-cream for all of them! If I haven't got
enough money, then none of them will get any! I often don't have the
money. On Monday, when the van came, I went mad! I spent over
two pounds on ice-cream! Other families always seem to have more
money than me . . . I don't know how they can afford to buy expensive ice-creams for their kids! I thought that I would treat my own just
this once.

M W   What would you say your greatest fear is?

J   Anything happening to the kids I think. Like them getting run over.
I have different fears for different ones of them. A lot of black guys
around here have said to me that Abbie has gorgeous hair and to
watch her when she grows up. Now, that would worry me in case she
got in with the wrong sort. The colour wouldn't bother me. I
wouldn't want her to go on the streets or anything like that, or be ill-
treated.

   I am also very frightened that I might die. I must go to the doctor's
next week for a test. I have not been well recently and something is
not right. My greatest fear is that I might have cancer. I was supposed
to have gone last week, but I was too scared! If anything happens to
me, what will the kids do?

M W   What would you like to be remembered for?

J   I would just like people to remember that I was a good Mom. That
the children were always looked after, that they always came first. I

am very slow to let anyone else look after them, in case they wouldn't treat them right.

M W   Of all that you have taught them, what do you most hope they will remember?

J   How to treat other people. I don't think Bijay has grasped it like I wanted him to. I caught him fighting today. I know the other boy was the same size as him. Bijay says that he was getting his own back because the boy had held him down and let five others beat him and so he wanted to see if he would be so brave when he was alone. But I said 'No! I don't like to see you fighting, no matter what the reason!' He is rude as well! He speaks his mind and it does come out rude!

M W   Do you punish your children?

J   I don't like hitting them, though I really belted Bijay the other day. Ranjet was teasing him and he took his bottle and threw it against the wall. There was milk and glass everywhere and Ranjet didn't have another bottle. I wouldn't normally hit him and it really shook him up.

M W   How would you like your neighbours to remember you?

J   Oh, I don't know. I heard the neighbours' kids talking about me the other day. They were saying 'She's mad ... She was dancing round the bins last week!' Bijay was out there, kicking his ball and I said to him: 'I'm ever so sorry about that but it happened when I was sick and I didn't know what I was doing.' I asked him if it bothered him and he said: 'No! I couldn't care less what they are saying about you!' and I said: 'Well, don't you think that I am mad, like?' He said: 'No! I know that you are not mad so they can say what they want!' It's not affecting him.

Right now I think that we are living in the Last Days and I don't want to be one of those who gets sent off somewhere else. I don't want to be one of those to whom he says 'Don't come near me!' That story in the Bible where Jesus says: 'I wanted water and you wouldn't give me any. I was hungry and you wouldn't feed me and if you are doing that to anybody else you are doing it to me' ... that story always sticks in my mind. If you are horrible to somebody, it's like you are horrible to him. I try not to be like that.

Here's coping: Joseph

MARGARET WALSH

JOSEPH: I was born in Nigeria in 1957 and brought to England when I was six months old. We were deported because of racial prejudice. My father is a full-blooded African and my mother is half Irish and half Scottish, so I'm a mixed breed. I'm a bit of a 'Heinz 57' I suppose! I am the fifth eldest of thirteen children. We came to live in Wolverhampton and my father had a job in the railway. I still go and have a look at our old home every now and again because we lived there until I was seventeen, when my Dad had his job transferred to London. I only lasted about six months there. I was so glad to come back because all my friends were up here. I hate the place. It is such a big rat race down there.

When I was young I copped most of the trouble. I was a little bugger really. However, I am now looked upon as the head of the family – especially since my parents died. If ever there is any trouble, they come looking for me, though there isn't always a lot I can do. Recently, I've had to change my name, because when the father dies, the head of the family adopts the Dad's middle name.

When I was very young, things seemed to be all right. We had plenty to eat and we used to get Christmas presents. It became more of a struggle after that – with a big family in a three-bedroomed house, it has to be a struggle I suppose. My Mum was ill a lot as well. She was very lethargic – having thirteen kids is bound to take it out of you I suppose.

I spent a lot of my early years in Children's Homes. When you get picked on as much as I was, you are bound to retaliate. I used to smash things up and run off. All the family seemed to pick on me, apart from my Mum. I used to get beatings off my Dad for nothing. I remember one time when I was about four, we had this cuckoo clock and every half an hour this bird used to come out. One day I tried to grab the cuckoo and I bust the whole clock. I ended up in hospital for a couple of months because my Dad beat me up so bad. His favourite

41

weapon was a poker. My old man nearly broke every bone in my body. Oh! I hated him so much.

I first went to a Children's Home when I was eight. My Dad came to see me once. He took me over to Rhyl, beat me up and left me on the beach!

MARGARET WALSH: Why did he beat you on that occasion?

J   I don't know! Maybe he missed doing it! After that, the Social Services changed my surname and moved me to a different Home so that he couldn't find me.

M W   What was it like for you in the Children's Homes?

J   Well, back in the 50s and 60s, full blacks were rare in those places and so you can imagine that half-castes were even rarer. I know that all kids can be vindictive sometimes, and they used to let me know that I was different. I used to retaliate and so that was why I was moved from home to home. I ended up seeing most of the country!

M W   Did you learn much in terms of formal education?

J   No, not really. I never bothered. When I wasn't in the Children's Homes, the only time I used to go to school was on Friday – to do double woodwork and double metalwork. The rest of the time I used to 'wag' it and go work with my Grandad – he was a painter and decorator. I learnt more off my Grandad than I did off anyone else. Anyway, I think that you can learn more about real life on the street than anywhere else.

M W   You seem to have been in trouble a lot of the time! When did you feel happy in those days?

J   Avoiding everybody else. I used to find corners – just to be on my own. When I was in a Home in Hereford, I used to walk around the woods, seeing the trees and the animals. I love animals. They don't shout at you and they show so much affection ... especially dogs ... they don't judge you. I used to run away a lot and believe it or not, I used to try and run back home! I was always caught.

M W   What happened after you finished in the Children's Homes?

J   At sixteen, I went straight into the army, mainly because I didn't want to go back home and I lost contact with the family for ten years. I also wanted to do something for peace in the world. I did three years – eighteen months of it in Northern Ireland. I was in the Falklands. I was actually there when we took Goose Green. That wasn't so bad. You knew what you could expect ... it was a war. In Northern Ireland, you never knew what would happen next. One of my mates got blown up when he went to investigate a doll's pram.

M W   Was your time in Northern Ireland one of a lot of fear?

J   Yeah. We was all scared. If anything, it brought us all close together because everybody was watching everybody else's back. The best friends I've ever had were my army mates. There was a lot of fear and our release was to get drunk. We would sit and laugh together and sometimes we used to cry.

I got married when I was in the army – to Sue, my childhood sweetheart. We were always together at playtime and we used to sit together in class. We kept in contact – even when I was in the Children's Homes. We used to write to each other and her parents brought her to see me. We began dating properly when we were about fourteen or fifteen. Once I ran away from a Children's Home and we tried to get a place together.

We finally got married in an army chapel. We were seventeen. Sue was pregnant and I suppose that pushed us into getting married. We had the consent of our parents. My daughter, Louise, was born the day after my birthday – that was the best birthday present I've ever had! I've got her photograph upstairs.

Sue was white and her parents hated blacks. They didn't hate me so much. When we got leave we used to stay with them. It was at her parents' place that Sue and Louise died. The gas cooker blew up. I was helping out a friend that evening ... it was Christmas Eve. The baby was six weeks old. I would have given anything for it to have been me, rather than them two ... I don't think that I would have been missed as much either. Her parents always blamed me for what happened ... they reckon that I should have been there. I think that I wanted to die then.

M W   How come the gas cooker blew up?

J   It was an old enemy of mine ... we were at infant school together. I gave him a pretty bad beating once because he used to pick on me. He always vowed from then on that he would get his own back, so on that night he decided to put a fire bomb through the letter box and it rolled under the cooker. He was not taken into custody at first because there was no proof of who did it ... no finger prints or anything.

One night, in a local pub, he was bragging about it, so the house didn't half go up, when I heard! I grabbed hold of him! I got stabbed ... I have still got the scar in my shoulder blade. I gave him a bad beating. It took six people to get me off him. He was in a wheelchair for a long time afterwards. It took twelve months to go to court. He got three months and I got three years. He admitted to it but the court put the deaths down to misadventure because he wasn't to know that the banger would blow the cooker up.

M W   What was your time in prison like?

J   Most of the time, three of us were together in a small cell. I was in with two other blacks. I think I learnt more in prison than I did anywhere else . . . like how to get into houses without leaving traces and so on. Most of the other prisoners had also been in Children's Homes and Borstals. For many, prison was a place to go – where you got a bed and three meals. They would break the law so as to have somewhere to go over the winter.

M W   Did you learn anything that inspired you for later on in life?

J   I learnt to have a sense of purpose . . . to get on with my life rather than to break the law . . . to prove that I was worth something.

I went back into the army after prison. I actually volunteered because I wanted to die so much. I didn't have the bottle to do it myself. Call it legal suicide if you like . . . get somebody else to do it . . . but it never happened.

M W   When in prison, you discovered a purpose in living, so why did you want to die in the Falklands?

J   Yeah, I did want to die but I began to also wonder 'Is it worth it? There must be a reason why I have been put on this earth?' If I had died then, I wouldn't have found my reason for living. When you lose your wife and child, you go through all sorts of emotions. One minute you want to die . . . when you can't do it yourself you look for other ways of doing it. I have come close a few times. After the army I had a pretty horrific smash on a motor-bike . . . I was in a coma for some time. When I came out of that, I began to realize that I didn't really want to die. My aim was to die but when it actually came to it I didn't.

It's scary when you go into a coma. You are in this dark tunnel and there is a light at the end of it and you are walking and walking . . . I think that the light is your life and you are trying to get towards that light so that you can start afresh . . . but the light seems to get further and further away! I was glad to be alive when I came round. I still am now. Bad experiences are sent to try us all I think.

I usually bottle things up. I don't talk like this very often! It's a load off my mind.

M W   When did you start taking cannabis?

J   I started taking it after my wife and daughter died. It was a form of escape. It relaxes me and then I'm not worried because I think that everything is all right when I am stoned! I am less aggressive too . . . I even laugh occasionally! Cannabis affects you in the same way as alcohol, but you don't have a hangover and you are more aware of what's going on around you. I wrote a lot of poems when I was stoned!

M W   How about the dealers and your own decision to become a dealer?

J I mainly started to deal to help me to pay my bills. You can't afford a lot of things, if you are trying to live on the dole. It's a quick way of making money and supply your own habit at the same time.

M W Was it a dangerous way of life?

J Yeah. I have now stopped dealing because I was robbed at gun-point, by 'crack-heads'. They took £600 and everything I'd got in the house. I expected trouble all of the time. I used to keep a pickaxe at the back of the door!

In any kind of dealing, there is always a risk, not just from the police but also from other dealers because they get jealous of your custom. I'll never deal again because I don't like the trouble it can bring. One of the people who robbed me was later stabbed through the heart. I had a nice home and was just getting going in a decorating business and because of what has happened, I have lost it all. The police have also put an injunction on me, so I can't go back to Heath Town ... otherwise I will be arrested.

I am having great trouble in getting accommodation also. Now I am black-listed with the Housing Authority and the Housing Associations. I have made several attempts to get a place of my own but they are all afraid of the trouble I might bring. I slept rough on a park bench for about two months after leaving Heath Town. It was better than the rented room I got later. That place was so damp! I now have bad asthma – one day, I collapsed on the street and spent a few weeks in hospital.

M W So, you have talked about friends in the army ... are there other people who have stood by you in life? How have you fared since?

J My friends have been few and far between. Since leaving the army, I have mostly been on my own. After losing Sue and Louise, I'm scared to settle down, in case something similar happens. I don't think I would be able to cope with it again. I did try to settle down once, with a girl called Ellen, and she got killed in a road accident!

M W And you suffered a tragedy also with your mother, didn't you?

J Yeah. During the latter years of her life, she had cancer and she had great difficulty in walking so she was house-bound. I used to do the running around for her. By this time she lived alone. My Dad beat up my Mum pretty bad when they lived in London ... bust her jaw, her ribs and her arm as well. If I wasn't there, my Mum used to get the beating. I got back in touch with the family after ten years. I bumped into my sister one day in London, this was after the Falklands and I was looking for some place to settle down.

When my Mum left my Dad, she came back to live with my grandparents in Wolverhampton. The youngest of the family was about ten at the time but she came back on her own. They all stayed with him. He kicked them out, as the years went on. Africans are very strict. They reckon that once you are sixteen you fend for yourself, whether you have somewhere to go or not. One of my sisters was pregnant, and he kicked her out as well! A lot of my family ended up on the street – homeless. They are all settled now and have kids of their own. Some are even married still! I've got forty-two nieces and nephews! One of my sisters has named her son after me! I'm god-father to twenty-five of them, so if anything happens to my brothers and sisters, I've got my own orphanage!

When my grandparents died, my Mum came to live in Heath Town. She had a one-bedroom flat and I used to kip on the settee until we got a bigger flat in Clover Ley. You remember my mother, don't you? Later, I got my own place, so that we both could have some privacy. I still kept looking after her. She needed a lot of attention but I had to get a job to help pay for her medicines . . . she could only get so much on free prescription. So she had to be left on her own a lot of the time. She died by suicide. She probably couldn't take the pain anymore. She started a fire in her living room. When I got back from work, I found her dead.

All my family who have died, are buried in Heath Town. I'm going to be buried with my Mum. I want to be close to her again, I suppose.

M W   And not with Sue and Louise?

J   There's no room. I only had it dug for the two. I could only afford a single grave at the time. When my Mum was being buried, I got a grave for the two of us.

M W   You have already spoken about some of the pressures that are on you. What would you say is the main one?

J   Memories. I have a few good ones but some are really bad. I have some really awful nightmares . . . about my family that I have lost, and the people who died while I was in the army. I can see their faces in my dreams. I've got to find a way to be more self-disciplined and stop the nightmares. I don't want to go and see a psychiatrist, because I'm not mad.

While I was in the army, a Chinese sergeant taught me a lot about their culture and the martial arts. It sounded terrific and since then, I've always wanted to go to China. If I ever get there, I hope that I may be able to learn more about self-discipline and so control my emotions . . . then I will be able to close myself off and the outside world won't hurt so much. I've just got to stop these nightmares! To a certain extent, I consider myself lucky – I've got bad memories but I am still alive . . . and I can still find out what my goal is, and that will be my next thing to win.

If I had enough money, I could do a lot of things that I can't do now. I would like to get my bike back on the road. I would feel like a bird again ... whizzing around! I could help others a lot more too. I like to do things for charity ... the hospitals always need help. One time I did a thirteen-mile bed-push and raised about £1,400 for a hospital in Redditch.

M W   In your present circumstances, have you much opportunity to help others?

J   Since the police placed the injunction order on me, I don't go out very much. Also, those who robbed me know that I am still in Wolverhampton, so I stay at home, in case I am seen ... I know that they would come after me. I hope to get accepted on a college course and maybe I'll be able to do a lot more then because I will be able to move away from this area. I would love to work with kids. Now, I stay indoors most of the time, except when I go to collect my Giro and do a bit of shopping. I am house-bound, to a certain extent.

M W   So how do you spend your time?

J   Just sitting here, watching telly, playing videos, listening to the radio, doing puzzles and jigsaws ... playing with the dog ... I'm sat here on my own most of my time, because my flatmate goes out. I sometimes find the day very long. I rarely have visitors.

M W   What gives you the courage to 'get up and go' again?

J   It's finding something to believe in. We are all put into life for a purpose. I haven't found mine yet. I'm still searching. I know what it is but it is hard to get there. I want to become a nursery nurse and work with children. I think that, through giving some love to kids, I will feel a lot better about myself and about life. I will have found that purpose and a reason to go on. It will be a long haul – because I haven't got any exams. I will have to begin by doing a City and Guilds Course, before I can start to train. And before that, I'll have to pass the interview for college!

M W   You are nervous about your interview at the college on Tuesday?

J   I'm shaking now! I'm ever so nervous. My greatest fear at the moment is that I might fail the interview.

M W   What is the worst thing that could happen to you?

J   I think that it already has ... when I lost my wife, my baby and my Mum ... and my friends in the army. Those kind of experiences made me back off from life ... made me stop and have a good look at what it's all about ... The people I have seen die, shouldn't have, and I wonder why.

M W   Have you a God?

J　Yeah! I'm Catholic. There's got to be a God, because nothing comes from nothing ... there's always got to be something there to start it. He's up there. He's watching us. It makes you wonder why he doesn't do something about the situation in the world, even though he has got the power to do something about it. He is the most powerful being ... I nearly called him a person then!

M W　You have said that the God you know is most powerful and the source of everything. Have you ever felt him close to you?

J　Sometimes. When I have been going through bad times I have felt somebody else there. It's difficult to explain. He is around everywhere and when you believe enough, you can feel his presence. It is stronger sometimes than at others. He has certainly been there for me when I have been really down. I have felt him when I have prayed. I've got my Bible upstairs. I read it sometimes.

M W　Is there any story that especially appeals to you?

J　Job. He was persecuted but he still believed. There are lots of Jobs about. Anybody who has had bad times and who still believes – that person is Job but in a different form. There are lots of Jobs in places like Bosnia and Rwanda.

M W　What do you think the end of it all will be? What's the point of suffering?

J　It helps you to find out your mettle. Only the strong survive. There are limits to everybody's beliefs. I think that that is why there is so much crime – especially by those with nothing to believe in ... so they find their excitement in other things.

M W　In what way does your God direct your life? Or does he?

J　I don't know how to put it. He does guide you in a certain way but he doesn't tell you what he thinks you should do. He lets you find that out for yourself but he does help you while you are doing it. He helps me with my decorating and with my poems. He gives me the belief in myself.

M W　You say that he guides you but that he doesn't tell you exactly, are there any markers that he lays down?

J　No, I don't think so. You have to find out what you really want to do yourself ... You have to be careful ... just plod along and take things easy ... don't rush ... because when you do, you tend to end up in cul-de-sacs. If you take your time, you will see which direction you are going in. Your inner self tells you. You begin to feel comfortable with what you are doing and then you know that you are on the right road.

M W　You said you prayed. Tell me more about how you communicate with your God.

J   It all depends. Usually, I just sit there and rabbit on to him – especially when I have had a smoke! Then I can't stop my lips from flapping! Sometimes I say formal prayers. I pray especially for peace in the world and I pray for other people.

M W   You describe God as being 'up there'. Do you meet him in any other ways? You talked about the Bible. How else do you get to know him?

J   I go to church sometimes. I usually go to Midnight Mass. My Sue and Louise died at Christmas and my Mam's birthday is on Christmas day. Apart from that I go . . . maybe two or three times a year. Do you really need to go to church to pray? I don't think so. Still, when I get myself sorted I will go more often. I'll feel more worthy then.

M W   How about the Heath Town Celebrations? Before you were run off the estate, you used to come regularly and were often involved in organizing them. What did they mean to you?

J   Yeah, they are a good idea. They show a different side of the church . . . it's more than just going, standing there and singing. The Hope Community has opened my eyes to what the church is about . . . that it can be in places like Heath Town. I think that if more churches did celebrations like ours, maybe more people would get involved in church.

M W   In what way do the Celebrations show a different side of the church?

J   When we do drama and things like that . . . and the ordinary people who run it. The Celebrations happen in the community, they are for the local people and are run by them. Almost everybody is involved in some way. I think that this is a better way of putting over what the church is about and it helps you to understand what it is all about. The only time you see a nun is in a church but you nuns are more involved in the community. A lot of the churches are cut off from the people . . . they are just there, in one place and if you need them, you have got to go to them. The Hope Community is there for us . . . people know where you are and you know where we are, so I think that this shows a real commitment to the community. I think that the church should be more community minded.

M W   Have you ever looked for help from the church?

J   When I was in the Children's Homes I did but not so much now because . . . I suppose I am used to fending for myself. I've never really known where to go for help. I've just picked myself up and carried on . . . but each time it has been harder. I've never had much experience of somebody listening to me – except to tell you my story! I've been shouted at a lot. I've tried to explain, especially to my Dad, but I was only beaten back. Now, it's not very often I ask for help. I find that people are really too caught up in their own troubles to really listen to mine and so I don't bother now. God listens to what I have to say and he doesn't butt in with his own problems.

M W   Does he ever speak to you?

J   Yeah. He sometimes says: 'Carry on the way you are doing. Do your best and you will be rewarded.' I think that the reward in life is death because then you will have peace and quiet and be well out of it. Maybe there is such a thing as reincarnation but I hope not. However, I sometimes think that I will never get to heaven. I'll probably end up stoking the fires of hell – maybe, this is just me being cynical. I don't think I am good enough to be with God. If I was any good I wouldn't have so many bad things happen to me.

M W   So the God you believe in, doesn't believe in you?

J   No ... Maybe I've still got to prove myself to him? I don't think I have yet. I believe that I am a good decorator and I believe that I am good with kids as well ... so I can't be that bad. My Grandad taught me to believe in myself even if nobody else does.

M W   You said that you had your Bible upstairs and that you read the Book of Job. What about the rest of it?

J   Well, it's such a long book! I think that I read what I am comfortable with ... the gospel might challenge me too much and I am not yet ready to change my life. I don't really feel that I am loved by God ... I suppose, that's because I have been pushed from 'pillar to post' all my life?

M W   Tell me again about your dreams for the future.

J   Well, if I get this college interview next Tuesday, I will begin to get my qualifications to train as a nursery nurse and my dream to work with kids will come true. I hope to be able to give kids some of the attention I never had. It's something I just gotta do and so I will keep on trying, no matter what happens with the interview at the college. Once I have realized my goal, I am not too bothered what happens ... I suppose I will die happy then. I also hope to go to China and already the college has told me of a student out there who wants an exchange. Maybe the nightmares will be over and that my real life will begin.

POSTSCRIPT: Joseph has begun his college course and recently has been offered a flat close by. He has stopped smoking cannabis. In a recent conversation he said:

It is the beginning of a new life for me. I am the only bloke in a large class and I get a fair amount of stick ... but I can handle it. I enjoy the study and I have passed all my assignments. I even got one distinction! Now, there is something to look forward to every day and the future holds out great hope. I now go to church every Sunday, though I still don't feel ready to receive communion. I must prove myself a bit more first. One day each week, I have a placement in a day nursery . . . I just love it. The kids call me Uncle Joe.

Here's hoping: The Hope Community, Wolverhampton

MARGARET WALSH

Returning to the sources

Our Institute, the Sisters of the Infant Jesus, has its origins in seventeenth-century France, when Father Nicolas Barré, a religious priest of the Order of Minims, heard the cry of those who were most neglected and abandoned in his country at that time. In 1662, some women, sharing his desire to 'bring the people together to help them grow as persons and come to know Christ', committed themselves totally to the same mission. A few years later he proposed to these women that they live in community 'without making vows or being cloistered', so as to be accessible to ordinary people and free to go to them 'in their surroundings'. Until 1789 the Institute continued to grow and spread throughout France. Then came the French Revolution. Faced with the threat of persecution and the guillotine, the Sisters scattered but continued their work of spreading the Good News among those most in need in whatever way possible. In 1806 they began to come together again, having suffered great losses during the time they had been separated. It was a re-birth. Trusting completely in the Lord, they were ready to go wherever they were sent. Expansion soon began, not only in France, but beyond the seas. The year 1852 marked the beginnings of new foundations outside Europe, first to Asia, then to some European countries, and later to all continents. The Sisters came to England in 1892 and to Ireland in 1909.

In 1966 the Second Vatican Council invited all religious institutes to 'return to the sources of Christian life, to the original inspiration of their institutes and to an adjustment of their communities to the changed conditions of our time' (*Perfectae Caritatis*). This led the Sisters of the Infant Jesus to look carefully at how they had been living this original inspiration. Consequently, in the last twenty years we have undertaken many new forms of the apostolate and have undergone the painful process of having to leave well-established areas of ministry. One such

52

new undertaking was the setting up of a community on Heath Town estate in Wolverhampton.

The mysterious call of God

Three of us, living in a community on the other side of Wolverhampton, were invited by the local parish priest of St Patrick's to undertake a census of the Heath Town estate in January 1985. When we met those who had the courage to open their doors and listened to their stories, the census became secondary, because we found so many people who felt forgotten by society, by the Church, and some even by their own families. They were lonely, full of fear, isolated and with little hope for anything better in this life.

It was difficult to leave them in the evenings and return to our community. It soon became clear that the Lord was calling us to find him in Heath Town, and to join these people in discovering him living among them. In October 1985, we became Council tenants on the estate. We now live in four maisonettes on a third floor near to the centre of things. When it became known that we intended living here, we had so many well-intentioned warnings that we were almost convinced we would be mugged or broken into in the first twenty-four hours. Ten years later, we have never experienced violence or hostility, and although we keep open house, we have hardly ever known theft. When we need to make a late night visit on the estate, there is usually one of our neighbours available if we need company, and we always feel well protected.

When we decided to become tenants, many of our friends wondered whether we could possibly fit in, or be accepted, as our backgrounds and professional training were different from that of most others on the estate. We were not even trained social workers, but teachers. We knew, too, that we could never completely identify with other tenants, since we came by choice, and therefore our identification must be limited. However, we also knew that God calls in mysterious ways, so we went ahead in faith, but also with some anxieties.

During our first twelve months, our community of three was extended to include others who wished to spend some time with us, sharing our faith, our community life and our ministry in the area. These are men and women from various walks of life and from different Christian denominations, who have also discerned a call to be with Christ and find his kingdom in the inner city. We became 'The Hope Community'. I think I can best describe our community now as a series of concentric circles. The central nucleus are those of us who belong to the Sisters of the Infant Jesus, the inner circle are others who have committed themselves to living with us for various lengths of time, and there are outer circles of neighbours and friends, who are involved with us in many different ways. Some of these so identify with us now that one night the police phoned to say that they had someone in custody who wanted to speak with the Mother Superior of his community!

The estate

Heath Town estate was built in the late 1960s. At first, people had to be vetted to come and live here, but it soon became a 'deprived inner area'. The reason usually given for the decline is unemployment and neglect by the local authority in doing repairs. Heath Town is now typical of most inner areas in Britain, where life is bleak for the many who live here. Over 80 per cent are on Social Benefit and nearly the same percentage are in rent arrears. In our immediate area there are 1,400 properties, of which 230 are empty at present. There are nine tower blocks, some 22 storeys high, and the rest are maisonettes, ranging from two to six floors.

Increasingly, Heath Town is becoming a dumping place for people who cannot be housed elsewhere: few wish to stay here permanently. Government policy, removing people from hospital to be cared for in the community, has increased the number of tenants who have been institutionalized for years. They are provided with very little after-care, although many are unused to fending for themselves, and are left feeling abandoned and isolated in empty flats around the estate. Sometimes, it is too late before they come to the attention of caring neighbours. Many suffering from psychiatric disorders do not know how to cope and express their frustration in socially unacceptable ways, making life even more difficult for themselves and those around them. Such large numbers of those who experience exceptional difficulties in coping with life have been housed here, that it is not even realistic to expect that they will find the kind of community support that they need, since many of their neighbours have the same kind of problems and are in no position to carry any extra pressure. Housing Authorities have an obligation to look carefully at where they place tenants and to liaise with other statutory and voluntary bodies, especially with regard to those who need special care in the community; the present situation for tenants on Heath Town estate would suggest that such consideration is not being given.

Since the 1988 Social Security changes, and then the Poll Tax, most tenants are very confused by the paperwork. Even when they do sort out their benefits, many go hungry for days before the cheque arrives. Friends and neighbours are forced to borrow from each other, or from loan sharks, and many are surviving on cups of tea, chips and jam 'sarnies', hardly a balanced diet. I have seen parents in tears because they are unable to provide a decent home for their families. One of them sometimes moves into another property in an attempt to gain a little more Social Security, since they are penalized financially for being a couple. Are the best of the Victorian family values only for those who can afford them?

According to Chris Pond, Director of the Low Pay Unit, almost 10 million adults in Britain earn less than the Council of Europe's 'decency threshold' for wages (set at £3.80 an hour in 1989/90). Most people who are in employment on the estate would certainly come into this category. We have our share of unscrupulous employers, whose workers soon find that they are worse off than when they were on Income Support. They live and work in the fear of being dismissed or of having to leave the job 'voluntarily', knowing that they will get little sympathy from the DSS since unemployment benefit rules may disqualify them from receiving benefit if they leave a job because its pay and conditions are unacceptable to them.

To set up their homes, newcomers must often begin by begging, for they can no longer depend on furniture grants. Loans from the cash-limited Social Fund are the privilege of those who can pay them back, an impossibility for many who cannot even feed themselves on the benefits they receive. Also, cash limits, discretionary payments and fourteen pages of paperwork are off-putting for even the most courageous. Some wait for weeks before acquiring a kettle or a cooker, and they understandably grow tired of a diet of cold drinks and sandwiches. We visited a new tenant recently and she had her baby sleeping in a shopping trolley. A Cabinet Minister's declaration, 'There is no poverty in Britain', must rank as the most fatuous public statement of the decade.

Others who are experiencing great frustration with new government policies are the far too few officials who have to implement them in areas like ours. While they try to make sense of the red tape and bureaucracy, the queues lengthen outside their doors. I marvel at their patience and understanding, as they try their best to give people time and attention, especially when they are often powerless to do anything about their plight.

It is not surprising that an increasing number are suffering from depression and hopelessness. For some, anti-depressants provide a temporary release from the burdens of life. Many drown their sorrows in the local pub and are an easy prey for the drug pushers. Others find their way into prostitution, and there are those who pin their hopes on a 'winning streak' at the local 'bookies'. Many here fall into debt; when they go to cash their Giro at the local Post Office, those from whom they borrowed are waiting outside! In recent months, we have seen an increase in the levels of aggression being expressed and experienced. This can too easily be dismissed as racial tension without addressing the underlying causes. The police maintain a 'discreet' presence, especially when it is a question of domestic disputes. However, they can show their determination to maintain law and order by coming in large numbers, armed with riot shields and supported by helicopter and search lights, as happened on the night of 23 May 1989, when we had what have become known as the 'Heath Town Riots'. People have lost confidence in such protection and defend themselves as best they can. We have to expect the occasional violent incident.

Option for the poor

We decided to come and live here because we were moved by the stories people told us as we were doing the census. Was this a call by God to live out our Christian vocation here? As we prayed, we became more conscious of Christ's preferential option for the poor, the teaching of the Church, and also of our Institute's original call to work alongside 'the deprived and the little ones'.

I now cringe when people say to me 'So you are working for the poor! All those drug addicts and prostitutes! Aren't you brave!' I cringe because it reminds me of my own attitudes before I made friends with our present neighbours. The most insulting and offensive attitude we can have is to be patronizing, even in such statements as 'We have come to live here because we have made this option for the poor' which can mean 'you poor souls need our help'. Of course they are all different and unique, each one of them with their own story, gifts and dreams. We deprive ourselves and society of the unique contribution which they can make, when we dismiss them with these soul-destroying labels, and the price we pay is well known: the 'problems' of the inner cities, which are of our own making. When people are not appreciated for who they are, and are regarded as worthless, many of them will react in socially unacceptable ways.

What do you do all day?

This is a difficult question to answer because like the prophet Isaiah: 'Each morning he wakes me to hear, to listen like a disciple' (Isa 50.4). Every day has its own demands and gives us plenty of practice in developing attitudes of true availability and involves us in a daily discernment of what to do. All our work on the estate is voluntary and so we are in the privileged position of being able to choose how we will spend our time. This freedom also brings with it a very real risk of 'burn out' because the temptation to meet every need and to be 'all things to all people' is very great. Some of us still have problems about not feeling guilty when we take a day off and we have to remind ourselves that graveyards are full of people who thought they were indispensable!

We try to be a loving and caring community ourselves and also to work with others to build up community on the estate. Many of our neighbours are very marginalized and socially isolated. They are a people crying out for a communion with others, so that their true dignity and self-worth is given recognition. Entering into this process takes a lot of courage, but by doing so their God-given gifts to reach out and show their love as brothers and sisters can become a reality. Including them, especially in decisions which affect their lives, and giving back to them their respect and self-esteem, is key to our undertakings. We therefore encourage them to be involved with us in our own community and in local organizations, which are trying to improve the quality of life on the estate. The most recent initiative is the development of an estate management board. This aims at improving the housing service and giving residents more say in how the place is run.

Attempting to do things for people tends not to be life-giving in the long run and perhaps is often a reflection of our own misguided need to be needed and our inborn tendency to dominate and so treat people as the objects of our charity. Only by walking alongside others and being with them, can we grow into the type of community that Christ envisioned for his kingdom.

We did not come with any prepared agenda. It was our conviction that it is more important to hear what people are saying, to see reality through their eyes and to make our response with them in the light of the gospel. We can learn this lesson from the Samaritan, who helped the injured man (Luke 10.29–37). He was able to do this because he abandoned his own road and moved into the path of the suffering traveller. The others kept to their own rules and agenda and passed him by. Had we had our own plans, we might not have gone to a Tupperware party during our first week here. Nobody was offering to host the next one, so we decided to open our house. This was to be the beginning of our having an 'open door' to anyone who wished to call. Our living room is now the place where many initiatives are planned and carried out, by ourselves and by the many who have become our friends, by dropping in for a chat and cuppa. We have also undertaken an official analysis of the estate, and informally we have many opportunities to get to know the needs of the people and to hear their story. We still do regular door-to-door visiting, saying hello to new tenants and inviting them to drop in; also, we do follow-up work from previous visits, or through requests made by the local churches or the statutory agencies.

Finding God

St Luke reminds us that the labourers in the vineyard are few and yet the harvest is so great (Luke 10.2). To me the harvest means that the seeds of the Spirit already exist. In other words, we did not come to Heath Town to bring God to the people – he was here long before we arrived! We are no messiahs! Max Warren puts it very well when he reminds us: 'Our first task in approaching another culture, another religion, is to take off our shoes, for the place we are approaching is holy. Else, we may forget, that God was there before we arrived.'

We find that many, despite the apparent hopelessness of their situation, are full of faith, which is a deep, childlike trust in a God who cares and who is in everything. A neighbour called late one night wanting to talk about her son in prison. After listening to her and praying together for a while, I turned to give her my full attention when I heard her say 'And now I want to talk to you, because you are a mother like me and you understand how a son can break a mother's heart.' I quickly realized that it was Mary, the mother of God, with whom she wanted to speak. After our prayer, we spent some time talking about our God. Speaking of the Holy Spirit, she said that she always prayed to her when she felt the need for guidance and wisdom. I pressed her to tell me more and she went on to recall that she always addressed the Holy Spirit with the name 'Winifred' because that was what she decided to call her when she made her confirmation! Working and praying with the people here has taught me more about what it means to follow Christ than any other spiritual formation I have ever had. I feel we are more evangelized than we are evangelizers, and we can rejoice as Jesus did when 'filled with joy by the Holy Spirit' he said 'I bless you, Father, Lord of heaven and earth, for hiding these things from the learned and the clever and revealing them to mere children. Yes, Father, for that is what it has pleased you to do' (Luke 10.21).

There are, of course, others for whom faith is an opium, an escape from life's harsh realities. They see their situation as God's will for them and look forward to getting their due reward in the next world. They are the religious fundamentalists, who pray for those of us who appear 'not to be saved'. They worry about our left-wing tendencies, which we prefer to call the promotion of justice and the reign of God. Another form of escape that we find is a type of psychiatric disorder which expresses itself in a world of fantasy. It is understandable that when people have never been truly loved for who they are, they will try to find that love and self-esteem in a land of make-believe. Medication which causes them to sit or sleep quietly in the corner may well be more socially acceptable, but it is not the answer to their hunger for human fulfilment. TV satellite dishes have sprung up like mushrooms around the estate over the past few years, and it makes me wonder if this is not another attempt to get lost in a land of dreams.

I had the opportunity to spend three months at St Beuno's in North Wales (a Jesuit spirituality centre) in the autumn of 1989, during which I made the full Spiritual Exercises of St Ignatius, which last about a month. The quiet, open spaces and the lure of the hills were a welcome break from the concrete and noise of the estate. However, I found that I could not forget or escape from the reality I have come to know here, neither did I want to, painful as it is at times. In one of my imaginative contemplations I was with Jesus during his wilderness experience. The parapet of the Temple faded away and I was standing on top of a 22-storey tower block. In a later contemplation I was hiding in the shadows of 'shame and confusion' and did not know how I would come out into the light of God's love. Suddenly, a wonderful scene opened up in front of me. There was Jesus, sitting in the company of a number of my friends from the estate – the biggest 'public sinners' I know! The sounds of friendship, ease and laughter drifted towards me. Then one of them caught sight of me in the shadows and called out 'Hey Margaret, what are you doing over there? I've never known you to miss a party.' There may be many mansions in heaven, but I feel sure that we will not enjoy the feast in the kingdom unless we are happy and at home in the company of 'the poor, the crippled, the blind and the lame' in this world (Luke 14.22).

Low self-esteem

Many here have been excluded for so long from any position of respect or influence in society, that they have a low self-esteem and little self-confidence. They feel they have nothing worthwhile to offer and this is sometimes expressed in feelings of guilt. How often we hear statements such as: 'I must have done something wrong to be so useless and such a nuisance.' It is true that they have little money or material resources, few have professional skills, many are broken in spirit. They have hardly any control over their environment and lack the means and opportunities to make choices – except for the ones they have to make between equally pressing financial demands. This powerlessness is the essence of the injustice that they suffer. It is also one of the reasons for their apathy in response to anything imposed from on high. They are well known for their apparent 'sins' – drugs, prostitution, fiddling the benefit system, etc. Living here has made it very clear to me that they are more sinned against than sinning. In fact, many of their 'sins' are the result of their having been pushed to the bottom for so long. This does not mean that we are all saints in the inner city and that all our sins are the result of our circumstances! The call to repentance and conversion must also be taken seriously by us as well.

Sometimes, when I am asked to write references for my friends here, I see very clearly the values which are most important in Britain today: classroom success, knowing the right people, a competitive spirit, white skin, an address in leafy suburbia. The Heath Town people abound in the gifts of the Spirit, in love, joy, peace, patience, goodness, kindness etc. (Gal 5.22) but employers do not seem to be impressed. It is challenging and exciting to find ways by which they can use these gifts in their own homes and in the community. This demands much lateral thinking and deconditioning, if you have been brought up to give priority to the values which this world promotes. Living here, one can learn much about the kingdom Christ proclaimed, and the meaning of his teaching on the Beatitudes, simply by observing the way people live and relate to one another. Our experience is that this is a kingdom which emerges daily and is full of surprises. Through them we have begun better to realize what St Peter means in his second letter when he writes:

> By his divine power, he has given us all the things we need for life and
> for true devotion, bringing us to know God himself, who has called us
> by his own glory and goodness. In making these gifts, he has given us
> the guarantee of something very great and wonderful to come: through
> them you will be able to share the divine nature and to escape
> corruption in a world that is sunk in vice. (2 Peter 1.3–4)

Friendship and solidarity

As I said already, we cannot fully identify with the people of Heath Town chiefly because we are here by choice and our backgrounds are so different from most. We know that friendship and solidarity can only be built on shared and mutual interests. Consequently, we are having to undergo a deconditioning process. Gradually, we are discovering more of our common humanity and developing friendships which are open to a deeper sharing of our true selves. As we work, pray and socialize with others, we try not to impose our own standards, values or customs. I find that I have to keep praying for humility, so that I can listen and learn. This is not easy, because I was brought up to look for success and to be in control, attitudes reinforced by becoming a teacher. It is hard to become a learner all over again. Many here are not interested in the competition or achievements that the education system promotes, neither are they impressed by status or power. Such persons they refer to derisively as 'snobs'.

When we cannot hide behind our accomplishments, we become very vulnerable and begin to wonder who we are and also to recognize our own brokenness. This invites us on a journey into our own need for healing and to a deeper awareness that Christ's good news for the poor is for us, when we place our own poverty of spirit before his healing touch. We start to recognize this as a real opportunity to find our true selves, to question our values and beliefs and to re-examine what we mean when we pray 'Thy kingdom come'. This can be both a painful and a confusing process, and the fear of losing our identity can be very real at times. We are challenged to be accepted for who we are, not for what we possess, whether material things or professional skills. Others here have so little that we are encouraged to live more simply and to share the possessions and skills we have. They are not happy about their material poverty; in fact, many feel angry and deprived, especially when they have not got the basic essentials which would provide them with a hot meal or a change of clothing. Perhaps we can help by showing that needless acquisitions are not the answer to a fuller life and that together we can allow ourselves to be challenged by Jesus' words: 'Do not store up treasure for yourselves on earth, where moths and woodworms destroy them and thieves can break in and steal. But store up treasure for yourselves in heaven, where neither moth nor woodworm destroy them and thieves cannot break in and steal. For where your treasure is, there your heart will be also' (Matt 6.19–21).

Closing the gap

One of our aims is to encourage local leadership. Many of those who have lived all their lives in areas like this have to be convinced that there is more to life and human wholeness and that they themselves can do something to bring this about. Finding ways to help a broken people to believe in themselves must always be part of our ongoing agenda. We sometimes worry about leading others into a process of conscientization because it often causes them to have greater feelings of dissatisfaction and hopelessness with their lot. It is also hard to assure them that they have a worthwhile contribution to make and that this will be taken seriously by those in authority. Attempts to bring about this 'empowerment' can sometimes be a frustrating experience. Efforts and organizations to build up the local community can seem to go so wrong, and are rarely run with the efficiency we expect.

Enabling others, by helping them to develop some of the skills required, can be very time-consuming. Great patience and creativity are required, if people are to be convinced that they have a role to play. It is difficult for them to slot into a time-table of meetings when for many, the only appointment they have to keep is their fortnightly signing on at the DSS, and this is a negative experience that they would prefer to forget! Also, even with the best of intentions, others are unable to cope with the extra stress of a meeting, when they already suffer from many emotional and social pressures. Others too, especially casualties of the education system, feel very threatened by the formality of meetings although we make many attempts to keep these informal and creative. Our efforts also can highlight our own position of power and perhaps of being 'do-gooders'. I believe that we still have a lot of thinking and evaluating to do before we can find ways to break down very deep-seated barriers. Our experience at this stage warns us that, when ten people sincerely intend to work on a project, we are lucky if half of them are able to turn up at the appointed time. The temptation for us is to take on leadership roles for greater efficiency. We have become very aware that it is much more important to liberate people from over-dependency, and to give them back some control over their own lives, than to offer apparently well-run community programmes.

From our Heath Town experience we can wholeheartedly endorse the declaration by Church Action on Poverty:

> We have seen with our own eyes our society being driven in a direction
> that contradicts the Gospel. Wounding effects are witnessed and
> experienced daily. They challenge us to seek a new social order
> founded on that vision and possibility of human wholeness which is
> contained in the Christian message and which speaks to all human
> experience ... the experience of the poor can contribute to the
> transformation of society and therefore to its salvation.
>
> (December 1989)

Our challenge here in Heath Town is to enable others to become a source of conversion for those with power and influence, so that they can redirect their energies for the good of all and so close the gap between the 'have lots' and 'have nots', not only in Britain, but also abroad.

I believe that the marginalized in Britain are also the lost and forgotten. Frank Field, in his book *Losing Out*, describes the government's censoring of sensitive data, particularly those which detail change in the degree of inequality in Britain. One cannot help wondering if this is deliberate policy, in order to keep the public in ignorance of what is really happening. It amazes me that people, who live only half a mile up the road from here, have no idea of the suffering and poverty of those who are so physically close to them. Occasionally, I have the opportunity to speak of our life in Heath Town and I always hear the same reaction: 'We had no idea.' These, of course, are those who want to hear and understand. The disheartening reality also seems to be that there are many people in our society who have the opportunity to know what is happening but are failing to open their hearts to the 'cries of the poor'. Even living here on an 'inner area' estate, those of us who are relatively 'comfortable' can be blind to the poverty and hardship on our own doorstep. In us the prophecy of Isaiah is again being fulfilled: 'You will listen and listen again, but not understand, see and see again, but not perceive. For the heart of this nation has grown coarse, their ears are dull of hearing, and they have shut their eyes, for fear they should see with their eyes, hear with their ears, understand with their heart, and be converted and be healed by me' (Isa 6.9–10).

I like to believe that Dives was unaware that Lazarus was lying hungry and in pain at his gate. It seems to me that the rich man was far more in need of help for his eternal salvation than Lazarus. Those of us who have the opportunity to hear the cry of the poor have, I believe, an obligation to alert others. It is usually my experience that once they hear about what is going on, they want to do something about the situation. There is much untapped goodness in people. Last year, I spoke to representatives of all the St Vincent de Paul conferences in Wolverhampton, and within a few days, six parishes were in touch with us, offering help of all sorts. The interesting thing is that I never asked for anything!

The story of life in the inner city can be disturbing and challenging at many levels if we listen to it with our hearts. I believe that real change will happen when people of influence in the mainstream of society find ways of making friends with those who have been pushed to the edges. When Dives and Lazarus will sit round the same table. Together they can question the root causes of inequality and can also share who they are and what they have in a non-patronizing way.

Our dilemma

The growing poverty leaves us with little choice but to be patronizing when people come to our door because they have no food or no electricity. Giving out food or clothing is a relatively easy task, which can make one feel very good, but it is only possible because we are also relatively powerful and free to make decisions. It does not solve the problem for the person in the long run and it certainly does not build up community and solidarity. Brothers and sisters do not beg from one another: they share. We find ourselves caught in a real dilemma. When hungry people ask for bread, a tin of beans or a blanket, the gospel imperative 'to feed the hungry and clothe the naked' seems quite clear. But is it the good news of liberation which Christ proclaimed for his kingdom, when you know that such patronizing charity only serves to condone a fundamentally unjust system? Because of the growing needs of those who are trying to survive, we also have less time to consider what is causing such injustices. It is difficult to 'act justly, love tenderly and walk humbly with your God' all at the same time (Micah 6.8).

Local liturgy

We are often asked whether we are getting many of the lapsed back to church and if we are teaching the people about God. Very few from the estate go to church, although the majority have a deep faith in God. It is perhaps a sad reflection on the Christian churches that so many feel alienated from them. Some say the church is too 'posh', or too middle class and that they do not understand its language or ritual. For the black people, the mainline churches are so 'white' and they feel uncomfortable and embarrassed when they find themselves one of the few non-whites in the congregation. For many, especially the children, church services are boring, although most have never been inside a church except for a baptism, wedding or funeral. Also, they are very conscious of 'sin' in their lives, and believe they are banned, or excommunicated, so that they will not even ask for baptism for their children. Some also believe that they must pay for weddings and funerals. One reason for not going to the church on a Sunday is that they have no money for the collection, or good clothes to wear.

We believe that we can best meet their needs by helping them to recognize God in their own experience before they can meet him in the sacramental life of the Church. To achieve this, we have developed a local liturgy, which reflects God's action in our lives and experiences. This is known as a 'Community Celebration' and takes place in the local community centre about every six weeks. The theme is decided by the local people; also its style, content and symbols. We choose our favourite gospel passages and hymns and make up our own prayers. The programme usually includes some drama, occasionally a slide presentation, and one of the adults gives a talk on what the theme means in their life, and there is always an opportunity for spontaneous contribution. Signs of peace and reconciliation also feature. It is interesting to note how many elements of the Church's liturgy have emerged since we began our local liturgy.

For one celebration, we worked on clay, a new experience for most of us, and it was very moving to see 'Mick', on the day of the celebration, standing before us and holding what he had made in his hands. He went on to tell us that working with clay made him think of God as the Creator, who had made us all in his image, and that we should use our gifts so that we could become more like him. We normally spend a few weeks preparing the celebration so that people have plenty of time to pray and reflect on the theme. For our Easter celebration this year, two people called Mary decided to contemplate what could have been the experience of the Mother of Jesus during his death and resurrection. They shared the fruit of their reflection in the following poem:

> I am angry, bitter and broken,
> As I watch my son, your son,
> The son you gave to me,
> Battered, bruised, despised,
> Hanging now upon a tree.
>
> Why, oh God, did you not tell me
> That in the future I would see,
> The son I reared,
> Dying now in pain and misery?
> Why me Lord? Why me?
>
> I brought him up, I taught him all,
> Watched him play games of ball,
> Saw him run, saw him fall,
> Watched him as he grew tall.
>
> I'd run to him, he'd run to me,
> When comfort he did need,
> Now, now I kneel beneath him,
> Unable to soothe his wounds that bleed.
>
> I cry out: 'Please my God, let this hour pass!
> Take him from this suffering,
> Grant him peace at last.'
>
> He looks down at me and I hear him say,
> 'Mother, do not weep,
> But ponder now, on the mystery
> I gave you to keep.'
> He cries out and breathes his last.
>
> 'He's dead', I hear them say,
> Dead! Dead! No that cannot be,
> Please, my God, give him back to me.

I cry out as they take him from the tree,
'Leave him alone! He was given to me.'
For a reason and a purpose,
Of which I am not yet sure.

Now, as I hold him in my arms,
I am bewildered, shattered, confused,
I even feel, by God, I have been emotionally abused.

I walk away from his resting place secure,
Believing in my saddened heart,
I would see him no more.

I am stopped by a voice that comes from deep within,
'Mother, do not weep for me,
Look and you will see,
The very reason why I died
Is the reason why I now live!'

Live! At that word I turn and see,
The son I lost, returned to me,
Standing there in perfect peace,
No anger, bitterness or signs of rejection,
Only love and forgiveness,
Peace and joy,
No signs of death or destruction,
For living now is my son,
In his glorious resurrection.

We provide help and guidance and during the planning meetings we come forward with our own suggestions, but we try to keep in the background for the most part. The local clergy from different denominations attend, but not in an official capacity. They are invited to take a pew!

The people enjoy coming together and have numbered over a hundred on a few occasions. They feel relaxed and at home in one another's company and in their own environment. The scene often looks a bit chaotic to newcomers, especially visitors, who are more used to orderly church services. Young children wander freely about, cigarettes are sometimes passed round, the occasional dog seeks admittance, etc. People feel free to talk and laugh and share the peace of Christ but there is always space for what is often a very profound and God-filled silence. For most, it is the only experience of church that they have. I feel I could well say to them what St Paul said to the Ephesians:

> You are no longer aliens or foreign visitors; you are citizens like all the saints, and part of God's household. You are part of a building that has the apostles and prophets for its foundations, and Christ Jesus himself

as its main cornerstone. As every structure is aligned in him, all grow into one holy temple in the Lord; and you, too, in him, are built into a house where God lives, in the Spirit. (Eph 2.19–22)

Another quote that comes to mind is from the first letter of Peter:

You are a chosen race, a royal priesthood, a consecrated nation, a people set apart to sing the praises of God who called you out of darkness into His wonderful light. Once you were outside the mercy and now you have been given mercy. (1 Peter 2.9)

Numbers attending these liturgies continue to grow and many are expressing a desire to make a commitment to Christ and to belong to Christian community. They know that they would be unable to fulfil some of the promises made in our baptismal services or keep many of the other rules. Because I have been so evangelized by these people myself, I am convinced that by listening to them, learning from them and by being creative in our response to meet their needs, the whole Church could be renewed. Many of our friends here are more free to explore new models of church and of liturgy, since they are not bound by norms and conventions which others of us may find hard to abandon after years of practice. For this to happen in Britain, I feel sure also that an inter-denominational approach is essential. While we recognize that Christian theology is in essence universal, it also has to be contextual to be truly relevant. We can learn a lot from what is happening in the Basic Ecclesial Communities (BECs) of Latin America, but it would be a mistake to try and copy what they are living and doing there, since our social, cultural and historical reality is so different. We have also got much to learn from the early Church which was primarily lay and where its leaders were those most ready to serve, following the example of Christ who washed his disciples' feet (John 13.1–20).

Faith Alive

'Faith Alive' is held on Thursday nights and begins, for those who want it, with Scripture, which is read and shared in the light of our experiences. Some are almost totally unfamiliar with the gospel stories and are hearing the Word of God for the first time, like those who heard Jesus, and it is refreshing to experience their reactions. Our friends here are wonderfully open and free in their sharing; they are unafraid to express both positive and negative reactions, no matter what others might think or expect.

Scripture sharing is followed by small group work with everyone who comes, during which we share our values on a chosen theme. After this, there is an opportunity to hear about some new legislation or local initiative which is likely to affect the estate, and we go on to discuss how we can respond to these developments. We also have a role for a foreign affairs correspondent, so that we can keep up to date on world affairs and perhaps see our own situation in a broader context. Matters related to the Third World and to situations of people which seem far worse than our own always give rise to lively discussion and real concern for brothers and sisters in greater need. Although we have little to give materially, we have responded by writing and signing letters of encouragement and support to prisoners of conscience and we have been in touch with various banks regarding Third World debt, etc. It is a great shame that the people here have not got the means to lessen the gap between the 'haves' and the 'have nots', because they are so full of human goodness and compassion.

Joyful mysteries

We believe in celebrating the joyful mysteries of life, so birthdays are remembered, new-born babies welcomed and cultural feasts are given due honour, usually with a multi-cultural mix, e.g. Irish coffee drunk to the beat of Reggae music! We also have regular 'shared tables'. Someone hosts the evening and we go along with food to share, and also with our Bible and hymn books. Many are slow to invite others into their homes because they may not be able to offer chairs to sit on or a cup of tea. Also, loneliness and isolation can leave people uninterested in caring for their homes. However, 'shared tables' can provide the necessary motivation for people to start home-making and offers others in the local community the chance to help them.

Some of the most joyful occasions we have had together have been on day trips and weekends away from the estate with groups of children, adults and sometimes families. The opportunity to leave the concrete and some of the pressures of life here is so re-creating! During much of the time we laugh and talk and sing but quite a lot of it is spent in silent wonder at the beauty and extravagance of God's creation. It is really great to watch the faces of the children when they see the wide open spaces. As soon as they get out of the coach they usually begin to run and run until they are exhausted! Many of them spend hours of each day cooped up in their homes here and very few go on holiday. On a trip through North Wales, one of my travelling companions remarked: 'What a lot of space God created! How come so little of it was used when Heath Town estate was being built?' These thoughts are also echoed in a poem written by someone who has lived on the estate for many years:

I sometimes through my windows stare
And see but concrete everywhere
Then I sit down and wonder what
Can be the answer to this 'lot'?
This mess that seems to spread all round
Weren't we supposed to dwell on ground?
Or were we meant to live like this –
A good idea that went amiss!
It might have worked if thought had gone
Into the things that would go wrong
It's now too late to start again
And so Heath Town slides down the drain.

(Carmen Brearley)

Another dilemma we live with here is that while our chief aim is to build community on the estate, we also find ourselves rejoicing with those who manage to leave because they have found a better environment elsewhere for themselves and their children. Our hope is that they will continue to work for the creation of community in their new locality. Some have found this too difficult to do on their own, and have returned to the estate, in order to find the friendship and companionship they had left behind. One thing to be said in favour of the 'concrete jungle' is that it gives such immediate access to people. We live so physically close to one another that we cannot step outside our own door without meeting our neighbour. Also we share a good number of facilities and many a friendship is begun in a discussion of common woes, such as a machine that doesn't work in the laundry or broken down lifts!

The New Jerusalem

In some senses I could describe my life in Heath Town as very exciting and it is true that I never like to be away from the place for too long in case I might miss something. I do not suppose that I have ever, in my ten years here, spent a whole evening watching TV, mainly because our living room is usually full of people who drop in. Actually, unless we do our housework and tidy up early in the morning, it just does not get done. Also, we keep deciding to do a survey of all the teas and coffees served in any one week, but we haven't yet done so. We must have the best used mugs in Wolverhampton!

We do not have to watch the soap operas because the human drama happening all around us is far more real and interesting, and taken at that level helps us to cope with it. However, in a deeper sense, when we attempt to meet people and enter into their situation with the compassion of Christ, there is very real pain and suffering to be shared. This can so affect us that when our friends are depressed, so are we, when they are angry, we share it. The temptation to hopelessness and despair is very real for us. When we began to recognize this real danger of losing hope, we decided to call ourselves 'The Hope Community' as a reminder of our task to stand ready to explain the hope that is in us (1 Peter 3.15).

The support we get from one another in community is vital to sustain this hope and it keeps us from giving in to the alienation and despair that is felt by so many. We have to work hard at being community and have many structures which help us to have common aims and the same vision of what we are about. As we come to know the situation better, we find we have to update our vision statement regularly. The fundamental characteristic of being community and of working with others to help build community has not changed, but how we go about this has to be re-evaluated constantly, depending on the particular gifts within the community and the ever changing needs of the estate. Living here has also made us very aware of our personal need for solitude and space and we always make room for this in our weekly timetable.

We in the Hope Community are very aware of the wonderful opportunity we have been given to live out our Christian vocation in Heath Town and to find God in the midst of it all. We find ourselves on a journey of true communion with others who are also willing to share their gifts and also their pain, in a spirit of love. It is a great privilege to be so free and available, to our God and to others. We don't have to worry about family commitments and because we live in community, our turn to cook or prepare prayer only comes around every few weeks! We pray much and contemplate him within and among us, God, who is to be found in the mess and confusion of life. Our hopes and our dreams for Heath Town and its community are well described in the Book of Revelation which serves as a guiding light when the way forward is dark and uncertain:

> Then I saw a new heaven and a new earth; the first earth had disappeared now, and there was no longer any sea. I saw the holy city, the New Jerusalem, coming down from God out of heaven, as beautiful as a bride all dressed for her husband. Then I heard a loud voice call from the throne: 'You see this city? Here God lives among people. He will make his home among them; they shall be his people and he will be their God; his name is God-with-them. He will wipe away all tears from their eyes, there will be no more death, no more mourning or sadness. The world of the past has gone.' (Rev 21.1–4)

Some of our friends still shake their heads and say that we are wasting our time and that we should be better able to use our gifts and training in the more traditional forms of evangelization. It is true that in ten years we have done little to boost numbers in the local parish register. We are blessed with clergy who do not condemn us for these poor results; like us, they believe that 'it is God who makes things grow' (1 Cor 3.7) in his own way and his own time.

We continue to agonize about structural sin and the root causes of injustice, and we wonder if we are making any progress in either understanding or changing the situation. The system is far too complex for us and sometimes we find ourselves standing silent before it, as Jesus did during his trial (John 19). The least we can hope is that we are making some head-way in the building up of the eschatological kingdom, although it might appear that we are not doing much to change the social order. Maybe there is a 'trickle-down' effect that actually works! What we can do is to continue to give witness to Christian community and to the hope that is in us. Perhaps it is far better and more creative not to have all the answers but to keep going forward with hope in our hearts and to proclaim the Good News when people are ready to hear it.

It would be a great mistake to believe that we already know the full message contained in the Good News, and so an attitude of being open to discover more of that truth by which we can become free is essential. If this is to be a journey of conversion, then our companions on the road are our friends and neighbours here, especially those who are willing to see their life in the light of God's Word and to recognize him as he walks along with us (Luke 24.15). We know that the more we deepen our understanding of the kingdom of God, the more effective will be our attempts 'to work for a social order which will incarnate its reality'. Our prayer is to be free to re-examine some of the values that we have held so dear; to let go of our desire for success and results and to say with St Paul:

> Glory be to him whose power, working in us, can do infinitely more than we can ask or imagine. Glory be to him from generation to generation in the Church and in Christ Jesus for ever and ever. Amen.
>
> (Eph 3.20–21)

Blowing bubbles: Poplar

Christian religious experience in the urban environment

LAURIE GREEN

I'm Forever Blowing Bubbles

We live in the East End of London where football is taken very seriously. It's also our custom to have very elaborate funerals with black-plumed horses and masses of flowers. When I officiate at a funeral I usually ask the bereaved family to choose a piece of appropriate music to be played at the ceremony. Little wonder then, when Charlie died – Charlie, who had lived for his local football team – that the family asked that we should sing the West Ham Football Club anthem, 'I'm Forever Blowing Bubbles'. And as we stood there with tears streaming down our cheeks, the words of the song seemed to sum up something of what it is to be a believer amidst the harsh realities of East End life.

> I'm forever blowing bubbles
> Pretty bubbles in the air.
> They fly so high
> They nearly reach the sky,
> Then like my dreams, they fade and die.
> Fortune's always hiding; I've looked everywhere.
> I'm forever blowing bubbles,
> Pretty bubbles in the air.

It will not be easy to analyse the religious experience of inner-city people. It is fragmentary, fragile and broken. It is born of suffering, hidden and evasive. It's very difficult to describe – but it is overwhelming in the experience.

Urban experience today

In *Inside the Inner City* Paul Harrison writes: 'The inner city is now, and is likely to remain, Britain's most dramatic and intractable social problem. For here are concentrated the worst housing, the highest unemployment, the greatest density of poor people, the highest crime

72

rates and, more recently, the most serious threat posed to established law and order since the second world war.' (A reference here to the riots or 'uprisings' which happened in so many of our Urban Priority Areas – and which no doubt will happen again.) Paul Harrison continues:

> And yet it is not a peculiar, exceptional problem. For all the deprivations found concentrated in the inner city are widespread throughout the country, strongly present in the peripheral northern and Celtic regions, and in scattered pockets almost everywhere. The inner city is therefore a microcosm of deprivation, of economic decline and of social disintegration in Britain today. It is not only a particular sort of place on the map, but a symbol and summation of the dark side of a whole society.

The inner city is riddled with the remains of old and often dying industry, particularly bad housing and dereliction. It is often a picture of squalor. You will find higher than average concentrations of manual workers, low-skilled, unskilled or de-skilled men and women there.

Harrison is also right in pointing out that

> The concentration of so many disadvantaged people in a single area produces other effects: local government, poor in resources and sometimes in the quality of staffing; a poor health service, since doctors cannot find decent accommodation or much in the way of private practice; a low level of educational attainment due primarily to poor home backgrounds and the low average ability in schools; and finally high levels of crime, vandalism and family breakdown; and wherever communities of divergent cultures live together, conflicts based on religion or race.

It is difficult to describe the terror and fear in some of these areas. My daughters have been mugged, my wife once hit rock bottom despairing of the filth and concrete façades of the place. I, like most, have had physical abuse and personal intimidation. Living in the inner city is not a romantic experience unless you find a way of cutting yourself off from its realities.

In my own area the abject poverty is frightening. I was asking a group of youngsters what they wanted for Christmas. 'Suppose you won the pools', I said, 'and had lots of money – what would you ask for?' One young lad replied 'Ooh, Sir, we could have the electric on all night'. For this young boy, the thought of being able to have the lights on all evening was the summation of his dreams.

A workbook from Poplar Methodist Mission says this: 'Living in East London . . . is to experience powerlessness, voicelessness and enforced idleness. People snatch at what is on offer, are politically cynical and emotionally hard because tomorrow is certain only in as far as it is

unlikely to hold any promise that it will be different from today'
(*Beatitudes in East London*).

And if the future looks bad, what of the past? Three weeks ago, I was
asked to lead a study group of local East Enders. After we'd got to know
one another, I asked them to draw a line on a piece of paper which
represented their life to them and then to think back over that life, the
characters, the places, the happenings. This we did so that we could
reflect on them. We were not long into the exercise before we were in
tears. It was such a painful experience for the group to recall what had
happened to them in their lives. As we shared those memories with one
another I was numbed into silence on hearing such horrific stories. In
the inner city it is often the case that people cannot think about their
lives without despair and pain beyond bearing.

Yet these same people give very little outward evidence of despair.
Often they seem vibrant, carefree, bombastic and ebullient. Wonderful
friendships and unaffected fun abound. So it is that pictures, statistics
and soap operas cannot do it justice, because so much of the reality of
inner-city people lies hidden. Hidden often from themselves.

And yet we can discern certain sensitivities which are evidence of
that deeper hidden life and it may be that reflection upon these
sensitivities will provide us with a way into understanding the bubbles
and dreams that inner-city people are forever blowing.

Spiritual sensitivity

a. A sense of PLACE: Like the people of the Old Testament, inner-
city people often have a sense that 'we belong to this place as much as
it belongs to us'. Life is very territorial. The longer you live in the inner
city the more you keep to those parts which you consider as your own
'manor'. To the outsider, Limehouse, Poplar and the Isle of Dogs are
much the same area but consider marrying someone from that other
place and the family will make tense jokes and want to know why it's
necessary to look so far afield. It's relatively easy to distinguish in the
accent of true cockneys the precise area within the East End from which
they originate. A sense of the history of the community and the place
abounds.

Travelling in on the Docklands Light Railway and observing the
urban landscape I sense a deep at-homefulness and a profound sense of
belonging, even though it all looks so disgusting. It is as if I have heard
other inner-city people say 'Take off your shoes, you're on holy
ground'.

I sense the majesty, energy and power of God in heavy industry and
in that a sense of belonging with God in a solidarity with God's

creativity. I feel delighted by a sense of wonder in industry that we have been given gifts to work with such complexity and find comradeship, worth and identity in the endeavour. In the service industries too I find sacraments of God's presence – hospitals, shops, sewers and dustbin collection – all gifts in their fascinating urban complexity. And with every such gift I sense too the challenge and anguish when we get it wrong. When industry becomes unjust; when political groups seek their own aggrandizement; when social services are badly resourced; I still feel God within it all, but now yearning and suffering with his children.

This could all come very close to a romantic pantheism if it were not for the fact that the landscape and the atmosphere are all so uninspiring and deplorable in their own right. It is not the thing in itself but the profound emotions it conjures up which seem to make the place holy.

b. A sense of GOD: The Afro-Caribbean and Asian communities in the inner cities bring with them a very evident theism, but a lack of overt religious activity among the white indigenous folk does not mean that they have no faith, but that in comparison with other faiths, Western-style Christianity has not offered them an easily expressible outward sign of belonging. There is no special costume to wear, no special prayer to make, no distinctive food to eat. And there is a history of institutional oppression which makes them reluctant ever to voice their faith in God through the usual church channels. But come Christmas Eve Midnight Mass, or the equally well attended All Souls Requiem for the departed, and even the anti-institutional will turn up to express their sensitivities.

Derek Waxham was ordained in East London in 1979 as an auxiliary minister after growing up locally. An anecdote from Derek's ministry focuses this last point very well.

> One evening when I was having a drink in the pub I suddenly found I was surrounded by three people that I was brought up to be afraid of because of their reputations. The one who was most known as a very villainous character said to me: 'I want you. I'll see you in the toilet', and he walked off. My stomach turned over but I thought: 'I'm a forty-six-year-old man; I've got to go out there.' So I went out and stood next to him. He said: 'You know I lost my Doreen?' So I said: 'Yes, Alfie, I know you lost your Doreen.' He said: 'I want you to do me a favour.' So the first tensions began to leave me and I felt relieved. He said: 'I want you to say some prayers on Sunday morning for me.' And he completely changed – his whole attitude changed. He was then a person asking a favour. Whereupon I said: 'Yes. OK Alfie. Why don't you come?' 'No, no', he said. I said: 'If you don't want to go to church

you don't have to. I'll still do it for you. I just thought you might like to hear it.' 'All right then', he said, 'I'll meet you outside the church at 9.25.'

When I got round there he was waiting. So I opened the door. But he said to me: 'No, Derek, sorry. Places like this are not for the likes of me. I'm going down to the flower market. You do the praying.' I said: 'Come off it Alfie, this is bloody ridiculous.' But he wouldn't have it. So I said: 'All right. I'll do it', and he went off. The service started and we got to the intercessions, and I looked up at the congregation and I realized that the door at the back of the church was open, and I could see a foot in the door. When it came to those whose loved ones were lost I mentioned his name and prayed for Doreen. As I finished I saw the foot disappear and the door close.

About a fortnight later I was in the pub and the governor came up to me and said: 'Blimey, you're honoured. What's all this about?' and he gave me a large scotch and dry. I said: 'Who gave me this?' He said: 'Over there', and nodded to the other side of the bar. When I looked, it was Alfie. He looked at me and without saying any words he just put his thumb up to say thank you.

Since then, on the anniversary of her death he still does the same thing – he searches me out in the pub, waits till there's nobody looking, or I go to the toilet, and he tells me would I please do the same thing.

In inner cities church-going is low (some 2 per cent of the population) but belief in God stands as high as 76 per cent (BBC, 1981). However, this is to beg the question, 'What sort of God is believed in?' There is a well-rehearsed story of the woman who, when asked 'Do you believe in a God who can change the course of events on earth?', replied 'No, just the ordinary one'.

The context of the inner city certainly affects the understanding people have of the God they give assent to. The situation is so very harsh for inner-city dwellers that God can be perceived by them as, on the one hand, the Loving Protector, who saves them from the worst effects of destitution and oppression, or at the other extreme, as the harshest Judging Teacher, who sends misfortune saying 'this will hurt me more than it will hurt you'. As an example of the first, there's George, who comes to church at All Souls-tide to remember the soul of his dearly departed heroine, Dame Anna Neagle. George, who has been coming annually for years, says constantly to me 'God is good, God is good'. Despite the torture of life, he has a Loving Protector in heaven who in the end will make all things well.

At the other end of the spectrum some, under the pressure of misfortune, will bitterly reject the God in whom they still believe. On a tombstone in my graveyard someone has scratched with a heavy crayon 'God is a bastard'. As I reflect on that I can only turn over and over in my mind the words 'My God, my God, why hast thou forsaken me?'

But third, in the inner city there is also a God of Last Resort. Someone will say 'We are at such a loss and so unprotected here that if we do not have faith then what do we have? Nothing!' There is the God of Last Resort, otherwise everything is loss. My Stalinist grandmother, who had suffered poverty beyond imagining, would say 'If there wasn't a God, there wouldn't be nothing. Not just nothing but not even nothing.'

In our doctrine of the Trinity these three different Gods find their rough and ready unity. For many, I suspect that God the Father is the Judging Teacher. There are many in the Sunday School who have no loving father around the home anyway, so father as judging teacher is about right in their experience. The Loving Protector God on the other hand is there in the figure of Jesus, the one who knows crucifixion and yet has the power to save. And the God of Last Resort who has simply got to be there, sensed inside and around by those who must have something, is to be found in God the Holy Spirit.

When I used to think of these things in academic terms I could never understand how it could be that, during the early centuries of the Christian faith, the doctrine of the Trinity was argued out quite vehemently in every street market. Now I begin to understand a little.

c. A sense of SIN: When one lives amidst the structural sin of the inner city it becomes clear that the real sin is not in the areas of poverty themselves but elsewhere, where decisions are made and where power resides. But it is experienced at its harshest where its consequences are felt, the inner city. I have never had to wait upon radical change in someone else for me to have a chance of reasonable existence. But that is the predominant experience of those we live amongst. It is an experience of being trapped by sinfulness.

Sometimes one has to stand silent before this structural sin just as Jesus did before Pilate at his trial (John 19). I was once involved in the work of a Christian advice bureau and I remember well the elation we all felt on one occasion when we had managed at last to secure Council accommodation for an elderly woman who had been made homeless. But our jubilation was soon quenched when it dawned upon us that all we had managed to achieve was some nifty queue-jumping. The root problem had not gone away, there were still too many homeless in line for too few homes. Structural sin abounds.

In the inner city I will often hear the sad complaint 'I must have done something wrong to be punished like this'. For many there is this inward questioning, but such a sense of personal sin, whether ill-founded or not, can also produce an accepting apathy especially in those who are in fact more sinned against than sinning. An acceptance of general sinfulness in oneself and in others can, when there seems no justice in it, lead to a ready conspiracy and repetition of the sinfulness. It becomes a self-fulfilling prophecy of degradation.

Frustrated guilt can itself produce powerful anger which is difficult to dissipate. Jacky, who has battered his mother repeatedly, often comes to the Rectory in a sky-high rage, demanding to enter the church with me for prayer. There he will stand at the altar screaming at God in anger 'Look after my mother! God, look after my mother!' It can take ages for his rage to subside.

Many are very conscious of sin in their lives and do not often sense forgiveness. Not so long ago, during a weekday Mass, Frank had wandered into the church and was sitting at the back nervously. When we came to the confession prayer he shouted out 'I topped a geezer. I really didn't want to do it.' He had served his time for the murder but had never opened up to me about it. As the absolution was pronounced I heard him say 'My God, I feel real cool now'. Sin, in all its aspects, is powerfully sensed in the inner city.

I have described the sense of place, God and sin to be found in inner-city people. But can we accept that such emotional resonances as these should be described as religion? Or is all that I've been saying about these sensitivities simply so much sentimental self-indulgence?

What is religious experience?

What is religion? Some will argue that religious interpretations of human experience are not what constitute religious experience itself. They would look for an awareness of the supernatural or the transcendent within the experience before they could pronounce it as religious. I have great sympathy with that thought but the limitations of such other-worldly expectations are boldly relativized by the Passionist Father, Austin Smith, who asks from the inner city 'Is crucifixion a religious experience?' By restricting our religious concerns to supernatural and not empirical events (like football for example, which has often been quoted as having strong liturgical elements) we could be denying ourselves an opportunity to hear what the Urban Priority Area has specifically to offer to the debate – that is, that there is real spirit in physicality! That things spiritual can be very physical indeed – hence incarnation and sacrament.

In the inner city there is a great warehouse full of spirituality which is often referred to as 'implicit' or 'folk' religion which is yearning for expression and which the Church is expected somehow to articulate.

There is also a tribalism to be expressed (as in football) which is to do with the affirmation and valuing of belonging and identity. But where in inner-city experience does all this become religion?

Folk religion is not systematic and is often self-contradictory. Church-going offers some possibility of orthodoxy in faith and super-stition, whereas the non-institutional nature of folk religion lets it get quite out of hand, unorthodox and muddled. Its muddled nature and its brokenness I take to be a more honest approximation to the real experience out of which the expression comes.

It is often the same with the folk language of the inner city. My mother tongue, the cockney language, is a good example. It is full of contradiction, ambiguity, word play, hyperbole and rhetorical ques-tion. But this style of speech it seems to me is a very fair representation and rendering of the situation out of which the language emerges. The inner-city experience, like the language, is also full of contradiction, exaggeration and conundrum. Rich minds give voice to a random flow of ideas, literal-mindedness, body language, question language, nonce words like 'innit', which in themselves have no referent at all. Some-times and often the religious expression in word and action is similarly random, literal, non-specific, questioning and brutal.

It would not be right therefore to look for a religious experience emanating from the inner city which was logically ordered, orthodox and systematic any more than it would be right to look for a language there of an ordered style. The language of the inner city expresses the inner-city experience and the religion of the inner city should likewise express the environment from which it comes.

But for all this I am still inclined to expect some yearning for a reference to the transcendent God, in a word or action, before I am completely happy to speak of it as specifically 'religious' – and it is therefore to that aspect of inner-city experience that I now wish to turn. And in this I am again helped by the work of Austin Smith. 'Where', he asks, 'does the resilience of inner-city people come from?'

Yearning for God

Where does the resilience of inner-city people come from? It seems to me that being 'human' in the inner city means reaching out for tran-scendence to survive at all! Sin, within and without, presses down upon the populace in every conceivable way. Stand in the street after the recent urban uprisings and witness the devastation – the results of the people's frustrated and unchannelled energies. Experience the silent groaning of alienation, sinfulness and powerlessness welling up from the pavements as the 'blood of our brothers and sisters cries out to God from the ground' (cf. Gen 4.10). And as we stand still alongside the poor we find ourselves at Gethsemane or at Calvary, for 'Where creation is sinned against, where human beings suffer, Jesus is crucified'. Jesus comes into the city and things are done to him. He has a certain style of acceptance of it. He works to remove injustice and suffering but where that is not possible then he transfigures suffering and uses it as raw material for love.

And I see the same style time and again in the lives of inner-city people. When I tell people that I meet Christ in the inner city I am saying that I meet with people who do what the transcendent does in the incarnation. They 'exist with and suffer'. There is no dependency on status, prestige or security, and yet they transcend – they rise above – they transfigure the suffering in love. And even more than that, for 'where causes are won for authentic freedom and power over destiny in the work of creation, Jesus rises again'.

The words of the First World War poet Wilfred Owen come very close to expressing this same insight:

> I, too, saw God through mud, –
>   The mud that cracked on cheeks when wretches smiled.
>   War brought more glory to their eyes than blood,
>   And gave their laughs more glee than shakes a child.
>
> Merry it was to laugh there –
>   Where death becomes absurd and life absurder.
>   For power was on us as we slashed bones bare
>   Not to feel sickness or remorse or murder. . . .
>
> I have perceived much beauty
>   In the hoarse oaths that kept our courage straight;
>   Heard music in the silentness of duty;
>   Found peace where shell-storms spouted reddest spate.
>
> Nevertheless, except you share
>   With them in hell the sorrowful dark of hell,
>   Whose world is but the trembling of a flare
>   And heaven but as the highway for a shell,
>
> You shall not hear their mirth:
>   You shall not come to think them well content
>   By any jest of mine. These men are worth
>   Your tears. You are not worth their merriment.
>   (from 'Apologia Pro Poemate Meo', November 1917)

The transcendent in that experience is no pantheism – seeing God in things – but is the intimate sacrament of Passion.

My fear, in speaking like this, is that I may be accused of holding out religion as an opiate to the people, for so it often is. But it is in the resilience of inner-city people, their courage, determination, immediacy, serenity, rage and numbness that I sense a yearning for transcendence which, when accomplished, issues in transfiguration – and sometimes, just sometimes, in resurrection. Perhaps that is why people turn up so enthusiastically to Candlemass – to see again the warmth and light of the purging and transfiguring fire.

But I am a romantic and so must quickly spin on my heels and announce that it is not always seen thus! Many, if not most, do not see it like this at all. And there are indeed many inner-city people who would not wish me to interpret their experience in these church-conjured terms. Theodicies are beside the point for the people of the inner city, for here rationalism is bankrupt. People learn to live by facts, stories and fun, for they are only too aware of evil. If you speak to them of God's so-called option for the poor they may well reply 'But there is no material evidence for it, is there? If God is on our side then we don't appear to have a very responsible ally. The whole experience is of fragmentation, shattered and splintered brokenness, and you won't be able to explain it to people who don't live here.'

Why empty churches?

The Church does not seem to most inner-city people to be the appropriate vehicle of expression for their religious beliefs. Joost de Blank, one-time Bishop of Stepney, once remarked 'They are wonderful people in the East End. They will do anything for you except go to church.' But church-going and Christianity are not synonymous. Most people never think about church – it's a foreign world. Most books about the inner city make no mention of it! By and large, UPA people know nothing of church and often have never been inside one.

Most do not see it as important nor do they know much about it. Whilst out visiting in the parish the other day, dressed in clerical collar, I was asked by a young teenager 'Are you a pope?' Engaging in a street procession of witness last Easter I heard two women in the street arguing about who we were. 'I think they're Catholics. No, I'm wrong. I think they're Christians.' When we were re-enacting the Way of the Cross on Good Friday in the local street market, one stall-holder got quite carried away and joined in the action. But what he had failed to realize as he joined in the play was that the man carrying the cross was the good guy and not the villain. He had never heard the story in his life before.

Some locals are interested to hear about the faith and I am always showing inquisitive youngsters round the church, but by and large what inner-city people know about church does not appeal to them.

UPA people come at it all from such a different perspective and it is worth investigating some of the assumptions that make inner-city people feel that church religion is not for them.

First, the Church seems to present them with *a fruitless hierarchy of values* which, whilst being called 'moral', do not convince them as worthwhile. The quest for a personal holiness and 'victory over tempta- tion' which denigrates feelings of aggression, sexuality and other important survival instincts with the stigma of guilt does not seem to be sensible. For the inner-city survivor, the Church 'teaches as doctrines the commandments of human beings' and pronounces things 'illegal' which are self-evidently not 'out of order'. There are problems about God's own morality too. It would be easier for inner-city folk to accept a God who is above right and wrong – one who simply demands assent and obedience. But, as Fred would say, 'God gives you a load of crap and then you're supposed to believe he loves you'. 'How can there be any happiness in heaven when there's misery in hell? – God expects you to be pretty selfish to enjoy heaven!'

Second, the Church wants *to wrap God up in abstraction*. To pin God down to systems of abstract doctrine seems quite contrary to inner- city experiences of an indefinable, ineffable God, a God you can chal- lenge but not deny. The New Testament resonates with this, for the discourse about text and doctrine which takes place on the Road to Emmaus does not turn out to be the time of disclosure of the living God. That only happens when the stranger is taken off the streets, given some warmth and a meal and participates in the very concrete act of sharing bread and wine (Luke 24.13–35). So the assumption of inner-city people is that they trust the truth of their senses whereas the Christian faith is so often presented in terms of metaphysical and subjective experi- ence.

The third assumption of inner-city people about Christian faith which conflicts with conventional church teaching is that *it is not necessary to find ultimate meanings*. Bernstein's work on language codes reminds us that when working-class parents answer children's ques- tions it is more likely to be in terms of assertion than explanation. If asked why leaves fall in autumn, Bernstein registers that the answers are likely to be of the order of 'because they do', or 'why shouldn't they?', or 'leaves do that'. So when the Christian theologian sees the faith as a way of finding answers to questions, searching for meanings, and making causal connections, they are working against the language system of UPA life. That system seems to prefer to focus in detail on the thing at hand and define it rather than to place it in relationship with other things. And yet this language system is quite adept at producing what Ian Ramsay called the 'disclosure situation' where a religious truth simply 'clicks' rather than being reasoned through.

Two months ago my Parochial Church Council had a discussion on the matter of the ordination of women to the priesthood. As the discussion meandered on I thought for all the world that the final vote would be a strong No. But I was very much mistaken. The argument, whilst seeming to me to be heading towards a No vote, had convinced the participants, I'm glad to say, of the good sense of the proposition at hand. They voted in favour. The subtlety of the language code can so easily be mistaken for naivety by those who do not speak the language.

This brings us to the fourth conflicting assumption. It is that *working-class language emphasizes belonging*. The need to stick together for survival is very strong and the language codes are used to sustain solidarity rather than to define the unique differences between persons, as it is in middle-class discourse. What would seem to be an over-indulgence in nonce words, repetitions, and rhetorical question, esoteric slang and 'in' phrases, is all geared to creating belonging and solidarity. The middle-class focus upon exclusive, private, subjective experience as the locus for encounter with God is often reflected in the language of the Church, and Christian professionals may thereby alienate the people of the inner city who, as in the Old Testament, see God especially in public observance, groups, families, and the nation.

So we come, fifthly, to *spontaneity*. Living for today and never minding the consequences for tomorrow is spawned of having a tomorrow which is so untrustworthy and beyond control that the discipline of long-term strategy proves always to be a nonsense. To save for such a precarious future is not a strong element in the culture! Many will lower their sights, feel happy with the life they lead now and 'have a laugh', whereas they see church people saying goodbye to the fun of today in order to participate in a life hereafter which doesn't sound much fun and, as with any future, may not exist anyway. Likewise with *prayer*. Inner-city people certainly pray a great deal but they sense that rather than the spontaneity of prayer, the Church prefers to indulge in an elaborate contorted self-discipline where all the anger and desire of prayer is seen as something to achieve mastery over rather than to be enjoyed. UPA people are more inclined to trust their feelings and instincts (it helps them survive on the street). But the Church expects them to subordinate these instincts to reason and sense.

Finally, there is the well-rehearsed *alienation* which the people of the inner city feel from the institutional Church in their midst. Urban

Priority Area inhabitants have every reason to mistrust authorities and the Church has often not served them well. Class, literacy, ethos and hierarchy have all taken turn to promote an alienation which can only be dispelled by the repeated efforts of clergy and lay people alike.

In all that I have said about inner-city people and their assumptions thus far, I have run the risk of making the crass mistake of resounding generalization. It seems to me that there is a certain inevitability in this, given the task set me, but I suspect that by and large these findings of mine tally in large measure with others' experience. I can only apologize and plough on.

Given all these reservations and conflicting assumptions, it is interesting that religious programmes and church services on the TV are not generally switched off in homes in the inner city. On the contrary, in some areas of the East End of London, where I grew up and now live and work, the Church is very much on the scene and finds its niche in the schema of inner-city life. Given a religious sense in the people of the inner city coupled with a strong suspicion of the institutional church, how do these marry up?

Folk religion and the Church

The Church has its part to play in establishing and giving voice to the experience of the transcendent in the midst of the inner city. It often tries to do this on its own terms but it is instructive to ask what aspects of the Church's life and expression UPA people themselves value and respect as a fitting expression of God's presence with them. How do the 'folk' approach the Church?

First, the constant help and availability of the Church, especially its clergy, is taken for granted *not as charity but as a right*. It may look to outsiders as if I pay Eddie to come to church. The fact of the matter is however that he receives alms from me after the service which is his right and which helps him through the week. If the free food which we give to the poor during the week is not of decent quality, the same rule applies and they complain with great feeling. And right that they should.

Second, there is *a representative quality about church attendance*. The priest is expected to pray daily for the parish and is often asked by the casual passer-by 'Say one for me'. Even when Granny goes to church, her family are often expecting that she is there on their behalf. In some respects she is even there as a representative of the other elderly people of the neighbourhood.

Third, *buildings are sacrosanct*. When our local St Matthias church fell into profound disrepair the local people were outraged. Outraged to such an extent, it has to be said, that whole sections of the fabric were carefully taken away by parishioners and built into their own homes. It is not altogether unusual in Poplar now to find stained glass in the bathrooms. 'The place belongs to us', they fume, 'and it's not right to see it wasted and falling to bits like that.' The local church building represents childhood memories, family ties, weddings and funerals. It is their holy place, a temple in which there is common ownership and a common sense of worth.

Fourth, I'm glad to report that in general *the presence of clergy* is counted as a blessing. Indeed, it has been remarked that there seems to be less anti-clericalism outside the church than inside it. We are often figures of fun to be japed at in the street, but when we are asked to attend at a family event or crisis we are reckoned to be affirming the presence and blessing of God, the God who is already at work. The clergy can be very close and yet they will always be regarded as different and separate. So it is that as theologians we clergy can never be there to make the story but only to tell it.

Fifth, *worship's task* is to affirm the continuing importance of the transcendence in the midst. Candles, smell, movement and music are all shared ways to touch on the numinous, whereas words seem to be less universal a vehicle. It is difficult to know what a more working-class liturgy would be but I suspect that it would have to be similar to the temple worship in a *Raiders of the Lost Ark* movie. The atmosphere is all important, with the right mixture of emotion and toughness. Medieval plain chant from a heady choir or the gentle strumming of guitars do equally as well, but it must be direct, moving and challenging.

Lastly, in the '*rites of passage*' the Church is expected to be present and affirm the transcendent moments of life – birth, love and death. But to understand what is happening in these rites of passage in the inner city we need for a moment to consider the relationship between belief and belonging.

Belief and belonging

Belief in belief is a preoccupation of the Western mind and culture. In the inner city to believe is a social practice, so even attenders at worship may not articulate their beliefs in quite the way we expect. Further, those who do not attend but still like to be termed 'C of E' to affirm that they 'belong', would rarely wish to assent to any of the doctrinal beliefs of the Church of England. This may appear to be a very cavalier approach to the sacred tenets of the organization to which one affirms allegiance but it is felt that a belief system is not necessary in order to comply with life's demands. It's an intellectual luxury that few can afford, whereas *you do need to belong!*

In the inner city the need to belong is paramount and secures survival. It is the most important way the UPA person has of transcending the brutal. It is a road to transcendence. It is a way of doing theology. Not to belong can mean loneliness and danger. There are therefore a number of important symbols and sacraments in the UPA language of belonging which we might mention here.

There is first the claustrophobic *intensity of the place*. The crowded concrete jungle of the inner city means we live within easy access of one another and this can sometimes be conducive to community, sometimes to stress. The crowded market can be a good place to belong even if it's not such a good place to shop any longer.

The extended family is another sign of working-class culture (both black and white) but it is breaking down under the pressures of the values of the dominant culture and economic persuasion.

And as with the family so also *class is important to a sense of belonging*. The logic of working-class awareness is that the oppressed should learn to stick together as much as the oppressors do, for experience tells them that the world is a fight for survival, and solidarity brings security. This form of security is at risk in itself however since more and more the less powerful classes are being convinced that there is no such thing as class at all. As the conservative commentator Peregrine Worsthorne once said, 'There is no such thing as class war, and we are determined to win it'. And so the people of the inner city have one less security, one less solidarity. They cannot belong to what reputedly no longer exists.

Unlike class, *ethnicity* cannot so easily be denied, but a sense of belonging along these lines brings dangers of disintegration and strife as well as solidarity and a sense of well-being. The black-led Churches are, for example, symbols of belonging and identity for those who feel alienated from the indigenous culture. Pushed aside by white groups they struggle to find a home and a theology which comes out of their own culture and experience. Some 'conventional' denominational churches have welcomed the black members and found a new expansive belongingness to share, but this is far rarer than it should be.

Amongst the white population there is correspondingly a growing realization of, and fear of, *loss of culture*. They look around and see new evident cultures of self-aware people who have distinctive food, dress, and rituals and there grows up an increasing wish to have their own children christened and taught the Christian faith so that they too may have a pride of belonging – a pride which at one time they could take for granted, but no longer. This pride easily spills over into race hatred, especially when there is an apparent taking over of the 'place' which has been part of their own sense of identity for so long. For place is another great symbol or sacrament which has operated in the inner city to promote and define the transcendence of belonging. The tribal white culture of the East End is territorial and exclusive, but it has helped to create their necessary sense of belonging. It has now become increasingly problematic.

As the environment of, and opportunities for, the inner city are yet further eroded and destroyed, its inhabitants feel more threatened. For although the need to belong is becoming more desperate, the opportunity to belong is becoming more intangible and illusive.

It is not belief and doctrine but belonging which is the key to transcendent experience in the inner city. UPA people believe in belonging – belonging to the place, to one another and to God. But there are fewer and fewer ways to express this fundamental experience. It is within the context of this discussion that we can now return to our consideration of inner-city 'rites of passage' and begin to make more sense of what we find.

Rites of passage

The family, its maintenance and its extension is of immense importance in the matter of belonging. The breaking down of accepted patterns makes it even more important to folk that the rites which are there to affirm and protect the family should not be taken from them. The creeping exclusivism of the Church of England with regard to its rites of passage is therefore most unhelpful and is highly resented.

A celebration of the transcendent miracle of birth, the naming and welcoming of the child into the community are all to be found in *the rite of baptism*. Some will also say when they come for baptism that they are wanting to 'put that little seed there', so that their child too may have a way into the transfiguration of its life's experience.

A *church wedding* means an expensive occasion but many locals will say it also signifies God's blessing. It is certainly about belonging and identity – belonging to one another, being someone in the family and in the community, and if you can afford it, even appearing in the local newspaper.

Funerals in the East End of London have to be experienced to be believed. No cost is spared on horses, hearse, flowers and the wake. On walking around East London cemetery you are accosted by a community relentlessly sharing its feelings of desolation, loss and solidarity. Here the local cultural love of rhyming and poetry comes into its own.

There is the enormous tombstone for 'Billy: Tragically taken from us 5th Feb. 1990 aged 24'. Atop the massive black marble tomb is a brightly coloured stone dartboard and the parents' words are inscribed beneath. The solidarity of mourners and readers is poignantly expressed in the challenging opening lines:

> Have you ever lost a son who was everything to you;
> One you loved so very much and miss him like we do?
> Have you ever had the heartache or ever felt the pain?
> We pray you never do.
> Because if tears could build a stairway
> And memories build a lane
> We would have walked to heaven
> To bring our son back again.

And despite all the sense of tragedy, God's will is not once questioned on all the stones you read. So for example,

> Those cheerful smiles, that heart of gold
> The dearest voice the world could hold
> A beautiful soul in a garden of rest
> It's true what they say
> God chooses the best.

There's even a shade of guilt that we should want our loved ones back –

> A wonderful Mum has gone to rest
> For each and all she did her best
> Please God, forgive a silent tear
> A silent wish that she was here.

I have quoted a few of these poems to give at least a glimpse of what an overwhelming experience it is to read inscription after inscription of shared community loss written in the language of the local people. To me they are eloquent and very 'religious'.

These rites of passage are communally embedded actions in relation to transcendent events. They affirm belonging, to one another and finally to God, just as in the incarnation God in turn says he belongs here too amongst the poor. In the parable of the sheep and the goats, as elsewhere, Jesus says of himself that he is to be found here, served here, and ministered to here among those who are considered to be the least (Matt 25.31–46).

There is no credal orthodoxy in this folk religion and the local people's use of the church and its rites of passage. It seems to me that it is more an example of the people of the inner city 'forever blowing bubbles'. But it may be that the bubbles are significant and worthy religious aspirations, even real experiences of the transcendent, but that they have simply not been caught and bottled by Roald Dahl's *Big Friendly Giant*. And for the BFG why not read CofE?

Nevertheless, some inner-city people will want to give more succinct expression to their experience of the transcendent. And some indeed will do this through regular attendance at the local church. Let us finally look together at the beliefs and practices of inner-city regular church members. It is here in church that the priest, the structures and the tradition will make the religion all the more predictable and Christianly orthodox, but the same primal experiences of the local inner-city people and the place will be the key elements to an understanding of what is going on for the people in the pews.

Going to church

It is certainly not easy in Poplar to make a clear distinction between those inside and those outside the Church. Demarcation lines are not always precise, but some clearly attend very regularly, and they attend in increasing numbers. Once in, the Church's traditions of Bible, liturgy, sacrament and so on, begin to resonate with people's felt experiences so that experience feeds the tradition and tradition feeds experience.

Like those outside who maintain that you can still be a 'good' Christian without going to church, those who attend will agree to some extent that ethics must play a large part in Christian faith. For it seems to them that to see religion as ethics, not merely metaphysics, is to root Christianity more firmly in the 'real' world of here and now. They are concerned that the faith should not just be reduced to a set of academic opinions but rather that it should cash out in fine action and brave community. (If you like, orthopraxis versus orthodoxy.) Yet for all the concern for ethics, there's still not all that much regard for middle-class values. It is not so much a concern for peace and justice as for contentment and judgement.

But for all the stress on ethics as a key to what being a Christian in the inner city is about, there is a strong contradictory stress on worship for worship's sake. And here it is grace not works which comes into its own.

Churches differ from street to street but from the many and varied expressions of faith let me just select four themes which I certainly discern in my own congregation.

Celebration: When that sense of transcendence in, and in spite of, the inner city is truly expressed in church life and worship, many inner-city people talk of their first visit to such worship as 'a home-coming'. I am then reminded of the words from the parable of the prodigal son:

' "For my son was dead and now he is alive again; he was lost and now he is found", *and they began to make merry.*' This profound sense of gratitude and transfiguration can be expressed in a flamboyant knees-up or in the traditional pomp and ceremonial of Anglo-Catholic worship. By and large, the black-led Churches are more celebratory in their liturgy and theology than sacramental and the excitement of their celebration is infectious. In the inner city where there is so little affirmation of the worth of human beings it is this celebration which can send the spirit soaring.

Community: The affirmation of the soul of the community is often one of the gifts of the Holy Spirit to the local inner-city congregation. There grows up, from the continuing awareness of the experience of transcendence among the group, a shared common wisdom and vision of what is best in the place and in the people. It gives direction for community action and a pride of the right sort, a pride which affirms but is not at the expense of the other. And with the empowerment of the community comes the liberation of individuals' gifts. In our own community we begin to glory in the talents of Jack the boxer who turns out to be a fine painter, of Benny the addict who has such acting talent, or Bristol Steve who welds so expertly. Often it is a community of disagreement, not sweetness and polite gestures to be sure, but it certainly is a community.

Sacramental discernment: The Cartesian dis-ease which many Christians have with the physical is not something with which the inner city feels at home. There is a ready appreciation of the spiritual depth of physical experience and this is taken up in worship in drama, pictures, processions, candles, statues, colour, smell, noise and so on. It is a celebration and a moving offering of who and what people feel themselves to be before God in all their humanity.

The intensity of devotion in an inner-city Holy Week speaks of a people who know transcendence and the numinous in the face of domination. The faces of those coming forward to venerate the crucifix on Good Friday speak volumes of experience and discernment of what Jesus was about in that self-giving action. And then in line came old Tom who couldn't quite kneel down to kiss the foot of the statue and so reached out to the crucified figure, patted him gently on the head and said, 'Well done Sir'.

And for many small congregations, the sacrament will be their own physical 'presence' in the inner city. Their own preparedness to stay true is a tiny but precious symbol of faithfulness. Sometimes such groups become the elderly guardians of a long-past style and forgotten era, but they still hold fast to that originating experience of the transcendent in their lives.

Acted parables: Many groups and congregations hear in the Christian traditions of the faith such resonances with their own life experiences that they are moved to respond in action in the community. This often issues in political engagement, pastoral or social work, care for the needy and so on. Rarely can one find an inner-city church where there is not at least some attempt made to respond selflessly to the needs of those around.

Some groups will respond to their at-homeness in the church by looking deeper together at the Christian traditions of Bible, liturgy and so on. The biblical stories which resonate however are not, in my experience, centred around the themes of exodus and renewal so much as the trials, temptations and crucifixion of Jesus, the promised land, exile and the beast of Revelation. I have written elsewhere (*Power to the Powerless*) about these biblical discoveries and the parabolic actions which they generated in inner-city groups in Birmingham.

In this way many find a faith to live and die by.

Paying attention

The inner city is a place of stories. There are many personal stories but more than personal story it is the community's story that I hear told. In our case it is the story of the place: Poplar, Limehouse and the Isle of Dogs; All Saints' Church, the constant bombing, the shipyards and dock-strikes, the coming of Docklands, the building of Canary Wharf, the closing of the hospitals, cinemas and shops – continuity and discontinuity. Story after story, all to prove that we are not absolute beginners but a people with a long history of survival. Remembering the past has its own pain but it reminds us of the values we hold dear.

The key to understanding the people and religion of the inner city is to *listen with rapt attention to the story*. For it sometimes occurs to the listener that they are no longer simply listening to our story but to The Story. It is in this same attentive manner that Jesus discerns God in the prostitute, tax collector, and foreigner. It is a spirituality of listening for God in the inner city.

I hope that the next time you visit the inner city, you too will hear the whisper of the transcendent in the story and you will sing with me the local anthem, 'I'm Forever Blowing Bubbles'. Or perhaps, if you prefer it, the similar sentiment of the final words of the *Te Deum*,

> In you Lord is our hope.
> Let us not be confounded at the last.

References

Geoff Ahern and Grace Davies, *Inner City God* (Hodder and Stoughton, 1987).
Beatitudes in East London (Poplar Methodist Mission, 1984).
John Bennington, *Culture, Class and Christian Beliefs* (Scripture Union, 1973).
Wesley Carr (ed.), *Say One for Me: The Church of England in the Next Decade* (SPCK, 1992).
David Cockerell, *Beginning Where We Are* (SCM Press, 1989).
Roald Dahl, *The BFG* (Puffin, 1984).
Laurie Green, *Power to the Powerless* (Marshall Pickering, 1987).
Laurie Green, *Let's Do Theology* (Mowbray, 1990).
Paul Harrison, *Inside the Inner City* (Pelican, 1985).
Ian Ramsay, *Religious Language* (SCM, 1967).
Austin Smith, *Passion for the Inner City* (Sheed and Ward, 1983).
John H. Vincent, *Into the City* (Epworth, 1982).
Margaret Walsh, *Here's Hoping* (UTU, Sheffield, 1991); see above, pp. 52–71.
Derek Waxham in *Building an Indigenous Church in East London* (START, Oxford House, Stepney, 1980).

Part Three

The sinews of an urban theology

Praise

DAVID F. FORD AND ALISTAIR I. McFADYEN

Week after week, congregations of Christians gather in Urban Priority Areas to worship God. They – and also, often, the wider Church – channel a great deal of time, energy and resources into this. Is it worthwhile to spend time building up a worshipping community? Is it a waste, carried on because of the Church's momentum from the past? Or a distraction from the real issues? Would it matter if the Church stopped worshipping? Should it do so, and devote its energy and resources to the many urgent and practical needs?

Is it not also striking how a great deal of Christian discussion, analysis and activity in these areas seems to have little or no living relation to the basic Christian activity of worship, and even to have no reference to God?

Our aim in this chapter is to explore the meaning of praising God and of sin against God as crucial for orienting Christian presence, understanding and action in Urban Priority Areas. It is not by any means accidental that the main focus for Christian identity and community is gathering together to praise and thank God. We do this not only because it is essential for celebrating the heart of faith. It is also vital for enabling personal (and communal) dignity and identity and judging what is right and wrong (and why it is so). Above all, it is about God energizing and shaping commitments, the use of time and resources, and active engagement with the realities of living in a UPA.

Scandalous praise

It may well be that in our culture the most scandalous thing about Christianity is not so much to do with the cross or death, but is in the area of goodness, resurrection and a God of joy. Urban Priority Areas fit the kind of evidence often quoted against the credibility of a good God who is to be celebrated, praised and adored without qualification. Even if this God is believed in, it might seem that in areas shot through with poverty, powerlessness and other disadvantages, the last thing that Christians ought to do is undermine the sense of the seriousness of the situation by being 'too joyful'. Does this not smack of escapism, 'other-worldliness' and even frivolity? And whose interests are served by such joy found in present circumstances? Against such attitudes it is not enough (though it is necessary) to place the whole tradition of Christianity and its most lively communities in diverse circumstances century after century. We need to penetrate what Christian praise is. For what is being asked here is how realistic Christian faith can be in its most basic mode of relating to God. No account of a situation is truly realistic if it is disconnected from the transforming God. We are saturated with accounts of reality that never mention God and implicitly deny God's reality. It therefore requires a drastic change in our habits of mind and imagination to 'think God'. Newspapers, television, our educational system and the rest of our culture deeply condition us to an agnostic or atheist 'realism'. This becomes normality, an orthodoxy which labels anyone taking God seriously as odd, or at best holding curious private beliefs of no public importance. The conditions of UPAs (at least as commonly understood) often lend themselves to reinforcing this. Christians in UPAs are in the grip of this false normality as much as any others. For those most concerned about the conditions, there is also the special danger of an activist, problem-solving realism which loses the life of praise and leaves them wondering what the significance of their faith in God is in relation to their commitments and the whole situation.

If God is as identified in the Bible and the mainstream of Christianity, he is the Creator who takes responsibility for the whole of creation. He enters into its distortion, brokenness, pain and suffering and takes those on himself in the world's evil, and the resurrection opens a future through evil and beyond it. The good news is that this is the truth of every situation, no matter how hopeless and dead to any good future it appears. The Spirit of this truth, this God, invites us to an equally radical and loving involvement with our world, through which unimaginable transformations are promised as we are drawn by God into God's future.

So praise of this God is the ultimate realism. What does that mean? It means first of all that it is about relating to an ultimate reality who is also intimate with us and is in solidarity with our tragic and intractable world. What is praise? Across the centuries the classic expressions of Christian praise have been the Psalms, the Eucharist and hymns. The Psalms gather all human life into conversation with God. Good and bad experiences, moods and emotions, personal and political life, confession of sin, the whole of creation, agonized questioning and ecstatic adoration, wisdom and prophecy – all are focused through praise of the living God. Here God is both horizon and centre. The Psalms are primarily public worship, affirming public truth. They shaped the faith of the whole Israelite community, allowing it to imagine reality differently from the surrounding nations and to order its affairs in line with God and his warnings and promises. 'Imagining differently' requires great intensity and creativity. The Psalms make it quite clear that only through the fullest engagement with this God, in word and action, can the required enlivening occur. In praise, reality is being shaped, not just in the world of the imagination or understanding, but concretely through the forming of a community.

The Eucharist is a gathering in thanks and praise to God. At its heart is the crucified God, the gathering around the body broken for the world. People can bring their whole selves to be fed and transformed – which means the whole of their situations, their sins, their joys and griefs, hopes and fears, tragedies and successes, the groups and institutions which help structure their world. The climax is the face-to-face sharing of peace, bread and wine, in memory of the last supper but also in anticipation of the feast of the kingdom of God. The conclusion is the dedication of all to the life of God in the world, being sent to live and work to his praise and glory. All of that needs to be worked through concretely for particular situations, but there is a strikingly strong stream of testimonies from UPAs (and, of course, from elsewhere) to the way in which such dimensions of the Eucharist are realized week after week.

What is at the centre of praise? Why praise God at all? At the heart of it is love. To be loved by one who is glorious beyond imagining, compassionate, just, wise, powerful, forgiving, more intimate to us than we are to ourselves – that calls for us to stretch all our being in response, and the most direct expression of that is in our worship. We can never cope adequately with the abundance of God: our immersion in it overflows in amazement and endless praise. And that praise itself is the dynamic of an overflow which permeates all the rest of life.

The distribution of praise

What does it mean to claim that this dynamic relationship, focused in praise, pervades the rest of life as well? It sets the horizon within which everything else happens. It draws us more deeply into that which, in reality, we are part of – the life of God in the world. To live before this God, to refer everything to God, to think of reality from within that relationship – that can be revolutionary for one area of life after another.

We praise God because he has honoured us, lifted us up, given us the ultimate dignity of being affirmed by him, set before his face in love. In praising God we actually receive our dignity afresh. We are set on our feet before God and other people; each of us is called by name to name God as the source of all dignity and worth – including our own. Our way of imagining ourselves and other people is (often very slowly and precariously) transformed by the amazed recognition of our dignity and theirs before God. God's way of giving us dignity does not just mean our being passive receivers. It can also excite us to all sorts of overflowing, generative activity. At the heart of it all is the one who invites us into a celebration of himself and his great act of resistance against all that diminishes our dignity and thereby constricts our capacity for joy and praise. It is realized in a thousand ways – we have been impressed by the rich variety of practice, ritual, expression and patterns of relationship in the UPA communities we know through which people are changed by participation.

Just as the praise of God involves a celebration of one's own dignity, it also requires celebrating the dignity of other people. Facing God in love means facing others in love – and it is in the faces of each other that we have most chance of glimpsing the image of God. The face of the other calls us to recognize his or her dignity and particularity and to draw the consequences of that in all sorts of ways – from smiles and truth-telling to the meeting of material needs and loyalty over many years. The shining of God on every face is the light in which no one should be permitted to be 'faceless' and marginalized, either within or outside the community of faith. The Church is called to be a community of mutual honouring and solidarity. There is an immense need for a culture of respect and dignity. The inner nature of this is, like God's love, to overflow beyond its own boundaries.

In this way the future is 'praised open'. Praise opens up the horizon within which present conditions can be seen to contradict the life and will of God; it energizes commitment to a new and different future; and it helps set an agenda for change. At the root of Christian resistance to the contradiction of God in conditions that impoverish, deaden and deface people is the community of praise that nurtures dignity. There is a vocation of the Church to be a sanctuary of transformation. Especially in bleak circumstances, there is an immense need for places of refuge and even asylum. They are 'signs' of transcendence and prophecy just by existing. In them there can be 'time out'. One can 'draw breath' in a different atmosphere. Time itself is structured differently. There is a rhythm to the week and year. We can be taken up into a different story from those we have learnt to inhabit through the projections that dominate our local and national cultures. We can discover new powers of speech and song. We can grow into new symbols, stories, ideas and ways of living. Our habitual ways of imagining and inhabiting reality can be transformed.

Serious suspicions

So the implications of praise extend, as widely as the glory, presence and love of God. But is this not sounding more and more like fantasy? How realistic has that account been? Can God be wholeheartedly praised? Is it possible to be filled with a sense of superabundant goodness without wilfully ignoring or at least downplaying the way in which people are daily ground down by misery, debt, noise, squalid conditions, uncaring institutions, erosion of self-esteem and the exhaustion of just trying to cope? Surely the praise of God here can only happen if we face away from the situation, escape into another world – 'heaven', an imagined 'solution', a salvation saying and doing nothing about present circumstances.

Another set of awkward suspicions arises here, this time not that praise is impossible in a UPA but that Christians typically wrongly identify what is praiseworthy. What is praised always seems to be outside the situation; the story into which people are asked to enter is disconnected from their own and fails to illuminate it. At worst it takes over completely and the effect is to ignore and silence people's own stories. Such suspicions lead to the desire to affirm people 'where they are' and to discern the good in UPAs – the resilience, under pressure, of people and culture, the many encouraging stories, habits and networks, and much else. Most crucially, these perceptions are generated within the locality, the affirmations are from within and grounded in ordinary life there – and it is quite possible that the wider culture, and especially the wider Christian culture, might regard much that is affirmed as undesirable, deviant or even criminal. At the heart of this suspicion is the apprehension that all talk of transformation into something better implies that what is to be transformed is seen as bad.

Those suspicions amount to a double possibility of praise being irrelevant fantasy; it might fail to do justice to the bad or it might fail to do justice to the good. Our response is two-fold.

First, the suspicions can of course be confirmed by many instances. Those are indeed two of the main ways in which praise goes wrong. Most good things are vulnerable, from children and marriages to eating, speaking and religious traditions – 'the corruption of the best is the worst'. But the corruption and abuse of good things should not discourage us from committing ourselves to their right use and enjoyment.

Second, the praise we are envisioning does precisely the opposite of what is suspected. Think of the last 26 chapters of the book of Isaiah. They are shot through with the language and experience of praising God and hoping in God, and because of that they illuminate the realities, good and bad, of ordinary life. This God resists being idolized or banished to some remote 'transcendence'. Worship and community well-being cannot be separated, and the truth of God allows a radical sense of how terrible the bad is. It is because of the glory and holiness of God that the awful depths of sin appear: they contradict the very source, meaning and sustainability of life. And there can be open-eyed recognition of this without giving in to despair, or even compromising by a stoic attitude which believes that 'coping is all that is possible'.

Neither can we be content with praise being so immersed in local life that discernment of the bad and the possibilities of transformation are compromised. It is not that there is nothing to be praised and affirmed in UPAs as they are at present. But if that is disconnected from God there are terrible dangers. Affirmation may be undiscriminating with-out a full conception of goodness, and may even conspire to reinforce the *status quo*. To see a situation before God may mean that at the same time we see it as part of a glorious creation, as deserving severe judgement and as open to fundamental transformation. Isaiah and the Psalms have all three in abundance. There need be no downplaying of the good: it is the occasion for delighted gratitude. But neither is there any pretence that goodness is not fragile, often short-lived and very fragmentary.

Sin and the idols of society

We have been describing sin as a contradiction of God. We now want to fill out the meaning of that and insist on a God-centred diagnosis of the pathology of our UPAs.

'Contradiction' is too thin and static a term. Think of what it means in relation to the trinitarian God. It means the possibility of the various dimensions of that richly generative, informative and transformative activity of God, as described above, being inhibited, constricted, dis-torted and dissipated.

Appreciating God is the only healthy context for interpreting and acting for the long-term good of the community. This by no means excludes the use of all sorts of analyses and frameworks of inter-pretation, indeed it requires them. But it prevents them having the effect that is often found: the particular secular framework becomes total, problems and solutions are defined in ways that implicitly exclude God, and it becomes even more difficult to worship in the situation. What Christian involved in the inner city has not emerged from another brilliant analysis of urban deprivation with the feeling that God must at best be some sort of add-on, or artificial insertion, in the world view of the analyst? The main problem here is that the forms of understanding and acting in the situation collude with disconnecting it from its own full goodness and possibilities. That is a subtle form of what is perhaps the most basic sin of all, idolatry.

The discernment of idolatries is a major Christian task in relation to what is wrong in our world. It has to take place at every level and in relation to the long-term dynamics of human life and institutions, dynamics with deep roots in the past and devastating consequences for the future. It is by no means a matter of indiscriminate naming – money, the market and capitalism; materialism and consumerism; liberal culture; comfort, health and security; status, success and power; science and technology; bureaucracy; the media, entertainment and pleasure; racism, sexism and nationalism; human and civil rights; family and friends; religion. Each has at times been called idolatrous. But each requires specific discernment, which needs to be up-to-date – to get hung up on the previous decade's prophetic discernment may itself be idolatrous.

But it is extraordinarily difficult to discern idolatries. Part of their definition is that for those involved in them they are encompassing and pervasive, comprehensive conditions of living which are often so 'normal' that they themselves ground our judgements and values. It is usually possible to justify them in the face of questioning and hard for anyone to say just when the line is crossed between 'good but imperfect aspect of creation' and an idol requiring the unqualified affirmation deserved only by God.

But idols around which a society is organized can only have their illusive goodness and efficacy sustained by concealing or marginalizing counter-evidence. This is done largely by lies. These pervade the entire fabric of society and we are all caught up in them. Our very ways of perceiving each other and ourselves and of orienting our lives are profoundly shaped by the images of our culture and the basic means of organizing and evaluating that we internalize. The best lies are, of course, those which use a good deal of truth, or deeply entangle themselves with truth, so the difficulty of truth-telling is immense.

Moreover, the Church is also implicated in the lies and idolatries – here, too, 'the corruption of the best is the worst' and so the corruptions of the good news in the Church may be most terrible of all. But while the Church still praises God, it embodies a witness to the ultimate contradiction to idolatry and sin. The crucified Lord shows that it is where God and people are despised, where an abyss of hopelessness has opened, that unimaginable energy and life are poured out – resurrection to new life and hope. The Church's discernment needs to be directed towards those places where the idolatries most obviously result in people suffering misery, injustice, oppression of all sorts, constriction of life and hope. Why? Because it is at those points where the consequences of idolatry manifest themselves in human suffering that the world is in most clear contradiction of God.

By identifying God with the crucified Jesus, the Church has the criterion for the direction of its praise and for its exposure of idolatries. But not just the criterion: it is also a matter of power. The power is that of the Holy Spirit which led Jesus on the way of the cross and from there opens up a transformed future. The energy to praise God springs from here and discernment of the idols is enabled through the dynamics of worshipping Father, Son and Holy Spirit, identified above all in the story of Jesus.

Urban Priority Areas are places where there is a specially intensive convergence of the negative consequences of our society's habitual idolatries – or, in other words, where there is a potent contradiction of God. Most people who can flee UPAs do so. Few live there from choice. They are places where the marginalizing that accompanies idolatries is focused in people who are marginalized. They represent what is *not* worshipped in society: failure according to the dominant norms of success and ways of obtaining resources; situations, summed up under general terms like poverty and deprivation, that make people shudder and want at all costs to avoid for themselves and their families.

One way of assessing this is that the margins can be a place of painful truth: here it can become clear what the dominant idolatries are and the points at which they fail. It is not, of course, necessarily so. In fact, the idolatries of society as a whole may be found in even more devastating forms here. Racial identity may become more vital when all aspects of self-esteem are being eroded and there are few sources of affirmation. Pursuing money and material possessions can become obsessive in the face of deprivation. The grip of images of status, security and pleasure can be intensified by exclusion from 'mainstream' ways of attaining them.

In the face of all that, it is even more urgent for the Church to relate its worship to UPAs (and, of course, to comparable situations). The issues are immense and fundamental. Who is God in this society? Is God the crucified Lord? What are the results of our idolatries and the ways they distribute and distract our attention? The distinction means that we cannot see or tell the truth about our society and ourselves. It also means that the Church is not worshipping the Christian God in truth, since its attention is drawn away from precisely those places where its faith teaches it to discern God.

So it is not enough to have concern and aid from non-UPA churches and the rest of society. Genuine worship in the UPA church is of fundamental importance both for those who live there and for the Church and society as a whole. What can open our eyes and hearts? What can resist the dissipation of our attention in many directions? What can hold to the essentials in the midst of deep and often trauma-tized confusion? At the heart of the Christian response is a riveting of attention on the crucified and resurrected Jesus: 'Follow me.' 'Do this in remembrance of me.' 'I send you.' 'My Lord and my God!'

Imagining differently

Can we be clearer about what this means in practice? One thing we cannot do is to work out some blueprint applicable in varied and complex situations. Discernment and action flow out of the community that is worshipping and constantly relating all the particularities together in that context. But that does not mean that nothing can be said. What we want to do in conclusion is to draw on our experience and that of many others in trying to distil, for the encouragement of local communities, a little of the wisdom that is to be found along the road of obeying 'the first and great commandment' in a UPA situa-tion.

Here are some 'counsels', brief statements of what might be involved in praise-centred attention and activity.

- Try to imagine how things might be different. God's abundant reality is decisive. That can be ignored or contradicted in situations which are sinful, in actions and in our thoughts.
- In each place find multiple ways of remembering who God is and who people are in God's sight, ways that are in tune with the abundance and generosity of God. We think not only of explicit worship but of forms of celebration and parties, rituals with rich symbols of identity, music and drama groups, protest and resist-ance, friendships, sharing in discernment, shared planning and responsibilities, solidarity in ups and downs, learning skills and so on. Listen: pay full attention to each person as of infinite impor-tance and in the image of God.
- Beware of developing a 'problem-centred' mentality. The dangers, when surrounded by problems, are of individual and corporate burn-out, of treating ourselves and other people primarily as prob-lems to be solved, and of reinforcing a constricted reality. Above all,

there is the temptation to idolize successful problem-solving and to despise failure.

- Practise analysing situations so as to expose the idols that dominate them. What is being seen as 'absolutely necessary', immovable, dominant? What are our deepest desires, assumptions, expectations? What are the ways of discerning and affirming and following through on the Lordship of God there?
- Worship and the community life that is centred on it help us not to despair when good things prove fragile or short-lived and fragmentary glimpses of hope do not seem to lead anywhere.
- How time is shaped and punctuated is vital for communities and individuals: the day, week, year, life, local history. Stories need to be remembered, told, learnt from. Worship is a point of convergence and interweaving between the Christian and other stories. Imagine time differently: sabbaths and feasts and fasts as the nodal points; the drama of the Eucharist is the decisive plot for all of us; getting beyond boredom and busyness; above all, worship is the main way in which the past is taken up in thanks and repentance, the present is lived in before the face of God, and we enter the future blessed.

Conclusion

This chapter on praise and idolatry has been deliberately downright in its recommendation of one big thought. We are convinced that that thought is actually the pivotal one for an urban theology that wants to connect with what goes on in UPAs, with the core of the Christian message and with the distillation of the practical wisdom of those who have been most deeply immersed in both.

The idols that consume the attention and energies of our society are voracious and are part of all of us. It seems a strangely weak gesture 'just' to worship. What are we doing every Sunday, every day, as we 'waste' time on this? We are resisting the most dangerous of temptations – to turn stones into bread, manipulate the world to suit ourselves, dazzle with successful gestures – in favour of a message that says to love God with all we have and are, and to worship God alone. And when we do that in the extreme situations of UPAs there is a sign of faith, hope and love that is desperately needed elsewhere too.

The body: physicality in the UPA[1]

LAURIE GREEN

One category of experience which demands our fullest attention in the inner city is that of the physical. The concentration of factories, noise, population, warehouses, high-rise blocks and vast physical structures presses in upon us. The physicality is raw and yet sophisticated, it is written in the concrete environment and reflected in the telling faces and the body language of the people. And in the Urban Priority Areas it is a category which forces its attention and speaks ambiguously of dereliction and power, of vitality and yet depression.

Each urban environment is particular and spawns a specific sub-cultural response to its physicality, which culture in turn affects the concrete environment. It is an interplay of physical structure and cultural structure. I am at home in the East London Boroughs of Tower Hamlets and Newham and this chapter therefore derives directly from that experience of an urban area swamped with youngsters, media hype, anonymity and physicality. I hope that my impressionistic account may resonate with the felt experience of other Urban Priority Areas, and encourage readers to reflect further.

In order to concentrate upon the dynamic interplay of the personal, structural and cultural aspects of the physical in urban life, I choose to focus particularly upon the body – with its evident physicality, sexuality, power, vulnerability and economic application, as well as its cultural self-expressiveness. And I want to look not only for aberration, as is so often the case when Christians write about physicality, but to do my best to seek out the more positive, in order that we may celebrate that and learn from it. So let us begin by considering sexuality; the body in its most supercharged and overt physicality.

UPA physicality: the image

If you ask the person in the Urban Priority Area pub about 'religion', you may hear that it's about not swearing, and no sex. You may hear that everything that sex is, religion is not. For example, religion is not spontaneous, not physical, not energetic nor exciting, but sex is! It would seem that sex, or sexual taboo, is a key element in the definition of religion offered by Urban Priority Area people.

Now, it is important to establish from the outset that this point of view that religion is basically a restrictive sexual ethic, like so much else that we will discuss, is not to be found exclusively in the UPA. We will discover however that what is certainly present in other parts of our society may be unwrapped and more publicly exhibited in the UPA. It is as if the blatant and harsh nature of the concrete environment prompts a more blatant and 'up front' expression of the truth.

In the UPA there appears to be an openness and apparent freedom about the physical which is born of a culture different from the one most clergy come from and with which they are at ease. For example, most of us, I suspect, have not had to encounter physical danger from a peer since we were children in the school playground. But that is not so in the UPA. It has been said that inner-city people are 'truth-tellers', and the ghetto the place where the secrets of all hearts might very well be revealed. A religious sister working in the tough inner city reports: 'They constantly assail me with two questions: the first is God, the other is sex.' It's all very forthright! It seemed quite natural therefore to the Ladies' Group in a parish I served to have their outing to see the Chippendales, whereas I'm sure that would not be true in every parish! Clearly, for many younger people in the UPA, sex itself might be seen now as a very natural, available and earthy thing, and it can be a great source of joy, a high-profile adventurous, exhilarating and exciting game. The media certainly promote that perception.

Those outside the UPA may, however, make more of this perception of the inner city than is warranted. For there is no doubt that within UPAs there are also those who for personal or for religious reasons would wish to keep sexuality and physicality very carefully suppressed and sometimes quite literally veiled. And, as anywhere else, in UPAs there are some people for whom the emotions surrounding the powerful physical forces of sexuality have led equally to hurt, frustration and repression. So it is that my conversations with single mothers in Newham tower blocks elicit a whole range of extreme emotions about sexuality. Some have been broken by it and reduced to oppressed objects whilst others absolutely glory in its frivolity and power. But

whilst guarding against hyperbole and projection, it would nevertheless appear that the overt spontaneity of physicality, and perhaps
also sexuality, is more evident in the urban scene. And it can be very
flamboyant and fashionably brassy in East London where it can be a
statement of strong personal and community identity against the overall repression of beauty and fun by the surrounding concrete drab
environment.

UPA physicality: the concern for control

Poorer urban people have experienced through many generations the
control by others of their physicality – their manual labour has been
harshly supervised and the physicality of their environment has been in
the hands of planners 'a million miles away'. Many UPA cultures have
internalized this suppression of the physical and made it their own,
retaining a staunch Victorian and sometimes even a prudish outlook.
But more and more, there seems to be developing a rebellion against
these controls on behaviour, and an overt 'up front' expression of
independent identity. More and more, 'anything goes' and the culture
encourages us to 'do our own thing' without too much regard for other
people or for the common good of society. There are a number of factors
that have encouraged this liberalization of societal norms almost to the
point of breakdown.

First, the dominant culture of individualism which is now promoted
in film and video, in advertising and in the cut-and-thrust mentality of
the market place economy, plays its part in encouraging a falling away
from more traditional societal aspirations, such as care for others in
community. And when this mentality is coupled with the energies
derived from the natural frustration inner-city people feel at their
powerlessness, then this helps to induce a breakdown and fragmentation of community cultures and leaves many anchorless and unsure
about what is any longer acceptable behaviour and what is 'out of
order'. Additionally, in the East London UPAs there is a feeling that
everyone has been equally jumbled together at the bottom, with UPA
people having little control of who is 'in' or 'out', with people being
brought into the area from mental hospitals, the arrival of immigrants
and refugees, and homeless teenagers descending upon the inner city
from the smaller towns and rural countryside. There is a resentment
about the lack of control over who gets council flats, or who gets jobs.
Indeed, they have little power at all to control anything which affects
their lives. And these frustrations of powerlessness help create the
physical tension which is everywhere evident.

Add to these pressures the anonymity of much of urban life where neighbours' opinions or legal restraint matter very little any more and we can understand why physicality comes readily to the surface on the streets of Tower Hamlets or Newham.

In order to be heard in the massive overshadowing environment one has to be loud and abrasive – to 'let it all hang out' – and there are few safeguards to restrain the unleashing of feelings which might be destructive and selfish. The threshold of tolerance can easily be breached in this 'do your own thing' environment, and minority groups and unattached individuals are abused and scapegoated. I was once set upon in a pub by a gang of lads who on seeing a dog-collar thought I was easy game for their physical and sexual abuse. Things became very violent.

But, of course, as always in Urban Priority Areas, the picture is more complicated and dynamic than these generalizations allow for and there are pockets of resistance to this 'anything goes' culture. People of faith, Christian and Muslim in particular, balk at these tendencies as do many older folk who prefer to remember a more ordered era – a time when people knew their place, knew the rules and were perhaps more scared to step over the line. And it is not only religious belief or age which induces a more controlled manner in many East End people. For example, many have experience of overcrowding which makes them more insistent on privacy to the point of apparent prudishness and we still recognize the remnants of very 'Victorian' attitudes which were ingrained in London's old East End white culture. You invade a cockney's space at your peril.

My abiding childhood memory of life on the streets of East London is one of fear of violence and the need to belong to a strong gang in order to preserve personal safety, and those who share that experience may have learnt to show outward physical bravado whilst actually wishing for a much more controlled and safe environment. Some will even have suffered sexual abuse and like so many others on the street, become fearful of and revolted by the overt physicality or sexuality around them.

Some inner-city religious groups actually major on physical and sexual repression or control, and often attract people who for whatever reason find this appealing. It can be a strong feature of the black-led churches and the mosques. It is interesting in this regard to compare the evidence of the New Testament Epistles where the mandate of uprightness in sexual and physical morality seems to have been a factor in the life-style of Early Church congregations which attracted urban people where the culture was under threat or was in process of disintegration, just as our own appears to be today.

The confidence of the body

In the tough Urban Priority Areas of Tower Hamlets physical things are for most people the main source of pleasure and power. Sheer physical strength, the turbo-charged BMW, success in football and games, the ability to attract people, the use of glamour and fashion wear, prowess in sport or the use of physical violence, can all be major avenues to power and success. In other cultures and areas of society the physical may be just as appealing but it is only one source of pleasure amongst many whereas in the UPA, where other avenues of expression, affirmation and success are less readily available, physical prowess may be the one sphere in which it may be possible to achieve one's dreams. Given the right physical attributes, it can be a readily accessible, agreeable aspiration and a cheap method of self-expression and affirmation. Indeed for many the *only* path to fame and fortune in UPA life may be through physical assets: becoming a model, or a rich man's or woman's plaything, making a rich marriage, becoming a prize fighter or sporting hero, or showing more endurance and panache than the average. Indeed, panache is a quality highly valued and applauded in most Urban Priority cultures whether it be expressed as a 'Jack the Lad' jauntiness or capitalized upon in the street market trader.

Physical attractiveness is seen by some as the one way to attract the elusive Prince Charming who, it is hoped, will save one from the drudgery of urban life. Women in Holloway prison were asked what they hoped for on release. Their ideas centred on attracting a man who would love them and treat them properly, give them a good home and plenty of money. The traditional pattern of pair-bonding was the path to everything desirable – love, the absence of violence, housing, lifestyle, money, security, identity. This of course can be the dream in other walks of life, but for many UPA women and men it has the lure of a deep-seated myth – a Cinderella story, if you will. And the typical East End wedding has all the trimmings of this illusion for both bride and groom.

Other women however tell me that they have opted for an altogether different path to security, having been let down or abused by men too often. They are content to remain independent of men in their mothering and treat the Holloway dream as the illusion it obviously is. Still others consciously or unconsciously make sure that they remain as unattractive to men as they can to keep them at a distance. Such UPA women do not buy the Cinderella myth but have gone to the other extreme and chosen to free themselves from a long-term attachment to one man and seek to become economically independent. Patricia Morgan gives figures in her *Farewell to the Family?*[2] to back her claim that a married father of two small children, working 40 hours a week, takes home £33 less than a single mother working for only 20 hours at the same rate. Tax and social-security benefits account for this. So for those single mothers who have the skills and backup support to go to work, if they are at the very bottom of the earnings scale, marriage partnership has been made an expensive luxury they can ill afford, even though single parenthood can prove a harsh and lonely alternative. Perhaps it is these pressures that lead to the increasing and sad trend in our UPAs for mothers to remain single but to take occasional supportive physical attachments.

Sport continues to be a vehicle by which to excel, and a reason for dressing in exciting sports gear, even if one is actually grossly over-weight! People in adverts on screen and bill-board, and the stars of the videos, all have well-built bodies, and body-building is promoted and seen as the fresh 'clean' physical activity for achievers. In the UPA, such physical prowess among the men has always been an aspiration and a status symbol, at one time the mark of a tough, useful and employable male, but now the mark of one who 'gets most out of life'. And, what's more, it's an outlet for the frustrated energies of life. And is there not something in this interest in sport which resonates with our Christian faith? Christianity is, after all, a thoroughly creational, incarnational religion. It holds to the belief that God has created the world and put humanity within it in a very physical way. For God, then, this physical creation is of utmost importance and to engage passionately in the glory of the physical might be a fitting celebration and tribute to its Creator. Our bodies are gifts to us, and sacraments of his love for us. So inner-city confidence in and brashness about the body is perhaps a good antidote to our usual Christian prudishness and denial of the physical.

For all that, these positive and sporty aspirations are not achievable for all, and it is the disintegration and degradation of society that is often more physically evident in the Urban Priority Areas, and in a bodily way at that. I can well remember, on first going to live in one of the most deprived inner-city areas of our land, being shocked and horrified to see the crippled, lame, bent bodies of many of the people on the street. And of those whose bodies had not been maimed from birth, some sought relief through alcohol and tobacco, or smothered their loneliness through eating to excess. In the heavily deprived areas, human bodies carry the very marks of poverty on society's behalf. The statistics of such health risk and deprivation in the UPAs are well documented, but coming personally face to face with it is another matter. With continuing lack of health facilities and qualitative environmental infrastructure, some people are physically stricken by the prevalent diseases of the urban environment whilst others find themselves emotionally unable to cope with it. Sometimes poverty itself will cause personal dysfunction, be it through malnutrition or the relentless worry of making ends meet. When we remember that it takes more skill to survive a tough UPA environment than a pleasant suburban one, then we are no longer surprised to find more people who cannot physically cope within the urban press. Coping too is contextual.

The body may turn out to be the only commodity a poor person has left to sell, whether he or she sells its manual power and skill, as in mining, dock work, furniture removal: or its strength and prowess, as in football, sport, or as bouncers and hustlers. Some may even turn to selling their 'sexual favours'. Such has been the experience of UPA people for generations and this situation will continue, as Shaw pointed out, until the day when people can earn a good living by other means. But for UPA young people it is hard, though not entirely impossible, to gain access to other professions – assuming that they actually want to. They have no inherited parental experience to help them choose, and little know-how to go about it. Their education may well have been interrupted by school cuts, ill health, difficult family situations, homelessness, or overcrowding. They must compete against others who have so much more going for them by way of supportive social wealth and personal and family contacts. So they are thrown back upon selling their physicality, if they can still find a buyer.

That such youngsters might ever become the subjects of their own history seems unlikely and yet Mary the Mother of Jesus sang a song of high revolt proclaiming that within God's redeeming salvation history this would indeed be so. The Magnificat holds out the promise that those who are oppressed by such circumstances will find that God upholds them, while the rich will be sent empty away. Jesus himself, time and again, addresses the poor with a similar promise of a new fulfilment which, appropriately for the poor of the UPA, finds its realization in the resurrection of the body. Earlier, God's redeeming Messiah is described by Isaiah as having 'no grace to make us delight in him; his form, disfigured, lost all the likeness of a man, his beauty changed beyond human semblance' (Isa 53, NEB). He appears like one of the oppressed of the inner city in bearing the defiling marks of oppression on his body, but this makes it ever more pertinent and telling that he is eventually crowned with the gift of glorious bodily resurrection.

Meaning and transcendence

Today, in all walks of life, sex is more likely to be held up as the main vehicle for an experience of human transcendence and the discovery of meaning than is religion. One might argue however that, on the contrary, sex is only illusory escapism which saps our energies from the real task of self- and societal fulfilment. But in making this accusation, we must remember that Marx laid the self-same charge at the door of religion when he called it the 'opiate of the people'. If we know that true religion need not be as Marx envisioned it, then perhaps we should also acknowledge that neither is sexual experience necessarily an opiate. In fact it has the potential of taking us onto a new plane of experience of love, and surely no Christian would wish to undervalue that possibility.

Sex can offer an experience of transcendence in a number of ways. For example, a loving sexual relationship offers an experience of transcending the self, of reaching out to the other. And in this way we can discover an awareness of the interrelationship between vulnerability and power – an interrelationship which exists between lovers and which in turn mirrors something of the divine. For just as human lovers play together in the joyful game of the dynamic of their own vulnerability and power regarding the loved one, so also it is a similar dynamic interplay which we see in the trinitarian Godhead. For on the one hand God is the almighty, the all-powerful Creator and protector, and yet on the other hand, his self-expression is in the Son, the vulnerable lover. Within the Trinity the three Persons are thus rapt in the passionate dynamic of those same forces of vulnerable love and creative power. So it is that the person who does not find religion fruitful may nevertheless glimpse something of the nature of the dynamic of divine love within their best experiences of human love. Sex, when it expresses a fulfilled loving relationship in this way, can therefore be a sacramental act.

So sex has the potential for moving people onto a different plane of experience, even though only fleetingly. Sex can offer a sense of fulfilment and creativity, of well-being and worth, of meaning and exhilaration. It is physically affirming, creative and fun. And what is important for us here is that it therefore offers socially powerless people an opportunity to experience real and loving power and to rise above the mundane even whilst remaining wholeheartedly in the physical world – to transcend their experience and play within divine love. Perhaps this is why, to quote Ken Leech, 'Patristic writers such as John Chrysostom and John Climacus insist that physical human love, eros, is analogous to divine love. God, says Chrysostom, is "more erotic than bride and groom". And Climacus speaks of the love of God as being "an abundance of eros".'[3]

But inner-city people sense that the Church is still caught up in its own fear of sexuality and physicality, as if to God matter did not matter. UPA churches which do become truly incarnational and creational in their theological life find themselves able to express their physicality with delight and thankfulness and through care for one another. It is often seen in those churches which have begun to own the physicality of liturgy, worship and church life and have warmed to the body language of the Body of Christ. We shall return to that point later.

We have spoken of loving sexuality as an opportunity to attain a sense of the self, rising onto another plane of meaning – an experience of transcending oneself. But sex offers the possibility of another experience of transcendence. It is an intense awareness of what could be – a new vision – a new potential. No longer is the drab concrete of the apartment block the only possibility. One senses a beauty beyond and a new potency to change what does not conform to the splendour once glimpsed. There can issue an awareness of the redemption of creation – even its political redemption. Sex transcends impotence and reminds us that the future is created and is not simply a matter of fate. For UPA people this can be a life-saving revelation.

Celibacy

But this gift of physical self-transcendence can be abused, for is it not true that a macabre self-transcendence is experienced also by the violent rapist who seeks to rise above himself or herself in the act of dominating and controlling the abused? Here the divine interdependence of power and vulnerability is thrown into foul confusion. This extreme case reminds us that with sex there is also a God-given ordinance of control and self-sacrifice if its sacramentality is to be realized. This is why the Church holds fast to the ideal that sexual intimacy should only be practised within a life-long married relationship. It is interesting therefore to find that we can learn more in this regard from the experience of those religious celibates, both sisters and friars, who live in amongst the poor of the UPAs.

The decision to lead such a celibate life is to go against the norm, and does require an extraordinary grace and call from God. It calls for a relationship with God which is so all-embracing and fulfilling that an exclusive commitment to another human being becomes incompatible with it. It allows the celibate to witness to the transcendence of God in everyone and in everything, and this witness causes many in the UPA to be intrigued by the religious' way of life. For its lack of exclusivity is, in one sense, quite promiscuous, and yet it is so profoundly different from the usual definition of sexual promiscuity as to be fascinating and intriguing in the inner city.

We must rejoice with the poor of Newham and Tower Hamlets and indeed marvel at the freedom with which many overtly enjoy their physicality and sexuality but we must also take care to notice that all too often sex in the inner city is not a self-sacrificial offering but a coinage for gain, a commodity to be bartered with, and the 'other' is too often treated as an object of lust, greed and violence. East London is alive with sexual hype and yet beneath this there is much brokenness of human spirit and loneliness beyond measure. But we must never lose sight of the fact that despite all this, the deepest hunger of all is still for loving and caring relationships and most of the time that is why sexual relationship is sought after. And often the celibate religious brother or sister brings the hope that the promise of relationship is not after all dependent upon commodity transaction, and holds out the hope that the sheer joy and vibrancy of sexuality, so obvious in the East End, is also of God. And if this is so, then it must therefore be honoured, treasured and treated as God's precious gift.

Commitment

In modern life, commitments seems less reliable than they were in the past. But in UPA life almost everything seems unreliable. Almost anything may be lost at any time, and the long-term view seems to be the privilege of the wealthy. Time was when sex itself was understood by all as a major bonding agent in society – allowed only within long-term, committed relationships. It stood as part of a nexus of home, marriage, children and economic interdependence, as a major plank of a stable society. This state of affairs largely derived from Christian teaching about sex and marriage, both affirming and enhancing long-term relationships, contributing to the growth and maintenance of trust and long-term dependability and commitment. And in the UPA as elsewhere we will find those who remain true to this understanding – indeed for some couples in Urban Priority Areas their marriage is the only reliable thing that remains amidst turmoil and change. But more and more there has grown up a lack of interest in the long-term and an idolization of the present moment. With that as the dominant motif, plus the particularly fragile nature of UPA life, there has developed in some lives a negative spiral of short-term relationships, leading to casual sex without long-term responsibility, and sometimes even the neglect of children. In these circumstances, gone is the sacramental quality of human love and sex of which we have been speaking. Here sex is no longer inextricably linked with marriage, children, home and stable economic life. This nexus which brought security to homes and families is slipping away, and the loss of full employment for men has even taken away opportunities for young men to learn financial respon-sibility for the family. These anti-bonding pressures lead to an increasing fragmentation of society – since a respect for society and the skills of building community have in the past largely been learnt within the family, even in families with considerable problems. Sex is therefore left to stand by itself, free of all the stabilizing factors that were formerly linked with it. And to the depressing breakdown of bonding, which is evident across the country, are added the pressures in the inner city of poverty and exploitation which simply aggravate and exacerbate these negative, fragmentary and isolating trends in society.

We cannot be proud of this absence of steady, long-term relation-ships, and we must acknowledge the sinfulness of a society which causes it. And yet may we hope that God can still be present and active in the fragmentary, just as he is present in the fragments of the bread broken at Eucharist? For someone who is in desperate need in an alienating, lonely urban environment, can God take even fragmented love and turn that crucifixion into resurrection? May we hope for their sake that God can still bring good out of ill? I have often known couples prefer to hang on to the little love that they do manage to find in what appears for all the world to be an intolerable relationship, rather than see even that little love evaporate.

Perhaps it is right to say that because the Church has not yet fully appreciated the wonderful sacrament that sex *can* be, so its ethical investigations into the abuse of sexuality can turn out quite lop-sided. God has created the world and the human being for love, relationship and contact, and when a sacrament such as sex focuses this well, then and only then can its opposite, abuse, be properly understood. For only then, when the good is identified and celebrated, can people identify abuse, by seeing what it is abuse of.

This requires a mature and confident sexuality, a maturity which our society finds increasingly difficult to attain. It is the kind of mature sexuality sometimes seen in the East End amongst those older black women who show a very strong wisdom and personal integration about their sexuality, often evident on the dance floor. They seem to be completely able to accept their sexuality as a vital part of themselves in a confident and mature manner. When this kind of maturity is attained, then the negative – its fall from grace – can be identified, but not really before! To understand the Fall you have first to hear the story of the Garden of Eden. So the Church is seen by the urban poor as largely unable to appreciate the abuse because it has not fully accepted the beauty of what is being abused. This fact puts us at a disadvantage when in the pastoral or counselling role.

Sexuality and elusive community

The inner security and self-esteem which a loving sexuality can generate also helps us traverse relationship boundaries and this in turn encourages the development of community. James Nelson has written of 'God's ingenious way of calling us into community with others through our need to reach out, touch and embrace, emotionally, intellectually and physically'.[4] Community, then, requires that we 'touch' one another in mutual respect and positive regard. Community requires communication and contact.

For many people, and not only in the UPAs, the body remains the chief vehicle of communication and 'contact'. As an East End child my spoken vocabulary was severely limited, but my mother tongue, in which I was very articulate and expletive, was body language. It was an almost tactile communication medium. It was a language in which the word became flesh. It was an embodied language which helped to create community by its intimacy and yet it veered dangerously near the ultimate East End taboo, which was the invasion of the space of another. Understanding when to touch and when not to touch was and remains one of the most subtle aspects of East End body language, which language thus maintains strict boundaries whilst introducing rich intimacy and passion. It is a physical and sexually charged community tool. Body language is the fleshy language of UPA community.

Building strong physical community requires the language of intimacy. In this regard, community building is like discovering qualitative sexual relationship in that both require human intimacy, trust and safeguards. They are intimate, generative acts of thanksgiving which encounter suffering, vulnerability, protective power and positive regard, all in dynamic with each other. As with sexuality, that most vital expression of physicality, building community requires the handling of intimate, sacred things. So it is that the intimacy of the UPA local or the club is treated with such seriousness and, dare I say, treated as sacred.

But a lack of qualitative physical or even sexual relationship can be crippling for individuals and communities. For in all of us there is a desire for relationships which honour and value the beloved, and in sex there is an intimacy which touches the most powerful motors of that need. This is gift, but if mishandled there can result profound dislocation and disintegration of the person and the community. For when persons lose this sexual integrity then their communities suffer the same spiral of disintegration, and passions are aroused which find no positive fulfilment, thus increasing the potential for depressive loneliness or destructive violence. Such is the power of sex in our communities.

Can the Church respond adequately?

As we said at the beginning, in the East End sexual taboo is a key factor in defining religion. It is believed there that the Church and religion are essentially 'anti-sex' and anti-physical. So it is difficult for UPA dwellers to feel that Christians mean it when they affirm that their religion is actually about a God of passionate love. And, to some extent, the accusation carries weight, for in our religious and theological circles talk about sex is likely to turn immediately to questions of abuse, domination, dissatisfaction, genetic engineering, and aberration. And I have tried my best to avoid being sucked into that trap of negativity in this chapter. I am reminded of the young couple who were sent away by the priest to select a Bible reading for their wedding. Since they had not met the Bible before, he had given them a series of texts to look up, but they came back to him full of delight to tell him that, although grateful for his suggestions, by chance they had stumbled upon the Song of Songs and had selected a particularly exciting passage from that. He was simply not able to cope with that overtly sexual Bible reading in the solemnity of his church. In the same way, the church lectionaries of daily Bible readings take great care to omit the overtly sexual passages.

But the UPA teaches us that a much more honest approach is needed. We must celebrate the God-given gift of physicality and sexuality with all our heart and not only bemoan its misuse. If for example we were able to acknowledge the important part played in our worship by the body in all its physicality we would perhaps be able to enact our liturgies with more honesty and with more human depth and sexual integrity. It might transform our ministries, for it would assist us all to acknowledge overtly that love requires painful and honest vulnerability. After all, the Bible uses the body as a very positive image. It is used by Paul as a symbol of unity in diversity (e.g. 1 Cor 12.12). It's a sign of the very presence of God in the eucharistic meal, as Christ's Body given for us (Luke 22.19). It is the Word made incarnate flesh – alongside our incarnate flesh, allowing us to celebrate the glory of being made in God's image, and acknowledging with gratitude that we are wonderfully made. 'You knit me together in my mother's womb' (Ps 139.12). At the biological level alone, the physicality of our creation is intriguing and miraculous, with DNA spiralling, cells dividing, and hormones racing. It is a wonder of God's creation and of our sharing in collaborative love and creativity. The Bible revels in it and sees, as in the Song of

Songs, how the intimate relationship of the lovers mirrors the longing that God has for intimacy with his creation.

The Christian faith is founded upon the physical revelation of the Divine in the incarnation of Jesus Christ in bodily form. Our response as individuals and as Church must be to honour the spirituality of the body and of the physical, to love God through it and in it, and to enter into an appropriate loving intimacy with our neighbour. We will then be so taken with a realization of the very presence of God in *everything*, including our physical universe, that we will no longer need to take refuge in talk of God inhabiting only a supernatural sphere. For God, being wholly other, is yet within all we perceive and comprehend – all, in that understanding, is natural and God is in it.

In the Urban Priority Areas physicality is a category which forces its attention upon us and for those with the gift of discernment it can be a sacrament of the very presence of God, the Body of Christ, divinely intimate, inspiring fear, fascination and fun.

Notes

1 This chapter develops ideas originally raised in an article by Ruth McCurry.
2 Patricia Morgan, *Farewell to the Family?* (ILEA, 1994).
3 Kenneth Leech, *Eye of the Storm* (Darton, Longman and Todd, 1992), p. 67.
4 James Nelson, *Embodiment, An Approach to Sexuality and Christian Theology* (SPCK, 1979).

A place of our own?

■■■■■■

MICHAEL S. NORTHCOTT

Religious experience and the experience of place have a strong affinity which is reflected in all the world's religions, including Judaism and Christianity. The history of Israel is that of a people without a home who seek and then find a place of their own as they are guided by the God of their nomadic ancestors. The Hebrew Bible recounts the story of their progression from nomadic tribalism to settlement in the promised land and the struggle for cultic and political ascendancy over the cultures and peoples of the region. Land was the key to livelihood, self-sufficiency and political freedom to the variously nomadic and enslaved ancestors of the Hebrews, and the abundant provision of the land is central to Israel's vision of the covenant community which is established between God, the people and the land.

When the Hebrews are exiled from the land, the prophets blame their loss of livelihood and freedom on their abuse of this abundance. The expropriation of land by rich from poor, the 'adding of house to house' by some at the expense of the livelihood of others is the cause of the eviction of Israel from the land. The abundance of the few leads to scarcity for many and so the people of God lose the privileges of abundant provision and political freedom which they had come to take too much for granted. The vision of redemption and return which the prophets construct is similarly oriented around the restoration of the land and of household self-sufficiency (Isa 62). This vision is sustained amongst the exiled Jewish people by its reorientation to the future: the sadness of singing the Lord's song in a strange land is overcome by the imagined city of Zion to which, one day, the redeemed of the Lord shall return, if not in this life, then in the next.

Even before the exile, the possession of the land is an ambiguous phenomenon for the prophetic and cultic imagination. Security and satiety bring their own dangers – of independence from God, of forgetfulness of God's redemption, and of denial of God's moral order for the land and for human community, hence the frequent contrast in the Hebrew Bible between the virtues of nomadism and travelling light and the dangers of settlement, security and accumulation. Isaiah finally resolves this ambiguity by universalizing Israel's sense of place: the temple is no longer the special dwelling place of God, nor the land, for all the earth is the Lord's:

> Thus says Yahweh:
> With heaven my throne
> and earth my footstool,
> what house could you build me,
> what place could you make my rest?
> All of this was made by my hand
> and all of this is mine – it is Yahweh who speaks.
>
> (Isa 66.1–2)

This latent ambiguity regarding place in the Hebrew tradition is carried over into the Christian religion. Jesus was a travelling prophet and miracle worker who set no store by land or houses or temples. He taught in the streets and desert places after being evicted from the synagogue at Capernaum. He frequently prayed and slept on hill-tops, in boats or in the wilderness to avoid the crowds and to commune with God. He celebrated the kingdom at the tables of tax-collectors, sinners and Pharisees, and rented an unfamiliar room for his farewell feast with his followers. Even his grave was borrowed from a well-wisher: 'foxes have holes, birds have nests but the Son of Man has nowhere to lay his head' (Matt 8.20). The writer of the Epistle to the Hebrews preserves this ambiguity about place and housing for 'here we have no continuing city' (13.14).

Christianity has not always retained this ambiguity concerning the significance of land and place. The focus on Rome as the predominant city of the new religion emerged sometime in the third century of the Christian era, and Christianity, like Judaism before it, took up in the Christendom era the identification of place and religion which is common in religious history. The third-century movement of Christian worship from private houses to purpose-built churches (basilicas) is one of the keys to this changed orientation to place. The new identification with place subsequently takes a variety of forms.

Parish and pilgrimage

We may observe this identity in the emergence of the territorial organization of ecclesiastical life and the parochial system in urban and rural life, which is preserved in the Church of England to this day. The identification of Church with the historical continuity of land and place, and with the diversity of the inner city, the city centre, the suburb and the rural village is enabled by the maintenance of the parochial character of the Church despite all the pressures towards congregationalism in this secular century. It is a central strength of the Church of England and other territorially organized churches, and gives an authority to the voice of the Church in relation to the social condition of divided England. The earliest forms of parochial organization focused upon feudal estates, and upon the lands, villages and spheres of influence of the monasteries. Both of these forms involved an identity between the Church and the working of the land, between worship and stewardship of creation, and between cultic identity and community life.

The predominantly rural structure of the parish system was adapted to urban life as the cities of England grew in the eighteenth and nineteenth centuries, though the process of adaptation has often created parishes which lack a sense of identity with recognizable urban neighbourhoods. Large numbers of churches were built in urban areas to provide accommodation for the new urban classes and parochial boundaries subdivided to create new parishes. But many of these buildings were never full from their inception and as populations have migrated out from city core to suburb and commuter hinterland so the Church is left with many nearly empty churches in places where few people actually live.

The close connection between religion and place is also revealed in the religious orientation of the architecture of medieval towns which were often built in precise and ordered patterns around churches and cathedrals. The labyrinthine layout of narrow streets in Canterbury and York is preserved until today. The labyrinth served the purpose of obscuring easy passage to the focal point of the town, heightening the mystery and significance of the last moments of the march of the pilgrims to their holy destination. The focus of medieval urban development on religious and cosmological criteria gave an aesthetic and architectural order to the premodern city which contrasts strongly with the rational, functional order, and the display of rampant individualism, which together characterize the modern city.

The articulation between place and religion may also be observed in the social and spiritual significance of pilgrimage in medieval Europe.[1] The places of pilgrimage were associated with the lives, actions, relics, and often martyrdoms, of great saints such as Thomas Becket of Canterbury and James of Compostella. The designation of these cathedrals as places of pilgrimage recalls in a fascinating way the articulation between settlement and nomadism, place and mobility which characterized the attitude to land and livelihood of the religion of ancient Israel and of the lives of Jesus, Paul and of many of the great missionary leaders of Christian expansion in Europe. As the paths and stories of the pilgrims reached into the spaces and cultures of regions far distant from the holy places, so the journeys of the pilgrims and the cult of the saints represented to the settled peasant and the landlord the romance and heroism of travel which transcends the time–space boundaries of every-day life.

Mobility and pathology in the modern city

This articulation between settlement and mobility, place and migrancy is also a key feature of modern and postmodern visions of the organiza-tion and culture of contemporary cities. The history of cities is the history of migration, often enforced migration, from country to city, and in the modern city from inner-city slum to housing scheme or suburb.

But just as mobility is the key to the origins of the city, it is also, according to interpreters of the modern city, a central cause of the pathology of modern city life. The medieval city-dweller celebrated the 'city air which makes people free'. But people in modern cities more often choke on the urban air, and dream of escaping the inner city to a garden suburb, or a commuter village. The triumph of mobility over settlement takes place in the real lived experience of motorway flyovers overpassing and dividing urban neighbourhoods, of traffic-laden roads destroying street community, of children's play space being restricted by the ever-present danger of cars. The modern city celebrates and facilitates mobility at the expense of settlement, movement at the expense of place. The result is the dissolution of the city as a place of settlement into what Manuel Castells calls the 'informational city' in which the flowing mobility of information, capital, people, traffic, and television images removes the sense of physical boundaries of place which are essential to human identity.[2]

Urban places, and place-based societies, consequently become dis-articulated: community, identity, neighbourhood, and culture are disrupted as human life is deterritorialized. The achievement of mass mobility in modern culture has the effect of compressing space, and of homogenizing place so that while tourists travel far to observe differ-ence, the universalism of mass travel promotes homogeneity and the 'McDonaldization' of the cities and places of the world. The global village creates a depthless and decentred world in which the human identification with locality, place and neighbourhood is often fractured or undermined.

Globalization and urban decay

The most important factor in the degeneration of urban places in Britain is not the mobility of culture or traffic, but the new global mobility of capital. The deindustrialization of Britain's former industrial cities is the principal cause of the decline of so many inner urban communities and places. The impact of the closure of heavy industry and manufacturing has been cumulatively greater in northern England and central Scotland than in any other part of Europe. Economic restructuring has an essentially spatial element as multinational companies, the majority of whose headquarters are located in the largest cities of Europe and the United States, have assumed a new mobility of labour and capital which has involved a quest for lower wages, reduced taxation, weak environmental and safety regulations and the maximization of profits. This shift to globalized production has disrupted the early industrial relationship between capital formation and the provision of livelihood, housing and other services in the places and communities of the metropolis. The control of most global industrial output remains in metropolitan centres such as London, New York and Paris. London for example contains the headquarters of 37 of the world's largest multinational firms. But the low-wage labour which is utilized by these firms increasingly resides in São Paulo, Bombay, Seoul or Beijing. Thus capital mobility is central to the economic and environmental decline of the inner cities of Britain in the last thirty years, and the linkage between capital formation and human well-being in particular spaces of the world economy is severed.

Globalization also produces another pressure which is reflected in the growing resistance of business, particularly in the US and the UK, to the social costs associated with the high wage, high tax, economy of the unionized welfare state. Corporate pressure argues for reduced government efforts to redistribute wealth from rich to poor, and for increased government intervention which favours business over local government or state spending, as instanced in reductions in corporation and managerial class income tax combined with cuts in welfare support, in public services, and in social and community programmes. The perception is sustained by governments and businesses that these things can no longer be afforded in the modern world, though a similar perception is not shared in relation to massive increases in defence spending in the 1980s (US), in security and anti-crime measures (US and UK) and in relation to tax-cuts for business and the rich.

The re-enchantment of the city

The urban policy of the last fifteen years in Britain has reflected this shift from public intervention on behalf of poor people, to public intervention on behalf of entrepreneurs and business. The new focus of inner-city policy in the 1980s and early 1990s on entrepreneurial activity, on making the inner city, or parts of it, attractive to investors and employers, reflects a strategy of competition in the global market for investment capital and jobs. But while the policy has brought about the physical regeneration of decayed urban spaces, this approach has not regenerated the communities of place which inhabit or surround these spaces, as invariably the large investments of capital have attracted external investors who in turn have shipped in workers and services which articulate hardly at all with the local community of lower skilled people. The extreme version of this is London's Docklands where the facilities and employment opportunities of the local population have not been improved, while the disruption of infrastructure, increased traffic flows and the influx of commuters have led to a further diminishment of the prospects and choices for many of the inner-city communities adjoining the Docklands area. Similar results have been charted in relation to the Quayside scheme in Newcastle, or Trafford Park and Salford Quay schemes in Manchester.[3]

The reorientation of planning and economic regeneration towards regenerating the appearance and environment of places also reflects a cultural shift. The postmodern attempt to re-enchant the city by urban regeneration strategies, with their references to premodern traditions and communities, is a considered response to the deracinated and disordered character of the modern city. The planners of the postmodern city have rediscovered place. The universalizing forces of mobility and modernism are addressed by a new respect for place and tradition, and a quest for difference and particularity: 'the postmodern city is then about an attempt to re-imagine urbanity: about recovering a lost sense of territorial identity, urban community and public space. It is a kind of return to (mythical) origins.'[4] Postmodern urbanity is about 'the attempt to restore meaning, rootedness and human proportions to place in an era dominated by depersonalising bulk and standardisation'.[5]

The residents of Britain's inner cities and peripheral housing schemes are certainly familiar with the problems of depersonalizing bulk and of the loss of a sense of place and neighbourhood engendered by the vast redevelopments of the last thirty years. But the postmodern re-enchantment of place is an essentially conservative response to the problems of urban poverty and decline which fails to engage with the real conflicts which arise in relation to power differences and economic differentiation in the increasingly global context of the modern city. The urban romanticism of the gentrified, cleaned up, cappuccino city is essentially a middle-class vision which above all serves the promoters of consumerism. The atria and malls with their stylistic references to a romanticized antiquity serve to insulate rich from poor, and to confirm the exclusion of inner-city residents from the modern version of the consumer good life.

The shift of focus in urban regeneration strategies from people to property and land is perhaps the most striking aspect of the change in policy with respect to urban areas. People are identified with communities of place. The focus on property has more to do with the commodification of space than the regeneration of communities of place. The largest single investment of the London Docklands Development Corporation has been in roads, closely followed by subsidies to the glass towers most favoured by the service sectors of international capital. This emphasis on roads is despite the growing evidence that roads do not create long-term jobs, and that without public transport infrastructure the new offices and enterprise spaces of Docklands and elsewhere cannot thrive.

The designation of urban development areas was a new form of industrial relocation policy, similar to previous government attempts to blend private investment with public inducement. However the difference with the 1980s urban development programme was in the size of the assisted areas. Instead of favouring Wales or North East England the policy favoured small pockets of land adjacent to poor housing areas, but also adjacent to large cities and suburbs through the transport system. Inevitably then the jobs shifted to the urban development areas were often not jobs created for people living in those places but jobs for incomers, or jobs for commuters. Large amounts of public receipts were spent by Urban Development Corporations (UDCs) which had formerly been targeted specifically at poor housing areas and social needs alleviation, with the effect of relocating the jobs of people who were neither unemployed nor poor.

A significant reason for the failure of the policy to address the needs of poor communities is that the UDC brochure ideal of an inner-city economy does not match the reality of a global economy, of international finance houses and service industries of the kind attracted to the developers' glass towers.[6] Inner-city areas and economies are not as tightly defined as the UDC strategy assumes. They are not homogeneous spatial entities. They are not confined to specific areas. Inner-city poverty is juxtaposed with affluence.

The focus on enterprise, space and property is presented as a strategy of empowerment, empowering the individual to change or demand change: local people as individual consumers gain trickle-down benefit from economic regeneration, and the policy is supplemented with support for inner-city entrepreneurs such as that given to young blacks by the Handsworth task force in the Midlands. But strategies to attract corporate investors, whether run by local authorities or UDCs, will not on their own achieve the sought-for reversal of inner urban fortunes. Many investors, attracted by subsidy, do not stay in the longer term. According to its critics, the enterprise strategy therefore needs to be refocused on job creation for poor, low-skilled people and on training and skills for low-skilled people.[7] If the same treasury receipts had been targeted more precisely on poor people, rather than on derelict spaces, it seems likely that the core problems of the urban poor – unemployment, unmarketable skills and consequent lack of civic power – would have been much more successfully addressed. Instead the shift of urban regeneration strategies from people to property exacerbated and accompanied the largest increase in wealth inequality in Britain since the late eighteenth century with the growth of the social, health and public order problems associated with extreme wealth inequality.

Landlessness and urban poverty

The biblical vision of place and economic livelihood is focused on the covenant community and the land. Access to land and livelihood are the key elements to the social and economic order of the covenant as interpreted in the law and the prophets. Isaiah envisions a restored land, a regenerated Jerusalem, and an outcast people once again returned to a place of their own:

> People shall build houses and live to inhabit them, plant vineyards and eat their fruit; they shall not build for others to inhabit, nor plant for others to eat. My people shall live the long life of a tree, and my chosen shall enjoy the fruit of their labour. (Isa 65.21–22)

Isaiah's vision of urban regeneration is focused on people and on land. God's people will once again have the freedom to live on the land in their own houses, to order their own communities and to enjoy the fruit of their own work. Urban regeneration for Isaiah means that the cries of help of the outcast and the exiles are answered, their children thrive, and there is land, work, shelter and food for all.[8] When this new social order is accomplished then Isaiah declares 'Rejoice with Jerusalem and exult in her all you who love her', for the Lord 'will send peace flowing over her like a river, and the wealth of nations like a stream in flood' (Isa 66.12).

In the Hebrew Bible land is a part of the covenant community. God not Israel is the owner of the land, and the goodness and fertility of the land is sustained when the terms of the covenant and the order of creation are respected. The people of God are entrusted with God's land but they do not become its outright owners. Land concentration and speculation is condemned as a denial of God's ultimate ownership of the land.

Landlessness, the denial of ownership of land, and access to land, is a central feature of life for the urban poor in Britain. Unlike subsidized mortgaged home owners, the considerable proportion of the poor householder's income devoted to housing represents neither investment in personal security, nor in the local economy, but typically a payment to an absentee landlord. Landlessness is as much of an issue for Britain's inner urban poor as it is for squatter settlers in Third World cities. Indeed landlessness in Britain is in many ways a more acute problem as British planning laws and tight policing of land use deny to the poor in Britain the option taken up by squatters in the Third World of informal settlement and the self-built city. The 1994 Criminal Justice Bill unjustifiably targets precisely those people – New Age travellers and squatters – whose response to enforced landlessness has been that of informal settlement in rural areas or in vacant city housing. The interaction of the property market and planning laws relating to urban and agricultural land commodifies land and produces a zoned pattern of habitation which effectively excludes a proportion of the population from participation in the standard capitalist route to economic security – property ownership. The sale of so much of Britain's socially owned housing stock in the 1980s heightened the problem for the poor as the remaining social housing was largely unsaleable because undesirable. Undesirable housing stock, typically high-rise and deck-access flats and run-down inner-city multiple-occupancy housing, is also the kind of housing which denies its residents access to land – private gardens, courtyards and children's play space are central elements of the sub-urban and gentrified housing of the more affluent zones of city housing.

The denial of access to land, and to ownership of land, is in biblical terms a spiritual and not just an economic issue. The exiled households of Israel mourned their loss of land and livelihood and their earnest prayer was to be able to plant again their own olive trees and live in their own houses. To this extent the Thatcherite vision of home-ownership might be said to have a biblical affinity. However the nature of land ownership commended in the Bible is very different from that associated with the 1980s shift from social to private housing. Land is held in trust by the community of Israel and its constituent households. There are legal limitations on concentrations of land ownership such that successful entrepreneurial farmers and traders may not acquire so much land that the marginal and unsuccessful are excluded from the land. Instead land is seen as a gift of God and a communal asset held in trust. In this sense the post-war vision of social housing may have been preferable from the perspective of a biblical approach to land. However the reality of controlled space, of absentee local authority landlords, and of mechanistic and inhuman planning did not commend itself to those who observed or experienced social housing. The break-up of public housing monopolies, the diversification of charitable and housing association provision, may therefore be seen as an important contribution to a more human-scale and communal approach to housing provision. But homelessness, rising private rents and the continuing horror of many housing schemes dating from the 1960s and 1970s continue to characterize the experience of urban space for the poor in Britain.

The denial of land and livelihood to the poor has still not been properly addressed by recent changes in housing provision, and in many respects the housing conditions of the poor have considerably worsened in the 1980s and 1990s. The rising incidence of diseases, most notably tuberculosis, associated with poor nutrition and damp and over-crowded housing in Britain's cities is one of the principal indicators of the further fracturing of an already divided nation.

Isaiah's vision of the exiled and marginal returning to their self-built homes and olive groves may seem a utopian irrelevance in the light of the current economics of housing and land in Britain. Perhaps we are no longer in a position where we can move people wholesale back into self-sufficiency on plots of land in rural areas, though there is clearly a considerable minority of people – New Age travellers, ecologists, Prince Charles – who believe that such a strategy is at least part of the solution to urban anomie, homelessness, unemployment and poverty. But Isaiah's vision does point sharply to the extremely concentrated nature of land ownership in contemporary Britain. The size of the housing and land estates of such people as the Dukes of Westminster and Buccleuch, or indeed Prince Charles, is the other side of the landlessness of Britain's urban poor. Britain experiences concentrations of land ownership which verge on those of Brazil and other very unequal Third World societies, and this is in a country with an already high concentration of population to land. Extreme concentrations of land wealth are a major element in the concentrations of urban poverty in some of the least desirable and most environmentally degraded parts of Britain's cities. Land is still the key to the economy of nature, the first product of nature without which economic development cannot take place. Unequal patterns of land ownership are one of the most common features of inequitable patterns of economic development and progress. Equally the fracturing of the relationship between human communities and particular places, particular land areas, is a key element in the deterioration of human life quality and natural environment which economic development so often brings in its wake.

The restoration of communities of place

Isaiah's vision of the restoration of urban Israel needs to be translated into an approach to urban community regeneration which restores dignity and livelihood to the marginalized people of the urban core and the housing scheme. Such an approach will be concerned with restoring the land and environment of the poor, making flowers and trees grow in the concrete wilderness, and clean air to return to traffic-free streets. It will allow the poor to help build and design their own houses and to live in them, to recover livelihood and a sense of self-worth. It will foster communal self-reliance and self-determination. Rather than relying on attracting the global forces of international capitalism back into areas from which they have departed, Isaiah's vision suggests a move to community-based strategies which involve the empowerment of people in a more collective and communal fashion than that implied in the enterprise vision.

Many of the best examples of urban regeneration have been those which have emerged from urban communities which have themselves sought to reclaim their own place in the world, to reorder their own housing and environment and recover lost dignity in new forms of economic activity and livelihood. Stories are emerging from around the world of inner-city regeneration where community groups have sought to regenerate their places, their housing and their economies by resisting, rather than enhancing or competing with, global economic processes and often also national or local government. In Baltimore and Finsbury Park, London, Community Business Trusts (CBTs) were established which enabled local people to draw private and public investment into community-designed housing and infrastructural schemes, and local job-generation initiatives. In Washington DC community development practitioners have experimented with Community Land Trusts (CLTs) where land is bought by the CLT and leased to individuals, groups and corporations who may own their houses or developments on the land while the land remains in the ownership of the CLT. The CLT helps the community to democratize land ownership, protect itself from absentee ownership and from the autonomous powers of planners and developers. CLTs have funded low-cost house-building, craft and home maintenance projects, and educational and care schemes designed to promote and recycle cash and wealth in poor urban communities, and to prevent the movement of money out of inner urban areas to distant landlords and businesses. Most of the CLTs in the United States were begun by alliances of churches or religious sisters with community and residents' groups. From the success of over two hundred CLTs a new vision of land reform for the poor in America has sprung in which it is proposed that a diverse range of subsidies, taxation and regulatory instruments be utilized to favour community and tenant group land acquisition over the acquisitive tendencies of property companies and private land-lords.

In Britain there are also a range of examples of communities taking control of their own place in urban areas. One such is the community architecture movement which was notably successful in a scheme in Liverpool where tenants employed the architect, chose the site, and designed everything from the floor plans to the landscaping. What people chose were simple traditional houses built around courtyards and gardens. Another was the community planning of a large piece of derelict former industrial land known as the Coin Street Site on the South Bank of the Thames. The area had been identified by government and private developers as prime office space but a group of local people lobbied for its development as a mixed site for private and social housing, community facilities, small business and recreational prem-ises. In a protracted battle between developers and a vociferous lobby of local people, the community finally won, albeit with the aid and intervention of the now defunct GLC. But the success of the Coin Street development pointed the way to a new paradigm of popular planning which is a significant alternative to the disasters of the bureaucrat-led planning of the post-war era and the business-led planning of the 1980s.

The establishment by community groups of city farms and gardens, and of vegetable growing co-operatives on derelict land is another example of a communally based endeavour to change the relation between people and land in urban core areas. City gardens have been established by local community groups on disused or run-down gar-dens such as Ashram Acres in Birmingham or in gaps between city blocks in the Bronx and Harlem in New York, in San Francisco, and city farms have been created in many vacant urban spaces in inner-city Britain. These initiatives provide opportunities for urban people and their children to experience growing plants and food, and caring for animals, helping to establish a new relation to nature, and opportunities for personal growth and development often denied to the urban landless and poor. In such schemes, people discover the pleasures of gardening and some have gone on to find employment in garden centres, or gardening work in the suburbs, from their first experiences on a city lot.

Another important example of communities re-establishing a sense of responsibility and control over their own neighbourhoods, their own land and living space is that of community organizing. Inspired by the radical community development ideas of Saul Alinsky, community organizing has become established in a number of urban areas in Britain where a broad alliance of predominantly religious groups – Anglicans and Methodists, Muslims, Hindus and Sikhs – have come together to identify the loci of power and influence in their areas, and to challenge economic, bureaucratic and political actors concerning the effects of their activities and decisions on poor people in poor neighbourhoods. One member of the Urban Theology Group, Margaret Walsh, described how community organizing in the West Midlands had enabled poor people to begin to retake power over their lives and to work for the health and welfare of communities with no effective voice in traditional party politics. A group on Heath Town housing estate in Wolverhampton was protesting at the siting of a poisonous battery recycling plant and a toxic waste plant in the midst of a large housing scheme. Using various forms of direct action and lobbying, local people discovered a new articulacy in confronting factory owners, environmental health officers and politicians with the scandalous pollution of the environment of a poor neighbourhood, which the beneficiaries and regulators of such activity would never countenance on the boundaries of their suburban gardens.

Many of these community-oriented approaches have a common element, which is the recovery of the vitality of communities of place, a renewed sense of locality, identity with land, even a quest for ecological harmony. There is also in many of these schemes an interaction between the regeneration of place and the recovery of livelihood. The local urban community becomes a place where cash-flows are recycled and wealth is collectively generated, supplanting the traditional mode of welfare subsidy and cash outflows of urban priority economies. Community-based economic and land-oriented initiatives challenge the traditional popular perception of urban priority communities as communities of dependence and subsidy. CLTs and CBTs have exploited the middle-class subsidies for mortgages and property ownership and maintenance, and small business subsidies in order to help overturn this image. They have also challenged the commodification of space and place implicit in deregulated markets in land and housing, and the destructive effects on community of the global processes of economic restructuring.

Resistance in the globalized city

According to recent studies of world cities, communal resistance to the community-destroying effects of global economic restructuring is a key aspect of the future of the globalized city.[9] As the global economy moves out of local scale, and beneficial relationships of mutual interest are cut between local communities and corporate actors, so the traditional work-association patterns of community empowerment – trade unions – have been weakened. Work-place-based resistance to corporate power is being supplemented or reborn in urban areas as place-based and neighbourhood-based resistance to the destructive effects of global capitalism on the communities and welfare of the marginalized. Connections of mutual welfare and benefit are re-established between economic activity and communities of place.

Community organizing, tenant power and local economic activity are all means by which urban communities are attempting to recover power over their own lives in the wake of the demise of traditional labour associationalism.[10] Another key aspect of this realignment of community empowerment is the growing informalization of local economic activity. Shadow work and the informal economy represent a growing proportion of income generation in the world's cities from the slums of Calcutta to the housing schemes of Coventry. Informal economic activity is typically that which is focused on communities of place, where individuals and communities which are excluded from the global economy, and from national and corporate employment and wealth creation strategies, find alternative ways of creating wealth and employment. These might be unregulated sweat-shop labour of the kind which typifies many Indian cities, and which have returned to Western cities such as Los Angeles or Birmingham. They might be home-based or street-based craft industries such as shoe or rug making. A growing and legal form of informal economic activity in Britain is the Local Exchange Trading Scheme also referred to in Peter Sedgwick's chapter on Enterprise. The informalization of local economic activity is part of a wider social shift arising from the failure of the partnership of the state and private corporations in the globalized world economic system to provide livelihood and housing for a growing proportion of the population. Community housing and land projects, and informal employment initiatives may all be seen as part of this wider trend to economic and political diversity in the global city.

For the move from dependency to communal self-reliance to become more widely established requires more radical changes in patterns of housing subsidy, land ownership and wealth sharing. The single measure most widely canvassed by theorists of a radical reorientation of the economy to the needs of human communities of place and the limits of nature and land is the idea of a guaranteed minimum income (GMI).[11] GMI is a sum of money, a basic personal income, which is paid to everyone in society regardless of their work status. It is seen as a direct means of distributing the wealth of a shrinking number of producer jobs in post-industrial societies, as a means of empowering the poor and removing the cultural and social stigma of welfare dependence, and as a means of reducing the need for intensive work on the part of those who would choose a lower-impact and more contemplative life-style were the opportunity available to them. GMI again recalls a central aspect of the Isaiah vision for urban and communal regeneration. Unequal access to livelihood, the denial of livelihood to some and its over-abundant provision for others, are condemned by Isaiah and other Hebrew prophets as instances of a social order which is in open rebellion against the pattern of covenant community which God ordained in the Torah.[12] The deleterious effects of wealth inequality on natural and human ecology, and on a nation's capacity to create wealth, are being increasingly well charted in the aftermath of the rises in inequality which characterized many advanced industrial economies in the 1980s, but particularly Britain. The provision of livelihood without means-testing is a vital aspect of the regeneration of communities of place as through GMI people are enabled to recover a sense of dignity and self-reliance. GMI need not involve a massive increase in taxation burdens on those in work. It would involve a major shift in taxation and welfare systems, which would remove the disincentives to work for families on housing and social security benefits, and possibly also reduce the need for full-time working in two-income households. For those in work the GMI would function as a personal taxation allowance while income above GMI levels would be taxed more highly than under current income tax arrangements.

Memory, ritual and eucharistic communities

What is the place of the Church in this recovery of local control over the economy in communities of place? As we have already noted, the place-based character of the Church of England is one of its principal strengths and opportunities. Its parishes and clergy remain in the inner core and the peripheral housing schemes of Britain's cities when many other agencies operate on the Urban Priority Area from outside. The local parish provides a significant potential locus for community regeneration strategies because the Church of England parish represents both building – place and focus for community organizing – and organizational base. Many of the charitable and trust-oriented initiatives recounted above rely on some form of pre-existing indigenous community base to become established. The parish church is such a base and can function in just this way as many of the projects supported by the Church Urban Fund testify.

Parish churches can revivify communities and localities. They can recreate patterns of communal self-reliance. But churches must also articulate the spiritual significance of a place, and why human beings find particular places evocative. This spiritual significance of place has a number of foci. It relates to the memories of patterns of human settlement, patterns of work and residence, events and communities which precede those at present residing in a particular place. Places may often seem to retain these memories, either physically in the marks of previous settlements or in some more mysterious fashion such as the strange sense of presence, and absence, in many a closed-down factory and dockyard. In premodern cultures and still in some places even in Britain this spiritual sense for the significance of place is retained. The spirits of Scotland's kings seem to hang over the small graveyard on the Isle of Iona just as the spirits of the pilgrims still seem to walk in the narrow medieval streets of Canterbury. But what of memory and a spiritual sense of place in Urban Priority Areas? Many of the residents of the inner urban core of Britain's cities have a particularly strong sense of place and memory. The London East Ender's 'manor', the sense for boundaries and territory of a street gang, the old lady who fought to the end the M11 extension which destroyed her urban terrace in Leytonstone, testify to a quasi-spiritual sense of place and a commitment to locale, over time and generations, which is a fading dream for so much of the West's mobile work-force. Some recent urban regeneration schemes and plans have sought to build on this memory of human settlement. In the wake of the dynamiting of the disastrous deck-access housing of Hume and Moss Side in Manchester the planners have projected a new street plan of terraced housing, shops and community facilities which is directly modelled on the old Victorian street patterns which the development of the 1960s destroyed.

This evocation and recalling of the significance of the memory of place, of a community's story of exile or home-coming, of oppression or liberation articulates strongly with the worship and rituals of parish churches whose sacralizing of urban areas is a vital element in the recovery of a sense of place. The paradigmatic sacred ritual of Christianity is the Eucharist where memory and present are brought together in the transformation of bread and wine and their sharing in the community meal. The Eucharist creates a ritual space where heaven and earth seem to meet, and the repetition of this event in particular places hallows the space and makes entry into worship easier for those familiar with the church and its story. Eucharist was the occasion for the development of particular places of worship in Christianity from the third century as the house assembly moved into the basilica. Christians at the Reformation sought to undermine this sacralizing effect of the Eucharist on space, and buildings. The vandalization of so many beautiful places of worship during the Reformation was an assault on this tradition which in many ways presaged the terrible sundering of the people from the land with the enclosure of common land and open fields by commercial farmers and the new landlord class. The Church signally failed to resist the enforced vagrancy and landlessness of England's peasant classes. The continuing experience of immiseration in city slums, though now so far removed in time from the harrowing events of the enclosures, is a constant reminder of the deep injustice and violence which preceded and enabled the modern social disorder of urban poverty and landlessness.

However, the Eucharist and the experience of Christian worship are not so strongly tied to holy space, temples and specific places as the rituals of pre-exilic Judaism or the Islamic orientation to Mecca. In this sense the Reformers were not entirely wrong. The Eucharist establishes a communion which though located and experienced in particular places, and frequently in various forms of holy space, nonetheless transcends the particularity of places and of settled communities or tribes and thus recalls the resistance of the prophets and of Jesus and the apostles to the idea that the people of God can ever rightly say they have 'arrived'. Christians are a pilgrim people and the Eucharist affirms their communion in pilgrimage as much as the identity of churches or congregations with particular lands, places or nations. The Eucharist affirms not just place as building or land but place as community, for in the Eucharist, wherever it is celebrated, the people of God are reconstituted as a community of believers whose meeting creates a sacred space, whether in a church sanctuary, on a factory floor or in the front-room of a high-rise flat.

The eucharistic transformation of the elements of human sustenance and livelihood perhaps loses some of its resonance in urban cultures where bread is bought in plastic bags and beverages in metal cans. Equally the sacred places built and set aside by Victorian or even 1960s Christians may become hollow shells, damp, cold targets for vandals as sacrality gives way to emptiness and economically-induced neglect. The urban church perhaps needs to find new ways of re-engaging the eucharistic ritual with the patterns of life and livelihood, and of life and livelihood's denial in the city. Many of the urban house churches which have sprung up in London's East End, in housing schemes in the East Midlands or in deindustrialized urban communities in North East England have actively eschewed the traditional sacrality of place associated with the parish church. Instead they choose to meet in school halls, community centres, even public houses. The strangeness, the otherness of the traditional church building is eschewed in a quest for a space which is made holy not by symbol and design but by the rhythmic singing, hand-clapping and testimony telling of this new style of church life. But whether in a school hall or a parish church, a housing scheme flat or a simple chapel, the place of community which is created in the Eucharist remains paradigmatic to the transformation, healing and community affirmation which the Eucharist represents, and which makes this ritual meal a vital element in the role of the parish and worshipping community in contributing to the regeneration of urban communities of place.

In addition to the sacred space which the community of Christians makes in its worship, and often in its buildings, there is also a need for specific rituals which link church worship to the land, to housing and neighbourhood. The old rural traditions such as beating of the bounds may be inappropriate in urban neighbourhoods, particularly where these boundaries bear no relationship to current patterns of settlement. Perhaps instead a shortened liturgy on an occasional summer Sunday morning might be followed by a form of service of the local environment such as cleaning up a river-bed, planting a garden on derelict land, or tree planting. Within Sunday worship a useful strategy might be to incorporate news about the neighbourhood and regeneration initiatives within the prayers, testimonies, readings, sermons and notices of the community's worship. The traditional house blessing, for which a form exists in the prayer book of the Church of South India though in no Church of England liturgies, is another means by which the Christian community can express a sense of the universality of God's blessing in every space, and also the particularity of his power and presence in particular places of human living-space.

By a variety of means of re-engagement with communities of place, economic, political, social and spiritual, the Church needs to reclaim the rule of God over the Urban Priority Area and the city, and to call forth the Spirit of God as the agent of the renewal of all the places and forms of the creation. Reclaiming land and place for human community and livelihood is not only an economic but a spiritual battle. The Spirit surely groans in travail with all those communities whose places have been ravaged by the combined actions of global markets, corporations, bureaucrats, developers and landlords. Our rituals, stories, sermons and prayers, as well as our community organizing and community development strategies, must recall the victory of God over the powers in the crucifixion and resurrection and the power of the Spirit as the agent of our renewal and regeneration.

The significance of land, place, neighbourhood and community is not just sociological and political but theological, moral and spiritual. Communal self-reliance, participation in community decision-making, access to power and responsibility, living space on the land, and a sense of sacred presence are all vital elements in the stories of the people of God and of their identity in both the Hebrew Bible and the New Testament. The denial of these elements in the experience of power-lessness, landlessness and community melt-down in many of Britain's urban areas is the cause of so much hopelessness, despair and aliena-tion. People need to recover a sense that together they can control what happens in their own place, that they are not at the mercy of unspecified powers and global forces. The authors of *Faith in the City* called for 'a process which will enable those who are at present in poverty and powerlessness to rejoin the life of the nation'. The strategies of commu-nity regeneration, tenancy co-operatives, community organizing, informal economics and popular planning all represent glimmers of hope that people, poor people, harassed people, formerly powerless people, can regain a voice, can participate in the future of their commu-nities, can rebuild a place which they may call their own. The maintenance of hope in the possibilities of human transformation, and of a theological realism about the strength of the powers which oppose the quest for justice and quality of life, are both vital to Christian rituals, songs and stories which can sustain churches and worshipping com-munities in their struggle from exile to the promised land, from the towers of darkness (often quite literal towers) to the self-built houses, gardens, roads and fields of which Isaiah dreamed in his vision of a regenerated Jerusalem.

Notes

1 D. Davies, 'Christianity' in J. Holm with J. Bowker (eds), *Sacred Place* (London: Pinter, 1994), pp. 33–61.

2 M. Castells, *The Informational City: Information Technology, Economic Restruc-turing and the Urban-Regional Process* (Oxford: Basil Blackwell, 1989).

3 M. Keith and A. Rogers (eds), *Hollow Promises: Rhetoric and Reality in the Inner City* (London: Mansell, 1991).

4 K. Robins, 'Prisoners of the city. Whatever could a postmodern city be?' in E. Carter, J. Donald and J. Squires (eds), *Space and Place: Theories of Identity and Location* (London: Lawrence and Wishart, 1991), pp. 303–30.

5 D. Ley, 'Modernism, post-modernism and the struggle for place'; cited by Robins, 'Prisoners of the city'.
6 B. Robson, *Those Inner Cities: Reconciling the Economic and Social Aims of Urban Policy* (Oxford: Clarendon Press, 1988).
7 N. Deakin and J. Edwards, *The Enterprise Culture and the Inner City* (London: Routledge, 1993).
8 R. Fung, *The Isaiah Vision* (Geneva: World Council of Churches, 1992).
9 M. Smith and R. Fagin, *The Capitalist City: Global Restructuring and Community Politics* (Oxford: Basil Blackwell, 1987).
10 P. Hirst, *Associational Politics* (Cambridge: Polity Press, 1993).
11 Ibid.
12 D. Meeks, *God the Economist* (Minneapolis: Fortress Press, 1989).

Children

MICHAEL S. NORTHCOTT

Children must come first because children are our most sacred trust.
They also hold the key to our future in a very practical sense.

Margaret Thatcher

While the British government signed the UN Convention on the Rights of the Child in 1993, it pursues policies which have systematically disadvantaged British children over children from other developed countries, and which have brought about a society in which the flourishing of children is increasingly undermined. Government research published in 1992 revealed that the number of children living in poverty in Britain had increased from 10 per cent to 25 per cent in the ten years of Conservative rule from 1979 to 1989.[1] Britain now has a higher proportion of children living in poverty than any other country in the European Union.

The causes of this dramatic worsening of the situation of Britain's children, and particularly of children living in Urban Priority Areas, are growing unemployment, increases in income differentials between high and low paid, increases in marriage breakdown and hence the number of children brought up in lone-parent households, shifts in the taxation system from progressive income taxes to regressive taxes on clothing, fuel, and other essentials, cuts in child benefit, reductions in benefit income and housing benefit, cuts in housing expenditure, and cuts in social services provision relating to children and young people. It is often claimed that as a nation we lack the money to improve the lot of children and the poor, but Britain spends less on health, housing, education and social security than almost any other developed nation.[2] Britain also taxes the low paid at punitive rates without parallel in the rest of Europe, and at rates much higher than top income earners through the interaction of taxation and income support.

139

Government ministers frequently intone that, despite reductions in child support and services, there is no absolute poverty in contemporary Britain, and that no child is forced to go hungry, or homeless, or without clothes or shoes in today's affluent society. But the following comments from parents living in public housing on supplementary benefit give the lie to the myth that there is no real poverty in Britain today:

> The little one is suffering, it's freezing cold upstairs ... We can't afford a heater, she's had a cold for the last two months. (Parents of an 18-month-old child sleeping in a damp bedroom with no heating.)

> I just have to sit with a lot of blankets around me and wear warm socks. In the winter, you feel like putting on the heating to warm them up but then I think about the bill and how I'm going to pay for it and I say to myself, leave it. Yes, when the children are here then I will put the heater on. They are small so you have to put it on for them, don't you?

> We can't afford to send the children on school trips, so they stay home for the day.

> We've got Christmas coming up. For me that's not any enjoyment, it's a nightmare. I look in the shops, looking at prices and it's a bloody nightmare.

> My eldest daughter (aged 14) has been saying that she wants to celebrate her birthday ... she's been crying all the time ... She's been saying she's going to have a birthday party but I'm saying no. I said to her 'You invite all those people, and they can come and sit on the sofa, but I won't be making anything' ... I just haven't got the money.

> I'd like to be able to afford to buy them new clothes without having to juggle and make them plod on but I have no choice.

> I only eat once a day, usually at tea-time, if I feel like it. But I've got to the stage I say to myself I'm not hungry, I can go for days without nothing ... because I want to put a bit of decent food in my bairn's stomach.

> I make sure the children eat first; if there's any left, I will. If not ... then it doesn't matter about me.

> I just worry about paying the bills ... I can't think about when the children grow up ... the worst thing is just not having enough money to pay the bills, buy the food and look after the children. It's too much from hand to mouth.[3]

The majority of poor families are concentrated in the residue of public housing which remains in local authority hands after the sale of council homes, most of it undesirable, poorly maintained or badly designed and therefore unsaleable. A recent survey of 600 families living in public housing in Glasgow, Edinburgh and London found that a third of their homes were damp and half had evidence of mould. Both damp and mould are associated with the rising incidence of bronchial disease and other health problems in young children: children born into poor homes are twice as likely to die in their first year of life than children born into middle-class families.

All of these pressures, of poor housing, inadequate diet, low incomes and unemployment, generate enormous pressures on UPA households and families. Many parents turn to alcohol or even drugs as a way of getting by. Many families break up. Children of unemployed parents live in fear of family break-down as well as fear of unemployment. Of families experiencing divorce, 50 per cent live in public housing, and 60 per cent of single-parent families live in public sector housing.

Government ministers frequently blame the high incidence of single-parent households for the high levels of poverty, and of child delinquency in UPA areas. However any correlation between delinquency and single-parent families is more likely to be related to the poverty which so many single parents experience, and to the pressures it places on struggling parents, than to the putative moral defects of the single-parent household. As Marina Warner said in her 1994 Reith lectures, the nation is not afraid that Prince William, raised by his lone mother, will turn into a delinquent heir to the throne, for he will have the comforts and privileges which will ensure he will most likely thrive.[4]

Poverty in childhood is the greatest single predictor of physical abuse in the home. It is also connected with the incidence of child sexual abuse although not so strongly. The feeling of powerlessness, of inability to perform as 'bread-winner' is a commonly cited trigger for male physical violence in the home. With sexual abuse, whose incidence is estimated by some UK social services departments to be 20 per cent for girls and 10 per cent for boys, poverty is again a factor, though the incidence of abuse is less strongly correlated with poverty than with physical violence in the home, and the presence of a step-father.[5]

Hazards outside the home are also much more prevalent for children living in UPAs, and the requirements this places on families for increased levels of chaperoning make it much more difficult for UPA parents to protect their children from the kind of experiences which are likely to ferment delinquency in later life: dangers from molestation by strangers, from fast-moving and heavy traffic, from drug-taking and soliciting behaviour, from offending and delinquent behaviour on the streets. Parents find that their local area is bad for their children, and that they are forced either to supervise their children more heavily than

children in other areas, or to leave them prey to undesirable influences. Children have to be accompanied to school, kept in the house rather than allowed to play outside:

> You can't go to the adventure playground over there because of the drug users, you can't go over there because of the neighbours, they can't play football in the streets because of the motors, there's nothing left for them . . . I feel rotten that I'm having to ground them for disobeying us, because they only want to play.[6]

Studies have found that it is those families who fail to supervise their younger children in this dangerous environment outside the home which later produce delinquent children.[7] The other key difference between families which produce delinquent children and those which do not relates to child-rearing practices, and in particular to the presence or absence of child-centred behaviour in the child's home environment, or, to put this another way, 'the willingness (of the parent) to take trouble for the attainment of aims in which the parent has no immediate interest'.[8] A more thorough definition of child-centredness would refer to such items as the availability of private space in which to play, dedicated conversation between parent and individual child before going to bed, parental participation in a child's play or hobby, and responsiveness to a child's feelings and demands.

The rising incidence of child delinquency in contemporary Britain, which is by no means limited to children from UPA areas, may then be accounted for by a general reduction in child-centred behaviour by parents. The reasons for this reduction might include the increasing tendency, and often the economic necessity, for both parents to work outside the home; the use of television and videos as child-minding equipment; the break-up of families and the high incidence of single-parent households where there is less time for child-centred behaviour. It might also indicate a weakening in moral attitudes and codes, or the prevalence of individualistic values and mores which are not conducive to the flourishing of healthy families where children are effectively nurtured. However, while recognizing the significance of parental responsibility for the increasing problems which children experience in contemporary Britain, we cannot easily isolate individual moral responsibility in relation to parenting from wider social, cultural and political factors, and this is particularly the case in relation to families in UPA areas. Most UPA parents face a series of impossible demands on their time and personal resources: the excessive demands of chaperoning because of dangers outside the home, the very limited space and resources in which to organize children's activities in the home, the limited emotional resources which parents have to draw on in the context of the daily struggle for the necessities of life such as warmth, cooked meals and decent clothing. Despite all of these constraints more than 80 per cent succeed in raising children who do not become delinquent. Rather than blaming single parents, and the putative 'underclass', for their inherent moral failings as parents, the key to supporting families in UPA areas, and to reducing delinquency, must surely be to develop educational programmes to improve the nurturing skills of parents, while at the same time increasing the income levels, and improving the housing and social conditions of families in UPA areas, so that they have both time and space in which to effectively nurture their children.

Educational attainment and expectation are also greatly reduced for children from UPAs. In an inner-city school in Edinburgh parents found that teachers were very pleased when children simply turned up for class, and even more so when they registered for and actually sat a public exam. However, expectations of achievement in such examinations were correlatively low. Poor accommodation in UPA schools is also a common problem. The National Audit Office found that deficiencies in school buildings were hindering the educational achievement and morale of one-fifth of school children.[9] Bullying in school is no worse in large cities than in rural areas. However there is evidence of more violence, aggression and bullying in schools close to or within UPAs. There is even stronger evidence that children from UPA located homes are often the victims of bullying, or engage in bullying behaviour. They may become the targets of bullying because of withdrawn behaviour or limited social skills, or because of poor clothing, footwear, health or appearance. Victims of bullying are typically anxious or submissive individuals with a low sense of self-worth.[10] They are also usually physically weaker than average, and also disinclined to use physical violence to defend themselves. Another group of victims of bullying are hyperactive children, and children with aggressive as well as anxious characteristics, again characteristics often associated with children from very poor homes. Children who bully are frequently the subject of aggressive, violent or extreme emotional behaviour in the home. They are also often from homes where parents have no emotional involvement with the children, and where there is little supervision of children's time or interest in their activities.

The increasing ubiquity of the motor-car means that children throughout society lead more confined and supervised lives than any previous generation, and fewer children cycle or walk to school or shops, or play on the street. Those that still do are at ever-increasing risk as more and more cars use the roads – some of them driven by parents taking children to school.[11] In one year (1990), 48,000 children were killed or injured on the roads in Britain, most of these accidents occurring in urban areas. Such accidents are much more likely to happen to poor children: children of unemployed parents are three times as likely as children of professional parents to be killed on the roads in Britain. British children are also much more at risk than their European counterparts, or than adults in Britain. Traffic danger and fear of road accidents contribute disproportionately to family stress amongst poor people as they live in the most cramped housing often adjacent to major arterial roads. Children kept in because their parents dare not let them play out add to family stress, they are less fit, they do not learn the skills of independent movement, and are denied a sense of freedom and responsibility in relation to their local environment.[12] They are also likely to engage in more intensive television watching as the only means of diversion or recreation that most poor households can provide, with the side-effects of passivity and reduced creativity and exercise that over-indulgence in television produce. It is a cruel irony that the children of parents who can least afford the blandishments of commercialized television – with its frequent adverts for children's toys, clothing, trainers, entertainment and sports equipment – are those who watch the most television.

The urban environment in which many children live is destructive of their spiritual and personal wholeness. Children's creative drives, their identity with and interest in natural processes, living and wild things, are undermined by the sterile and denatured aspect of so many urban landscapes.[13] The Tarmac school playgrounds which most urban children play on are notorious for creating minor injury, but they are also associated with aggressive and less natural behaviour than that which children practise in wild or less controlled spaces. Vandalism and the destruction of the few things – such as trees – which do grow in UPA areas may be a reaction to the excessive control of space imposed on inner-city and UPA children, as much as an indication of poor self-discipline or weak parental control.[14]

But children in UPAs find other survival strategies than vandalism. More than half the children from poor and deprived backgrounds in contemporary Britain achieve a better life for themselves as adults. Children in UPAs learn to be 'streetwise', they pick up methods of self-defence, they find waste ground on which to play, they develop skills in challenging adults who may wish to do them harm, and indeed in challenging authority figures and others who may wish to unduly restrict their lives and freedom to play. They may also challenge the fears of their parents about the risk of abduction or other dangers on the street. Children want and need to play with their friends in and around their local neighbourhood. Safe space for children to play in is the single

resource most commonly requested by family residents of UPA housing schemes and inner-city areas. Children under ten play within a few
hundred yards of the house and the poor provision of play space means
that most children are forced to play on narrow pavements, in stair-
ways and walkways or in the road.[15] Outdoor play is tremendously
important to children because through it they build a bridge from the
family into the neighbourhood community. The over-supervised child
is a child who fails to discover an identity with place and the local
environment. Play requires freedom of movement and action, exploration and privacy. Children experience their locality more intensely than
any other group. Adults come and go, to work, for shopping or to visit
offices or public buildings. Children rarely leave large housing estates,
except on occasional bus trips to town-centres. It is all the more the case
then that children need, and seek, the opportunity to have positive
experiences of play, exploration, freedom and movement within their
local areas. Where the dangers are so great as to necessitate the denial of
all such freedom, then truly this leads to a diminishment of all that we
understand as childhood.

There are those who claim that childhood is a social construct rather
than an inalienable state of innocence, freedom and play without the
responsibility of work. In other cultures and other times, it is said,
children were required to work, to till fields or work in factories, and
children did not have the protected space from adult responsibility and
experience that modern societies provide. The loss of innocence or
freedom to play of the UPA child may then be no great cause for
concern. Most children in most centuries did not conform to the modern
romanticized view of childhood. However, this sociologically fashionable view has been discredited by more recent historical studies, and
indeed if we look at that most influential of documents in relation to
Christian Europe, the Bible, we do find a special place given to childhood, not over-sentimentalized but nonetheless distinct, which is in
sharp contrast to the picture of premodern European childhood as
presented by some modern sociologists and historians.

The enduring popularity of the Andrew Lloyd Webber and Tim Rice
musical *Joseph and the Amazing Technicolor Dreamcoat* is a reminder of the
significant role that children, and stories about children, play in the
Bible, in both Old and New Testaments. The dreamy child with the
wacky coat who becomes Prime Minister is a story with a lot of modern
appeal to youngsters who dream of winning the national lottery as the
only escape from their own poverty and fears of unemployment. The
stories of the childhood of Samuel and David are equally significant for
a theology of childhood, reminding us that God calls and speaks to
children, and that the purposes of God are served by children as well as

adults. The story of Naaman is another child-centred story, which tells how a captured and exiled girl, playing the role of servant in her captor's house, was instrumental in bringing about his healing from leprosy. The girl was far from home and her faith in God very stretched but when she suggested a meeting with Elisha for her master's cure, her faith was instrumental in bringing about Naaman's healing.[16] Again many of the prophets including Jeremiah and Isaiah were called not as adults but as children. To the young Jeremiah, God said 'Do not plead that you are too young; for you are to go to whatever people I send you, and say whatever I tell you to say. Fear none of them for I shall be with you to keep you safe' (Jer 1.7).

The most striking biblical reference to a chosen child is of course the birth of the Christ child, recounted in various forms in all the gospels, and the stories, few though they are, surrounding this child's growth into adulthood, his flight into Egypt, his attendance at the Temple, his growth in wisdom. The message of these stories, that God intends to redeem humanity through the birth of this vulnerable child, is central to the gospel, and to the biblical concept of goodness as vulnerable and gentle, a goodness which overcomes evil not by force and violence but by the power of sacrificial love. The attitude of Jesus to children is also quite striking. A number of the recorded miracles involved children – Jairus' daughter, the (young) man born blind, the boy with the five loaves and two fishes. There are also the famous sayings concerning children: 'Let the children come to me; do not try to stop them; for the kingdom of heaven belongs to such as these' (Matt 19.14); 'Truly I tell you: unless you turn round and become like children, you will never enter the kingdom of heaven. Whoever humbles himself and becomes like this child will be the greatest in the kingdom of heaven, and whoever receives one such child in my name receives me' (Matt 18.3– 5). Again we read of how when Jesus came to Jerusalem it was the children who acclaimed him in the Temple while the chief priests complained at the noise they were making:

> When the chief priests and scribes saw the wonderful things he did,
> and heard the boys in the temple shouting 'Hosanna to the Son of
> David!' they were indignant and asked him, 'Do you hear what they
> are saying?' Jesus answered, 'I do. Have you never read the text "you
> have made children and babes at the breast sound your praise aloud"?'
>   (Matt 21.15–17)

The unambiguous recognition by the children in the Temple of Jesus as the Messiah reminds us that it is children who so often express con- troversial views of the adult world, who identify hypocrisy and see

through falsehood, and conversely who are attracted to genuine goodness, to the compassionate leader, and express their exuberant joy in
shouts of acclamation.

Jesus' frequent child-centred sayings and actions are not without
echo in the early Church. The controversy over the centuries concerning
child baptism seems so often to have missed the point that the early
Church baptized children because they were members of one household and all shared the faith of the household, and were seen as
legitimate members of the community of faith. It is a mark of our more
individualistic concept of selfhood that so many Christians no longer
find this idea of collective faith acceptable. But we should not forget that
Jesus displays a much more ambiguous attitude to the family than he
does to children. Unlike other rabbis, he actively welcomed children,
but again, unlike other rabbis, he frequently dissociated himself from
his own family and discouraged too much focus on familial responsibilities and ties, preferring instead that people should give their primary
loyalties to the Kingdom, to following him and his way to God.

This positive focus on children is also a reflection of a wider
orientation in the gospels to marginalized people, poor people, to
women and children, to people who in the adult and male-oriented
world of the Jewish faith and of Roman society were typically on the
edge. The Kingdom of God is already present among the poor, the sick,
the children and the slaves.[17] Indeed we may speak of a divine bias to
children, a child-centredness, which contrasts so dramatically with the
apparent bias against children which is so evident in British society, not
only with respect to children in UPAs, but with respect to children
generally. There can be few countries where children are more often
made unwelcome and excluded from hotels and restaurants, their
games banned from so many open spaces, their lives put in danger by
adult driving habits, or their very existence ignored in the design of
housing estates and transport schemes. After returning from living in
Malaysia my daughter Lydia, who was eight at the time, commented on
how adults in Britain rarely address children except to tell them off, or
to stop them doing something, while adults in Malaysia frequently talk
to children as people, ask them about themselves, or welcome them to
a meal, a church or their homes.

Neil Postman argues that children feel especially unwelcome in the
modern world because childhood itself is disappearing.[18] The heavy
use of media by young children introduces them to the adult world of
violence, fear, eroticism and horror, and induces passivity and cynicism
about the world they are growing up in. Children grow up in fear of the
nuclear bomb, of AIDS, of unemployment: because of television they
are no longer protected from adult information by the barrier of reading

which protected older generations from information about the hazards and threats of life in the adult world. The commercialization of childhood through television and video advertising is another feature of this loss of innocence and of the growing exploitation of children in contemporary Britain. The disappearance of childhood is even more a feature of children's lives in UPA areas. The over-supervision, or the dangers on the streets, which children in these areas experience threaten both freedom and innocence, creativity and play. Too little is done to support the family and hard-pressed parents in our culture. Far too little is done to ensure that the most vulnerable members of our society – children – are respected and protected as the future citizens of our increasingly fragile social order.

Instead of protecting and investing in our children as the future of our society, politicians, newspapers and the media have tended to blame disadvantaged and disturbed children as the cause of society's increasing disorder. The murder of James Bulger by two ten-year-old boys in 1993 led to a pattern of worry and blame about the condition of childhood in Britain in which violent children, children out of control, and lone parents, were represented as the scapegoats for many of the problems of social disorder and moral decay which Britain had experienced in the preceding fifteen years (see Al McFadyen's chapter on crime, pp. 178–90). The Bulger case encouraged newspaper leader writers to condemn the mini-adults who had acquired rights without responsibilities in the 1980s. It led to calls for tougher sentencing and new security regimens for young offenders under the age of fifteen which the government is now enacting, and a general culture of blame in which children were not the victims but the causes of society's ills.

However, behind the rhetoric and tabloid hype, the reality of children's lives, particularly in UPA areas, has dramatically worsened in contemporary Britain in recent years. There can be no doubt that a major element in this worsening picture, as a recent United Nations report on Britain's children recognizes,[19] is the widening gap between rich and poor which government policies have generated since 1979, combined with cuts in welfare and social programmes, which have resulted in a threefold increase in the number of children living in poverty between 1979 and 1995.[20] If individual failure of parental responsibility were the primary cause, as government ministers so often argue, we would have to ask why parents in Britain are so much more morally failing than their counterparts in other parts of the European Union. The New Right rhetoric of the disorder of contemporary childhood, with its stress on the moral failings of single parents and of irresponsible mini-adults, ignores the ways in which neo-liberal economics and the attack on welfare in Britain have damaged the family, and have disadvantaged so many of our children, and especially children living in UPAs. It is children in these areas, the most vulnerable members of already vulnerable communities, who have borne the brunt of the vast social experiment of Thatcherism in Britain.

The Bible does not present us with a picture of childhood innocence, other than the Garden of Eden, nor a sentimentalized account of childhood. But children, and the right guidance of children, are seen in biblical cultures not just as the products and responsibility of their parents, but of society as a whole. The community of the people of God bears the responsibility for the actions of the child until the child reaches the age of moral responsibility – thirteen in Jewish tradition. This collective understanding of the relation of children to society is an important corrective to the individualistic view pronounced by government ministers and others that parents alone are responsible for the financial security and moral guidance of their offspring. Thatcher in her instincts was right, if not in her social policies: children are *our* sacred trust and this is why we must put the children first. They do not belong to their parents alone, which is why we now recognize the rights of children, and the Children Act of 1989 enshrined their right to be heard in British law. But if society confers rights on children, over against parents who may sometimes wish them, or do them, harm, society cannot simply wash its hands of children whose families its policies have broken apart, whose homes are damp, whose streets are dangerous, and whose schools are in a state of disrepair. The warning of our Lord in the gospel of Matthew is instructive: 'If anyone causes the downfall of one of these little ones who believe in me, it would be better for him to have a millstone hung around his neck and be drowned in the depths of the sea' (Matt 18.6).

The Church, particularly the Church in the UPA, needs actively to begin to put the needs of children first. Children's ministry is a diverse and even contested area. A parish priest in Edinburgh closed down all the uniformed organizations of his new charge because they were not as he saw it serving the specifically Christian mission of the Church. Other parish clergy argue the need to establish boundaries between the Church and the secular society by insisting on long-term membership of parents before accepting their children for baptism. But it is doubtful that such policies express the kind of divine and human child-centredness which we are called as Christians and as a society to express.

A UPA parish in Easterhouse, Glasgow opened up its church hall after school with the help of volunteers so the children would have somewhere to go and something to do, instead of returning alone to watch television in cramped and often empty houses. Other UPA parishes sponsor summer play schemes, mother and child groups, subsidize holidays for city children in the country or on the coast, or put on special services where the culture, music and styles of young people are affirmed and explored in singing, ritual and preaching. In Heath Town the Hope Community have developed self-help groups in which members of the community and parents work together to develop parenting skills, and in particular the child-centred activities and involvement which are so crucial to a child's sense of well being and self-esteem. The connections between religious faith and the nurture of children may also be explored in such skills sharing. In Leeds, church families are developing a response to the growing problem of homelessness amongst young people. Young people sleeping rough on the streets are offered a bed for up to five nights in the home of participating families. After five nights they may move on to another home or, ideally, into a young persons' hostel where they can get a room of their own and begin to put their lives back together.

Many UPA churches live in fear of the children. Our church in Leith had a problem with children climbing on the roof, smashing windows, and occasionally breaking in. But persevering youth work by members of the congregation, and the maintenance of uniformed organizations, is a more characteristic mode of the church's relationship with young people in the area. The authors of *Children in the Way* insist that the Church cannot simply abandon children who have no church connection through their parents, but must continue to find new ways of reaching out to children, of drawing them, and perhaps through them their parents, into youth groups and church activities, and ultimately worship.[21]

Children in church also need to have a greater sense of relationship with worship, rather than being restricted to the odd action song, or singing in Sunday School. A central component of welcoming children in worship is their participation in the Eucharist. The growing number of parishes which now invite young people before confirmation to receive the elements of bread and wine alongside their parents marks a significant inter-generational reorientation of contemporary Christian ritual practice. Another key area in relation to children and worship concerns cultural style. Young people are very much oriented to music and dancing in contemporary culture but in church we expect them to sing along to Victorian hymn tunes and to stand in serried ranks, unmoving in pews or rows of chairs. Music, rhythm, dancing are of course dimensions of church life in many Pentecostal, charismatic and black-led churches: they are much more attractive to contemporary young people than the quiet traditional worship favoured by many parish churches in the UPA or in the suburb. Changing the culture of worship, or of some worship services, is a necessary part of the Church's missionary response to the advance of secularism.

Helen Oppenheimer suggests that the greatest temptation of the Church in approaching children is in presenting the faith as either too simple or too unambiguous for contemporary children to believe in.[22] In packaging God for children we are often in danger of reducing God to certainties and to simplicities that children soon find unconvincing as they encounter the adult world in the mass media, or on the streets. But God's providence is close to dangerous risk, God's grace close to blind love, God's truth close to that sharp childlike ability to see through hypocrisy, God's power is dangerous, fearsome, as fearsome as any horror book or video.

The Church, locally and nationally, should also be active in pressing, lobbying and organizing for children to find a safe space, a wild place, in which to play, for in children's play are repeated the timeless and culture-transcending themes of the mythic struggle between good and evil, the stretching risks of adventure, the power of role play, drama and the social skills learnt in the game. The diminishment in contemporary Britain of safe space in which to play is the biggest single threat to the freedom and creativity which are the secret of a full childhood. Why not build an adventure playground in the churchyard or a children's nature study centre at the diocesan retreat house? Perhaps this would be better than keeping the children out of the graveyard or off the grass.

Above all the Church needs to be actively working to create within its own parishes and congregations communities where children, and the vulnerable of all ages, are welcomed and nurtured, sustained and supported, and drawn to personal and spiritual maturity. In the context of all the threats which children may face, from increasing poverty, from abusive or neglectful parents, from hazards on the streets, from environmental degradation and pollution, or from government cuts in social provision, the Church has a spiritual and a moral responsibility to seek to build communities which welcome and nurture children, and to sustain parents in their efforts to raise and nurture children in a morally ordered environment. Such communities are a counter-sign to the disappearance and impoverishment of childhood in money-obsessed and car-mad Britain. Communities which welcome children must seek in their worship and in their life together to sustain the magic of children's wonder, the spontaneity of their happiness, the tears of their vulnerability, and the trust of their love: 'Suffer the children to come . . . for of such is the kingdom of heaven' (Mark 10.14).

Notes

1 Department of Social Security, *Households Below Average Income* (London: HMSO, 1992).

2 *Children Now* (London: The Children's Society and National Children's Bureau, 1993), p. 5.

3 Parents on social security benefit and living in Urban Priority Areas cited in R. Cohen *et al.*, *Hardship Britain: Being Poor in the 1990s* (London: Child Poverty Action Group, 1992).

4 M. Warner, *Managing Monsters* (London: Vintage, 1994).

5 L. Segal, *Slow Motion: Changing Masculinities, Changing Men* (London: Virago, 1990), pp. 256ff.

6 Parents in Urban Priority Areas cited in *Hardship Britain*.

7 H. Wilson and G. W. Herbert, *Parents and Children in the Inner City* (London: Routledge & Kegan Paul, 1979).

8 Ibid., p. 168.

9 National Audit Office, *Repair and Maintenance of School Buildings*; cited in M. Rosenbaum, *Children and the Environment* (London: National Children's Bureau, 1993), p. 73.

10 D. Olweus, *Bullying at School: What We Know and What We Can Do* (Oxford: Basil Blackwell, 1993).

11 Rosenbaum, *Children and the Environment*, p. 54.

12 Ibid., pp. 59ff.

13 D. Nicholson-Lord, *The Greening of the Cities* (London: Routledge & Kegan Paul, 1987), p. 133.

14 Ibid., p. 140.

15 Fewer playgrounds are provided in Britain than in any other European country and Britain has no government recommended standard for play space provision.

16 2 Kings 5.

17 J. Moltmann, *The Way of Jesus Christ*; cited in *Children in the Way* (London: Church House Publishing, 1995).

18 N. Postman, *The Disappearance of Childhood* (New York: Laurel Books, 1982).

19 *The Guardian* (30 January 1995).

20 *Children Now*, p. 4.

21 *Children in the Way*, ch. 4.

22 H. Oppenheimer, *Finding and Following: Talking with Children About God* (London: SCM Press, 1994).

Labouring for a new birth: the black experience

NOVETTE THOMPSON

When the Los Angeles uprising erupted in April 1992, I was completing a Master of Arts in theological studies in Dayton, Ohio. A year earlier, the video recording of a young man being brutally beaten by a gang of Los Angeles police had been flashed across the world's television screens. No one could comprehend how those policemen were then acquitted of using 'unreasonable and unlawful force' in order to arrest a single man. My first lecture on the morning following the verdict was Corinthian studies. The professor, using the various disciplines of biblical studies, wanted to see what the text had to say about the conditions of urban America in the 1990s. Needless to say, that class was extremely emotionally charged as those of us of African descent questioned whether anything had changed for black people, whether in North or South America, Britain, Europe or Southern Africa over the last century.

There has been a lengthy waiting going on for black people across the continents these past 500 years. A waiting and a labouring for a new birth, and a new life when we shall be seen as people who are also created in the image of God. We labour for the day when we shall view ourselves with honour and dignity. This intense labour-pain that we are going through is shared by people of colour all over the world.

Whenever we see and hear of the suffering of people of colour – Middle Eastern, Native Americans, aboriginal Australians, Indians, Asians and Africans – there is an identification and resonance with those people. I shall, however, be speaking from the particular experience of black British people who are of African and Caribbean descent. Although I shall be talking in general terms, I recognize that amongst black people there is a wide range of experience.

The sense of alienation

The sense of being disadvantaged is a feeling that pervades the world of most African-Caribbean and black British people in Britain. The evidence for this comes from many areas of life. This sense of not belonging was conveyed way back when Elizabeth I expressed her alarm in the sixteenth century that there were too many blacks on the streets of London and wanted to send them back to Africa.[1] This intensified in the 1950s and 1960s as larger numbers of African-Caribbeans began arriving in Britain. There was no equivalent to the United States Civil Rights movement of the 1960s in Britain, particularly because most African-Caribbean people saw themselves as guests in a host community, and were aware of the threat of deportation.

In Britain today, the African-Caribbean community has the largest proportion of unemployed people. A report published in January 1995, noted that young black men under the age of 25 were three times more likely to be unemployed than their white counterparts. There is a disproportionate number of black British people incarcerated within the penal system – 'One in seven prisoners in British prisons is black; one in five of all people held on remand is black and one in four female prisoners is black.'[2]

Black British children have been failed by the British education system. For many reasons African-Caribbean children do not achieve as well as children in other groups. Some teachers do not have a high expectation of black children's academic achievement. Inner-city schools which are largely attended by black children are under-staffed and ill-equipped. In recent years there have been attempts to acknowledge the culturally diverse backgrounds of children within schools, but even these small attempts are now under attack. Having gone through this education system myself, I remember that nothing was taught of my history as an African-Caribbean black British child. There was always that puzzling question, 'Well, where do I fit into all this?' But at nine years old one did not know how to frame such a question. At that time the curriculum was entirely Eurocentric, and largely remains so. Today I hear young relatives of eight, nine, ten years old tell me how the teacher never responds to them for the answer, no matter how long they have their hands up.

Black British people are acutely under-represented within the universities. One will find more African students in British universities than black British students.

In the workplace, as civil servants, nurses, lawyers, teachers and on the factory floor, black people are constantly overlooked or frustrated when they strive for promotion to more senior posts.

These realities shape the way that black British people experience the world. When one adds to this blatant cases of racism from across the world, one can understand how most people of African descent perceive themselves as being part of a struggle for new life.

It is important however to note that the black community is not only made up of inner-city people. People of African-Caribbean descent are not a socially homogeneous group. Black British people can be found across the economic social groups. Their economic status may not change their experience of abuse or rejection, such as experienced by people like Lenny Henry or John Taylor (Cheltenham Conservative candidate), though it may provide other avenues for them to deal with it.

We groan together in travail

Black people within Britain are striving to be born again, to rediscover themselves in the face of disadvantage. The labouring for rebirth is enhanced by using many instruments; the Church, the arts, economics and business enterprise, through critical and self-critical education and within the family – amongst men, women and children. With these instruments and within these arenas the black community seeks to discover a new self-perception. These are the arenas through which many people within the black community will shake off negative stereotyping and discover the self, historically, spiritually, culturally and politically.

A substantial proportion of black people in Britain today are home-owners; single women, married couples and particularly older people who were refused council property when they came to Britain in the 1950s and 1960s. A number of black businesses have grown up in the food and entertainment industry, financing, fashion and hairdressing. Many black women are returning to full-time education after several years and are being more successful in securing a career.

As with any ethnic group, there is a proportion of black women and men who are involved in the arts: literature and poetry, the theatre, music, fine arts, fashion and designing. Black writers, film- and programme-makers still battle with the media for space on television; for the opportunity to produce serious and culturally relevant work for the black audience by black producers and directors. Black theatre is an instrument through which young and old are educated and inspired. From grandmother to grandchildren, and from across the social groups, all are present at a production. Black theatre is not a spectator/audience art form. It is always participative and emotive. Black theatre or poetry is spiritual because it addresses and comments upon the condition of black men and women. By debating issues using theatre, opportunity is given for reformation to continue.

Spiritual and religious expression has formed an important part of black self-expression. In the 1970s the Rastafarian Movement awakened in many young people an awareness of their African identity. Today in the 1990s, the rise of the Nation of Islam Movement is providing for many articulate young black British people a spirituality and a framework for political analysis of the African condition worldwide.

As the Church has opened up, there has been a steady rise in the number of black women priests, ministers and deacons into the ordained ministries.

These are some of the social, cultural and spiritual environs that black people are using to redefine themselves.

Spirituality for regeneration

St Paul equates the development of the spiritual life with life itself: 'Those who live according to the Spirit set their minds on the things of the Spirit ... to set the mind on the Spirit is life and peace' (Rom 8.5–6). It is through nurturing one's spiritual life that the new birth will eventually take place. Paul expanded the vision of birthing from the personal to the universal when he said,

> We know that the whole creation has been groaning in travail together until now, and not only the creation, but we ourselves, who have the first fruits of the spirit, groan inwardly as we wait for adoption as sons ... (Rom 8.22–23)

The spiritual life is of great importance to many black people. An emphasis upon our spirituality and religious expression must be maintained if social and cultural regeneration is to take place.

Historically, the Church has been the foundation upon which people of African descent have based their rebellion against social injustice. Far from being an organization for escapism, the black Church in the eighteenth and nineteenth centuries, in the United States of America and in the Caribbean, represented a culture of resistance. It was the black Church which fashioned people like Martin Luther King, Jr to lead the Civil Rights movement in the 1950s and 1960s. The God that black people met in Scripture did not support their enslavement or any form of dehumanization. And in response the spiritual songs they sang reflected this understanding of Scripture.

There is a view that church religion particularly in Britain has 'domesticated' many black people to the extent that they have accommodated social injustice. There is a view that black spirituality is too otherworldly and void of social awareness. On the contrary, black Christians are acutely aware of the burden of simply making a life in Britain. They are aware of the pitfalls that are strategically placed to hinder the social and economic development of their children and young people.

But there is a waiting that has to be done. The kind of waiting that a labouring woman does in between contractions. In the meantime there is intense suffering. Tremendous patience must be exercised. Janet Morley expresses this when she says that to wait is part of the struggle – knowing when to wait and when to push is part of the work of bringing in a new life. Part of black spirituality has been this lengthy waiting 'with eager longing for the revelation of the sons of God' (Rom 8.19).

In my experience as a Methodist, and a minister, I have seen black spirituality expressed most clearly in the corporate worship of African-Caribbean people. African-Caribbean people practise a variety of spiritual expressions. Some enjoy a contemplative style of worship, some prefer worship that is energetic and vibrant. The Methodists of Neasden Church who are Ghanaian, Nigerian, Sierra Leonean, Caribbean, Malaysian, Sri Lankan, Scottish, English, Philippino and Welsh enjoy a mixture of rousing Methodist hymns as well as quiet Taizé chants.

Crucial to most black Christians is the proclamation of the gospel. The sermon must be engaging, intellectually stimulating, emotive and speak to the people's life situation. After years of hearing friends and relatives complain that they came out of church as cold as when they went in, I knew that the challenge to preach the gospel would never be an easy one. Preaching from the Old Testament as well as from the New is important, and, as I have been reminded by some members, do not neglect books such as Daniel and Revelation; the themes of judgement and the return of Christ.

The prominence that black Christians place upon eschatological events serves to remind me that a people under trial needs to be assured that its testing in the fire will not go on for ever. The Old Testament prophets not only spoke God's words of warning, and sometimes condemnation, but also spoke words of hope and restoration. The close identification that black people have with the Old Testament covenant people of God, makes the preaching of a message of hope vital.

I have noticed that the very presence of a black minister makes a difference to the way that a black congregation approaches worship. There is a sense that permission is given, both to the minister and the congregation, to 'be yourself'. Comments from the pastor of the Pente-costal church that shares our premises have revealed to me the kind of impact the presence of a black minister has upon a worshipping community. The presence of a black minister is a sign to the black congregation that some small progress is being made in the wider society. That there is some recognition that black people are present and participating and are less invisible to the wider society.

I have found that people gain a greater sense of satisfaction if they are allowed to participate more fully in worship. Participation takes place when, for example, visitors are recognized by asking them to stand and introduce themselves. Opportunity for open prayer during worship, lighting candles as we intercede for the world. A time of testimony and thanksgiving suddenly opens up and relaxes the whole congregation, and people are able to speak of God for themselves. There is a richness within worship that the preacher alone cannot provide.

Black Christians believe that worship on a Sunday should have an impact upon one's life for the rest of the week. Therefore, for black Christians, there is often a strong ethical element to faith – faith affects the way you live your life. As is the case for black or white Christians in the city, Bible study discussions cannot remain with the text. Discussion of the text is always related to people's living experience.

Our pastoral care of one another is closely linked with our worship and ethical duty. My formation as a Methodist minister has continued since leaving theological college. In the area of pastoral care I has learned an immense amount from the Christians at Neasden. The strong cultural influence of African and African-Caribbean patterns of care has been illuminating. On occasions of the most distressing kind of bereavement, the bereaved is never left alone. He or she will feel free to go and lie down and get away from people, but there will always be visitors in the house over the entire period.

I have learned that, essentially, pastoral care is more about presence. Yet prayer should never be left out. Prayer turns the attention away from our human finiteness, to the Infinite One who can hold us together emotionally, physically and spiritually.

Ministry amongst black Christians

Black ministers, pastors, priests, lay and youth workers, deacons and deaconesses are called to operate in a variety of settings, but always called to be themselves. Ministry for black Christians is always multi-layered. There is the vision for the worshipping community – to strengthen the bond of pastoral fellowship, and to grow in spiritual insight and expression. But there is always the vision towards the wider community; how a family is holding itself together when there is a disturbed child in it, or when a marriage is breaking down. Added to this are the obstacles presented by welfare and educational institutions, legal institutions, the lack of employment. The vista of the Christian must be wide enough to take in all the variables that impact upon the life of African-Caribbean people.

The ministry of one person will not be able to address all these variables overnight. There needs to be consistent work over a period of years that will enable black people to chisel out for themselves a way of life that has advantages and opportunities, not only disadvantages. This is a lengthy operation which calls for intense attention to the birthing process of the black community.

For the time being, I feel that the place for most black ministers and priests is within multi-cultural settings. Possibly in the future, we will perceive a need for us to be in rural areas. But for now our work must be with our people because of the sign of hope that we represent for them.

'Claiming The Inheritance' – a practical model of regeneration[3]

Community regeneration begins with spiritual regeneration.

The 'reasoning' sessions of the Rastafarian tradition are character-istic of African culture. These are sessions where people meet together to discuss and try to understand the events of life and to place some meaning to them. The event may be some personal experience, or it may be some current affair affecting the wider community. 'Reasoning' is the model which some black Christian organizations are using to address their own issues. The activity of reasoning, perceiving wisdom, talking and explaining reality is an important part of black culture.

Claiming The Inheritance is a multi-denominational Christian organization formed in 1986 and based in Birmingham. Its focus has been upon consciousness-raising, education and the empowerment of the black community, all within the light of black Christian experience of God.

The name 'Claiming The Inheritance' arose from the sense that we are reclaiming our rich heritage as people of African descent and as people loved by God. Claiming The Inheritance is about doing theology from the context of black people's lives. That means examining our role within the Church, and confronting racism, sexism and classism.

Similar organizations that exist around the country have sprung up out of black Christian congregations – Anglican, Methodist, Catholics, Baptists, United Reformed Church – to do similar work. Conferences and seminars provide the forum for ordinary men and women, with the help of professionals within the fields of education, the social sciences, literature, the health service and the Church, to explore the Christian response to the conditions of the black community.

These seminars have been vehicles of education for black Christians. They have acquainted people with changes in the education system, alerted people to the treatment of black people within the mental health service and penal system. These forums have awakened people to the call to more involved church ministry, and challenged others to the possibility of starting one's own business.

Claiming The Inheritance has awakened local congregations to spiritually support other areas of black concern by going out to them. For example, by making contact with supplementary schools set up to enhance the education of our children culturally and historically. The Church could also encourage one group to support another, e.g. black businesses and enterprise to become more closely involved with supplementary schools. Other creative strategies need to be put into action to help empower the black community.

Black-led churches and black congregations within white-led churches need to examine their faith in relation to the condition of the black community. This is what organizations like Claiming The Inheritance seek to encourage. All the instruments for rebirth – the Church, the arts, education, economics, politics and the family – are areas in which black people are active, and are therefore areas to which the Church has a spiritual responsibility. That spiritual responsibility is expressed through involvement, support, self-education, and criticism.

Conclusion: *emerging as full sons and daughters*

Under the cover of darkness Nicodemus went to Jesus, and was told that he had to be born again if he were to see the Kingdom of God. 'That which is born of the flesh is flesh, that which is born of the spirit is spirit' (John 3.6). In the night of our experience in Britain, black people also need to be reminded of the need to be born again if we are to see God at work in our lives.

And yet it must be acknowledged that the struggle for rebirth involves both the black and the white community. The whole creation groans in travail TOGETHER. At a recent Methodist conference organized for black church stewards, once again the question arose, 'Why are we excluding the white people from our meetings?' The thing that struck me about this question is the fact that both black and white people are having to struggle with the issue of racism in our society. Often white people feel threatened and guilty that black people are meeting together and trying to work out the meaning of their presence in Church and society. But also some black people feel guilty that they are excluding their white counterparts and may perhaps be sending a message that black people are 'against' white people. The labour for new birth has to take place both within the white community as well as within the black community. It is necessarily painful for both.

My emphasis upon spiritual rebirth throughout this chapter is, I believe, crucial for the survival of black British people. Further self-examination and assessment of our place and role in society under the spotlight of faith must continue. But that self-examination must go on for our own sake as well, not only for the impact that we shall have on the rest of society. We need to find meaning in life for ourselves as black people.

Some black people have interpreted our experience of struggle over the past 500 years as a medium through which God has been able to speak to those who do not suffer. That we have been brought to this place in history in order to prick the conscience of the world, and call it back to justice and righteousness. That black people are to be a spiritual light in a dark world that has lost consciousness of the spiritual. The figure of Job also holds a lot of meaning to many black people in Britain – the one who suffered and who was eventually vindicated. These are some of the ideas that have sustained black people in the midst of life.

Black people, like any other ethnic group, are simply trying to make a life for themselves and their children. But that effort to make a life is weighed down by the sense that one is not at home in one's society.

Being born again for black people in Britain will not mean being accepted by others, but will mean being accepted by ourselves. As long as we try to remake ourselves in the image of other people, we shall never be at peace. Being born again must mean celebrating and reclaiming our own cultural and spiritual inheritance. That process of being born again is a long and painful one; but labour pains do come to an end. Then new life comes into being, and that is not the end. It is the beginning of growth and development, of learning and the search for wisdom. Now we 'groan inwardly as we wait for adoption as sons' (Rom 8.23). But once adoption has taken place, we are given new names and a new identity. Then it will be revealed that we did belong to the rest of creation and to God all along.

Notes

1 Peter Fryer, *Staying Power: The History of Black People in Britain* (London: Pluto Press, 1984), p.10.

2 *The Black Parliamentarian Magazine,* vol. 1, issue 3 (Winter 1991) (The Black Parliamentarian Publishing Group).

3 Evangelical Christians for Racial Justice, 'Claiming The Inheritance', *Racial Justice,* no. 6 (Spring 1987) (Birmingham).

Enterprise and estrangement

PETER SEDGWICK

Introduction

In this chapter I have tried to weave together two themes. On the one hand I have sought to reflect further on my study of social change published as *The Enterprise Culture*[1] and the profound difference in the way we now live compared with twenty years ago. On the other hand I have also sought to explore the shocks caused by the murder of Jamie Bulger, the election of a far-right councillor in East London, and the periodic outbreaks of riots and violence in many cities. What unites this list is not simply the fact that cities now have examples of both enterprise and violence. More profoundly, enterprise is an example of individualism, and the individual entrepreneur was the hero or heroine of the last decade. However individualism can also be a very destructive force when society breaks down into violence, and communal bonds are broken. This indicates a deep estrangement at the heart of urban life. The exploration of individualism will occur later in this chapter. Can a Christian vision of urban life (*Faith in the City*) say anything about the search for individuality and individual self-realization found in enterprise on the one hand, and the collapse of urban life into individualism and isolated individuals on the other, which would enable enterprise (individuality) and estrangement (individualism) to be held together? Giving an answer to that question is the object of this chapter.

Enterprise

Enterprise has been classically defined this century by the Austrian economist Joseph Schumpeter as self-reliance, innovation, risk-taking and creativity. Leadership and the acceptance of uncertainty become crucial factors. Enterprise behaviour has both skills and attributes: skills include problem solving, creativity, persuasiveness, negotiating and taking decisions; attributes would be self-confidence, autonomy, dynamism, versatility and resourcefulness. Flexible response to challenges and the achievement of goals become all-important.

Why does this matter in urban areas? The answer lies in the fact that people who live there are just as resourceful as anybody else, and there are endless stories of personal creativity and problem solving in coping with poverty, and a harsh environment. However the environment offers little chance for people to exercise creativity and innovation outside day-to-day living. What chance of creating your home exists when all the accommodation is rented, and there is no possibility of building your own? What chance of starting your own job is there when the expectation was for decades that you would work for a large employer, and now those employers have vanished like mist? What is the chance of self-confidence when there is high unemployment and no role models of successful self-employed people exist? All this has been true of urban areas for the last thirty years at least. People may be very resourceful in a family, but still have very little chance of a job on an outer estate or inner-city area.

There is now a substantial body of behavioural literature on entrepreneurship. Equally there is also a considerable amount of research on the 'key essences' of self-employment, including informality, and the personal commitment to success. People learn by interaction with their environment. There is a continual emphasis on learning under pressure, which produces self-aware individuals who see change as fundamentally exciting.

The essence of enterprise, then, is the acceptance of change, the understanding of self-reliance, and the belief that things can be different. Schumpeter argued that the entrepreneur acts beyond the routine tasks understood by all. Acting with that confidence requires skills present in only a few people. Enterprise is not the same as wealth-creation, resourcefulness, or small businesses. It consists, in Schumpeter's memorable phrase, of 'the perennial gale of creative destruction' that renders old methods obsolete, old institutions redundant, and old ways of thinking irrelevant.

Enterprise is important in urban areas because it can offer a concrete example of hope, innovation and self-reliance. There are many examples of entrepreneurial activity in parts of cities where there had been no change and no self-reliance for many years. Part of the decline of urban areas has been the gradual disappearance of small businesses, community ventures, pubs and even shops. While a few remain, there are many outer estates with apparently little entrepreneurial activity. However, it is worth noting that on outer estates in Hull there are still some self-employed people, such as garden contractors and builders, and community activities. There is also a distinction to be made between formal entrepreneurs (e.g. small businesses) and informal ones (perhaps in the black economy, perhaps in crime). There can be hostility to small shopkeepers in urban areas: 'they take our money' can easily be added to 'Paki shopkeeper'. Racial prejudice unites with populist anger. So too Korean shopkeepers were targets in the Los Angeles riots. But a chip shop can be a community venture, with a working person creating things for people. A small business that actually manufactures things for the local community, taking risks and building up the self-reliance of people, is a particular example of urban enterprise; and so too are some retail ventures, some trading outlets, some service activities such as music, or recreation. Role models can be created: the first initiative by women, the first small business, the first ethnic enterprise. The criteria of success may not be financial, but personal: it may lead to individual exploration of new values. However, two cautions remain. First, it is unlikely that such activity will generate enough wealth to regenerate an entire area. Good though examples of such practice are, the economic base of many Urban Priority Areas is too low to be regenerated by such means alone. Second, there must be a real fear that individualism will be fostered by enterprise in a way that is indifferent to moral considerations or accountability.

There are, however, signs of real hope in Urban Priority Areas which are worth mentioning. Hansib Publishing, which publishes the *Asian Times* and *Caribbean Times*, trains young black workers who were unemployed and lets them use their experience as a springboard into employment. Arif Ali, who began the enterprise, saw the fragmentation and hostility of society as the main problem. Black businesses kept their links in the black community. The role of the churches was to open up society, and enterprise in this example was socially beneficial. Ali had become successful by seeing the need for black newspapers (innovation, self-reliance), but had used his publishing business both to promote good news about the black community (or highlight the problems which it faced) and to use employment as a means of empowering black youth. Another example is the Church of England's Linking-Up Scheme which relates community ventures in one city to another. The work of Linking-Up is separate from the work strategy of the Inner Cities Religious Council (ICRC) which is an arm of the Department of the Environment, but the ICRC will contract with Linking-Up to follow up their regional conferences. Chris Beales has been important in relating the two bodies. Community businesses, credit unions, tenants' co-operatives all provide both social cohesion, foster the sense of local responsibility, and prevent the development of amoral individualism. It is through examples such as these, as through the Hope Community in Wolverhampton, that people can regain the skills of civic participation, responsibility and moral worth. In Hull there is the strategy of the local council to develop community forum, credit unions, local exchange trading system (LETS) and neighbourhood enterprise schemes. Hull City Council appears to be developing some of the most imaginative schemes of any city in Britain. It is significant that the leader of the City Council, Pat Doyle, is a Roman Catholic deeply versed in liberation theology and the option for the poor. The vision which he promotes is, on the one hand, the redevelopment of the city centre with shopping centres, trade with the Continent, local business parks and housing action trusts; but, on the other hand, a commitment to involving all the faiths in social and economic development (the ICRC held a conference in Hull in 1993), and as much communal participation in Urban Priority Areas as possible. The aim of community participation is both economic and social: the low level of voter turnout on outer estates in local elections (9 per cent in one case), the high degree of poverty and long-term unemployment, and the estrangement often felt from the rest of the city all illustrate the argument made at the beginning of this chapter. Interestingly, the response of the churches has been to work closely with the Council in the regeneration of these estates.

One example is OPNHE, which stands for Orchard Park and North Hull Enterprises Ltd. It is more than a small business centre on an outer estate, for it is managed by a combination of city councillors, the private sector and those from the local community, elected at community meetings. It has created some local self-employment on a deprived outer estate, but it also promoted a skills survey of the estate. It is linked to an advice bureau, job centre and a small café; and will in future develop a large social centre, community businesses and explore the possibility of training. In a fragmented, individualist society, OPNHE links together both enterprise and social regeneration. Ten per cent of the estate is made up of lone parents, so again the provision of childcare is a future aim. The effect of such a centre, partly economic, partly social, must be to allow the regaining of responsibility for the residents of an estate that has suffered long-term unemployment on the very edge of the city, surrounded by fields and roads into the city. OPNHE is also supported by industrial mission.

Those are small, practical examples, but they illustrate that economic decline can be overcome, even if only in part. Enterprise need not be individualist, but can be communal, and socially responsible. The rediscovery of civic participation remains a long-term problem, for the examples given are largely social and economic. Political activity lessens with each decade, the turnout at elections is very low as is party membership, and the sense of responsibility to society is not easily discerned. Nevertheless, a start has been made with such examples. There are also private small firms which take an interest in the neighbouring society.

Estrangement

There is however a major problem with the preceding analysis. The urban areas in which economic decline is so pronounced also suffer from another, far more deadly disease. And the problem is that the promotion of enterprise may make the disease worse. The disease is literally a dis-ease: people no longer feel at home in urban areas, but ill at ease and dissatisfied. However deep their roots are – and the white working class can have long memories across the generations – those who live there can now feel quite a sense of estrangement. It is one of the most striking features of Urban Priority Areas. Although there is much that can be affirmed about the degree of involvement shown through clubs, voluntary activities, etc., there remains a pervasive sense of estrangement. Crime has become so common in urban areas that many people who live there demand that the government should be far more ruthless towards criminals. There is a repeated demand for 'getting tough on crime', 'cracking down' on young offenders and a belief that social order is disappearing into a black hole. Civic society becomes made up of strangers. This is true of many parts of our society, but is especially the case in Urban Priority Areas. It is hard to find examples there of civic society becoming stronger. Citizenship is not a concept which has very much cash value, and it is easily prone to trivialization by the media. It is far easier to talk of violence, dependency, and the failure of institutions. Equally the failure of public bodies to serve the citizens who use them is often exaggerated out of all measure. We are a very long way from the appeal to 'Citizens!' that marked the French Revolution two centuries ago. Perhaps the only civic act is the receipt of benefit. There is a sense of crisis that bedevils the argument, compounded by an endemic trivialization and contempt for many who work in the public sector by the tabloids.

In this dissolution of the civic order, there has been a repeated call for a return to 'ethical voluntarism'. This abstract phrase refers to the way in which groups take it on themselves to do something about (or, preferably, alongside) the deprived, the have-nots, those who have little stake in society and few resources. The churches have a very long track record in this area, especially in Victorian England, and more especially in East London, and other urban areas. But it is not clear that such a move has actually had much success in strengthening the civic order against yet further dissolution, despite the undoubted success of the Church Urban Fund projects.

If you begin in this way, by looking at civic society as the context in which enterprise is set, any discussion of enterprise looks very different. Enterprise can be an economic or a cultural phenomenon, but it is part and parcel of the society in which we live. And if that is itself in decay, if not yet in crisis, then appeals to 'do one's own thing' may render the disease worse and not better. Quite apart from the economic problems of self-reliant enterprise on a depressed estate without much wealth, there is also the fact that the complex web of rights, privileges and duties which make up citizenship may be further broken by the emergence of random forces of 'enterprise behaviour' which do not enhance the social relationships of those who live there.

The aim of this chapter is to ask how a Christian understanding on the one hand of civic order, mutual help and social duties and on the other of enterprise, innovation and risk-taking can be held together in a single vision. It is clear that there have also been many examples of Christians taking profound risks (enterprise?) on behalf of their faith: the Pilgrim Fathers would be one obvious example, or the courage of missionaries across the centuries. What is not clear is how these two aspects of social action can enrich each other.

An essay on enterprise cannot simply add up examples of resourcefulness, but contrast this with the lack of available jobs. That is a perfectly proper argument, which shows that enterprise can create wealth but has little chance of doing so given the impoverishment of many Urban Priority Areas. What is a much deeper argument is how enterprise might relate to the intricate network of duties, rights and responsibilities that we call 'society', or 'civic order'. And the theological questions which arise are related to this tension of enterprise and civic order. For instance, consider the strong, self-determining will rooted and grounded in faith, which is so much a feature of Protestant theology but is also central to the enterprising self: this raises the question of individualism. The vision of an interdependent society, where each person serves her neighbour and builds the just city together, has been a feature of much Western, Christian social ethics this century. The former view, stressing the autonomous individual, appears paramount today, while the latter is in decay. Can a Christian vision hold together the reality of the will and the social order in a way which allows room for both? And if this seems a descent into rarefied metaphysics, look at the second booklet of the Commission on Social Justice, entitled *Social Justice in a Changing World*:

The welfare state ... failed to make citizens feel it was theirs ...
individual problems were to be solved by experts and there were few,
if any mechanisms for ordinary people to participate in decisions
affecting their own lives ... Greater personal independence,
paradoxically, means increasing social interdependence ... The
challenge to the Commission is to develop new mechanisms of
collective action which will at the same time meet common goals and
liberate individual talent.[2]

There is a lengthy task in rethinking how individuality might be
strengthened in a mass society, while meeting the common goals of an
increasingly polarized and fragmented society. Poverty deepens each
year in such a society, while individuals complain of having their
aspirations stifled. But the Christian task is also to see how individuality and the common welfare of all can be held together.

The argument can now be set out. First, a deeper consideration of
civic duty and moral responsibility must be undertaken. What does it
mean to say that 'the buck stops here'? Then the nature of enterprise
and individualism/individuality will be explored. Then, and only then,
do we move to a theological understanding of this tension, in which the
will and the social order are held together through the dynamic activity
of God. Enterprise is a perfectly valid activity, which can do much for
those who engage in it; it might also create wealth for society. But unless
it actually contributes to the strengthening of our social fabric, the place
of enterprise must be questioned.

So urban society needs a strategy for economic renewal, and enterprise can help here. But it also needs greater social bonds, and ways of
cohering together. The danger of enterprise as a strategy is that it might
create many self-sufficient people, who weaken society. That is the
paradox. What we have seen in recent years is the subservience of civic
life to economic prosperity, and the attempts to centralize a national
economic strategy. Although cities have fought back with their own
economic plans, often involving considerable expenditure, a combination of multinational companies, the decline of other companies,
government centralization and world economic forces all degrade the
local economy. Beyond the local economy, the character of the local area
becomes problematic. Politics becomes the management of economic
life. The regeneration of urban life is a theological task (it is what *Faith
in the City* was all about, after all), but it must involve a theology of civic
life, and the integration of political and economic life, where the
economy serves the city, not the other way round. Within the city, the
importance of local groups must be emphasized, as the key foundations
for a flourishing civic life. Here the contribution of Christians becomes
crucial.

Civic duty and moral responsibility

Citizenship is composed of rights, privileges and duties. Rights stem from the Enlightenment stress on the autonomy of the individual, although a theological understanding will want to question this emphasis on autonomy. There are rights to vote, organize and speak freely, which are rights stemming from the struggles of past centuries. Civic relationships were born out of struggle, and civic rights were forged in conflict. Privileges are a different form of rights. Out of the right to life there comes the privilege of the receipt of welfare. Some may consider these as of less importance than direct rights, such as the right to speak: others will argue that they make talk of rights more concrete in everyday life. This raises theological issues, which are discussed at the end of this chapter. Duties are required both from the state (the protection of the individual) and the individual. However, talk of rights, privileges and duties is now elided into a confused speech of claim and counterclaim. There is no consensus at all on what is meant by rights and duties, but instead an endless debate, which is frequently bad-tempered and acerbic, of aggrieved groups and threatened officials in positions of responsibility. Each claims benefits for its own group, and the state abdicates its own duties: for instance, there has been almost no attempt by the state to provide adequate low-cost, public housing in the last decade. Even the redistribution by local-authority housing bodies of money from the sale of council houses is forbidden. In this world the temptation to do one's own thing (enterprise) becomes overwhelming. The duties of each individual to society are literally meaningless for many people, corroded by either mass, long-term unemployment or the privatizing forces of affluence.

Responsibility to the civic order thus falls into disrepute, whether through the desire for lower taxes from the right (why pay more to have better education?), or the denial of personal responsibility from the left (it is the fault of the system). Yet even at this nadir, one can point to Vaclav Havel's emphasis on responsibility, or to the feminist critique of the male lust for power without the caring spirit of nurture and responsibility. Marxism's greatest failure was perhaps the lack of guidance on how power should be used once appropriated, and on the relationship of truth, responsibility and state action. Sakharov's moral critique of the Soviet Union stemmed from this point, but an equal critique from the left can be made of the amorality of the market. Both a critique of Marxism and of the market require the linking of an individual ethic to that of communal responsibility. It is this which it is hard to find in our often corrupted and amoral society: following the chapter by David Ford and Al McFadyen, UPAs are 'places where there is a specially intensive convergence of the negative consequences of our society's habitual idolatries' (p. 102); more simply, they focus the corruption and alienation to breaking point. This is not to impugn individuals, for the amorality is often found equally, and more so, in white-collar fraud, but to highlight the sense of estrangement so often found there in UPAs. In all this confusion, an expansion of individual freedom ('enterprise') may justifiably be seen as the final inflammation of the body politic, creating greed and callousness. Yet economic and social freedom can be joined to libertarian permissiveness. While I am aware of the underlying prejudices which can easily stereotype and caricature minorities I would argue that permissiveness and social-economic freedom can lead to greater egoism, and indifference to social order.

The reaction to anti-social acts is not helpful either. It is under-standable that the heated response to appalling crimes is one of moral outrage and a call for greater discipline, social enforcement of society's norms, and the assumption by the state of the individual's own sense of responsibility. In a world of estrangement, alienation and moral abdication, there is a very rapid swing from freedom ('the enterprise culture') to social compulsion. This only further removes the connection between responsibility and individual or communal action. The crucial factor is surely re-establishing responsibility at a local level, through heightened individual or communal awareness of what it means to have both duties and rights.

Otherwise, society will evolve to a point where the sanction for anti-social actions will be the withdrawal of civic benefits (no welfare) or even the loss of civic rights (no right to vote). Workfare, compulsory community service, and the imposition of obligation are the harbingers of social compulsion. This is one strategy for rebuilding civic order, but the cost will be terrifyingly high. Those who defend this strategy argue that it links duties, rights and privileges together, in a manner which illuminates the necessity of social obligation by the individual, but they ignore the consequences of social compulsion.

The alternative is a combination of individual responsibility where possible, but collective responsibility where necessary. It is not helpful to place all the weight of responsibility on the weak, so collective action remains important. There is however great justification in stressing individual responsibility because the emphasis on letting people take responsibility for their own lives is not a way of rolling back the state further, but of recognizing that without exercising moral responsibility people will not learn how to use it. The community can help people take responsibility for their own lives, if the local community is so empow-ered (education, training credits, etc.).

The development of a sense of mutual obligation is the crucial factor. It is not an easy panacea: women who carry the main weight of domestic responsibility anyway will ask how empowerment might be made meaningful. But the crux is Augustine's recognition that freedom is no freedom at all unless it is the freedom to do the right thing.

The practical implications are vast, but it is not the burden of this essay to argue them out. It is enough to point in business ethics to the 'stakeholder' theory, where the community as well as the shareholders, the employers as well as the managers, have a stake in the company, and so the company has responsibilities to them all. In local government the failure to deliver a service could be made accountable. Frank Field has long argued for the importance of the responsibility of pension funds. And, at the individual level, there is the fostering of community involvement, civic education and a duty to take responsibility for one's future, in response to training credits. (This holds true, even if, as at present, there is grossly inadequate training.)

Responsibility and civic order hold together freedom and the wholeness of society: the individual and the collective. But the tension is not easily held, and the childlike nature of utopian ideology promises liberation without demanding anything. It is in this context that 'enterprise' must be seen: and only from this perspective can 'self-reliance' and the 'liberation of individual talent' be recognized for the ambiguous slogans which they are.

Loneliness and individuality

'Enterprise' has something of an artificial nature. It was a phrase of the last decade which attracted both opprobrium and hyperbole. Given such a history, careful definition is necessary. Individuality also suffers from a confusion with individualism. Individualism is seen as the affirmation of the autonomous self, often resulting in an atomized social order. Individuality, which Mill prized so highly, values the distinctive qualities of an individual, and the importance of preserving self-realization against the tyranny of mass society. In our own culture, individuality may seem a means of placing the individual above the estrangement of civic life. Dress, sexuality, and life-style all contribute to the sense that a person makes their own world, celebrating difference and selfhood above the mundane banality of the modern world. Enterprise and individuality often go together, as the fashionable role-models of the last decade suggest. Urban Priority Areas are often places where individuality flourishes with enormous vitality and a celebration of human life. Against the estrangement there is humour, enjoyment and a heightened sense of self. Urban areas are seldom dull places.

There are four senses which can be given to the meaning of the term 'the individual'. The responsibility of the individual is a biblical notion, but is held alongside corporate relationships. Even the phrase 'Son of Man' which expresses the uniqueness of Jesus by himself refers in the Old Testament to Israel as a whole. The accountability of an individual before God, *coram Deo*, is not separate from the accountability of the community. What emerged out of this in Western theology, however, was the concept of the individual accountable only to himself, able to maintain his course by a strong inner morality. Authoritarian religions often produce such people, driven by high ideals and the need for success. 'Enterprise' can often be associated with such people, but the isolation and autonomy of such people make them both vocal advocates of authoritarian measures in a fragmented society, and yet paradoxically inadequate leaders of society. There are dangerous implications for urban areas in such a role-model. A third meaning of the individual is the inner-directed person, who lacks a highly developed moral sense. Assertiveness and self-advancement are the goals for such a person, lacking any inner, moral coherence or external roots. Again the authoritarian nature of the developing consensus in society to deal firmly with deviant, urban behaviour can be found here. A fourth sense entails self-expression, authenticity, where self-expression, hedonism and independence hide the lack of any real content to life. Such is the emptiness of much urban life.

Each of these meanings slides into the other. Consumer society draws its success both from consumption as a mark of self-advancement (type three) and from consumption as a definition of the ego (type four). Yet the creativity which might be found in the first three types is lost in the final one, where there is a continual redefinition of self in personal behaviour. 'I am what I wear' becomes the watchword. But the inner moral sense, related to God and the community, is increasingly lost as we move from type one to type four and a brittle consumer society emerges. This is the economic correlate of the fragmented political society described in the previous section. The weak in such a society are brushed aside, for self-assertive individuality has no moral sense. Egotism becomes rampant. The lack of responsibility is allied to a passive video culture, where both participation and the moral sense are diminished. This is not wholly negative: there can be, as noted above, a sense of enjoyment and pleasure in this individual egotism.

Urban Priority Areas are societies that are both politically fragmented and deeply estranged. They are also places where the individual can be found, often in great loneliness, sometimes in author-itarian guise, sometimes with great self-assertion, style and confident sexuality. They are paradoxically centres of enormous poverty and need, alongside conspicuous consumption and gorgeous displays of hedonism:

> Proudly rise our modern cities, stately buildings, row on row,
> Yet their windows, blank, unfeeling, stare on pitted streets below,
> Where the lonely drift unnoticed in the city's ebb and flow,
> Lost to purpose and to meaning, scarcely caring where they go.

Urban society looks increasingly to a resolution of the individual's pain by the pursuit of happiness as a marketable commodity. This society does not encourage maturity: pain-avoidance, adolescent longing and the illusion of happiness as easily attainable are the flip-side of an uncaring, power-driven world. However, neurosis is created by the social structure, and the achievement of true individuality is very difficult. Achieving maturity requires personal, Christian stoicism and the recognition of social damage which destroys human relationships; only out of this insight can new, caring relationships be sought.

The issue can also be expressed in terms of personal integrity. Personal integrity is deeply tied up with 'integration with the public domain of communication and relation with others. Genuine person-hood is primarily derived from one's fidelity and commitment to others. Fidelity and commitment to oneself do have a rightful and important place – but they are secondary and valid only in so far as they are required by commitment to others.'[3] Equally, personal identity is built up from personal interaction, and a distorted relationship results in a corrupt individualism.

Enterprise, estrangement and Christianity

Justice is about the restoration of relationships, where goodness is seen as right relationships in the Christian vision. The relationship with God and the neighbour is an interdependent one. It is not the case that fairness, or following the legal processes, can be equated without any further argument with justice.

Where relationships fail, there justice is weakened. Central to the biblical account of God's dealing with humanity is that one cannot speak of a just society where there are bad relationships. The implica-tion for a broken civic order is that from a biblical point of view the situation becomes less and less just, even if 'due process of law' is followed or there is fairness. Estrangement means the breaking of relationships, and justice is weakened.

Justice is also expressed in structures of political and economic life. Such structures are easily perverted and become sinful. An unjust political order can perhaps be grasped more easily than an unjust social order, where relationships are weak and people are estranged. Yet neither of these expresses God's will for humanity, where there is a mutual valuing of people.

God is not found in a perspective that doesn't belong to anyone in particular. God takes the risk of belonging to an order of slaves that will become Israel, in a totally estranged civic order called Egypt, where slaves are forced to make bricks without straw. At other times Israel is forced into exile, as a society without hope and full of despair. Rowan Williams argues that there is no avoidance of risk if God is to speak, even if the risk of speech is that it is turned into the idolatry of its hearers.[4] Such a risk is necessary if estrangement is to be overcome by the self-giving of the divine love.

Risk in the divine self-giving accepts the inevitability of change, and the possibility of a catastrophic ending. Nevertheless, resurrection is part of Good Friday: the cross is not simply defeat, for Jesus still speaks beyond the corrupt trial, the false witnesses and the painful death. A church, or a secular body, that takes risks to overcome estrangement is following the pattern of divine action which is a commitment to justice and the establishment of true relationships. This action challenges idolatry and frozen situations where the outcome is predetermined. We may say more: it is hardly possible to encounter God in situations where the possibility of risk is absent. That is a painful message for a church or civic body. If the alienation that is so prevalent in our society is to be changed, a church or city council must risk failure, and the loss of credibility.

Transformation itself is a risk. But the affirmation of dignity enables a person to survive risk. The energizing of relationships through the presence of Christ enables a trinitarian understanding of change. There are decisions, risks and responsibilities. Each can be related to a person of the Trinity: the creation of the world by the Father, the risk of incarnation by the Son, the responsibilities which the Spirit brings to the Church where she dwells. Practical idolatry is the isolating of one aspect without the other. But a civic body, or a church, can hold all three together in a wonderfully enhancing way.

Examples like OPNHE could fail, just as those involved in the businesses created by OPNHE have no guarantee of success. If the risk is not taken, however, there is no real possibility of hope for a community. Hope is rooted in moral convictions. It thus returns this argument to the idea of the individual, or community, which is both morally aware and accountable to God and to its neighbour. Faith, hope and love are the theological virtues, but they grow in the soil of prudence, wisdom, temperance and courage. This is a theology of virtue, where the community can shape character if the community is itself formed by faith, hope and love.

There is no glorifying of risk here. Too much risk, and more failure, could lead to estrangement on a greater scale. The issue is what sort of risk is appropriate in a complex world, and under what conditions is it an appropriate strategy? Risk is only appropriate where those who take such decisions have a character fashioned in such a way that it supports duties, and enables one to offer rights.

The task of the church in an urban area is to be a place where moral strength can still be found in a compassionate identification with its local community. The local community must flow in and out of the church, which is a problem for churches which are not part of their local society but have a gathered congregation. Equally a local church should cultivate intermediate institutions. It should stress the value of related-ness, participation and responsibility. Moral strength is found in a myriad of small-scale relationships where there is a genuine under-standing and sharing. Alongside that moral strength there will need to be an encouragement of risk. Enterprise is a proper arena for displaying that moral sensitivity. Urban areas need people to take risks, and show what is possible. Nevertheless, those risks are only meaningful if they enable the existence of hope in a brittle, consumer society which is politically estranged.

The creation of wealth in society (enterprise in one of its forms) is closely related to a social understanding of wealth. Just as creation embodies moral values, as in the Psalmist's interpretation of creation in Psalm 139, so enterprise which creates wealth must embody civic and social worth. The regeneration of society is one task, politically, eco-nomically and socially. Just as God continually re-establishes light and not darkness, so the Church, in support of political bodies such as a local city council, must again and again seek the overcoming of estrangement and sheer individualism.

Peter Kellner, a political journalist, has put the point well: 'we are enriched by things that economic statistics either ignore or fail to measure fully.' The creation of social wealth in an innovative way is a true form of enterprise. The final conclusion must, however, be ambig-uous. Political activity diminishes and individualism increases: the dissolution of civic order is greater than it was a decade ago. God empties himself into this world, and is present in self-giving love.

The relationship of enterprise to estrangement remains as ambig-uous as ever. It turns on what it is that enterprise creates, and how that creativity mirrors the creativity of God, who embodies in the life of Jesus moral worth and the overcoming of all estrangement.

The steadfast love of God, *hesed*, is associated with God's faithfulness to the promise that he will be present in the most estranged situations where human beings no longer trust one another except as consumer, customer and perhaps as casual visitor. Sin describes those who suffer misfortune through no fault of their own, but who experience life as marginal. Enterprise can represent the possibility of change in a society, but alongside this possibility there is the need of a new relationship which is not based on estrangement. The identification of Jesus with sinners in the table fellowship, which is such a feature of the gospels, establishes that relationship.

The political implications are found in the links between worship and a vision of citizenship. Worship must be related to the acceptance of public responsibility, where the pluralism celebrated in 1 Corinthians 12.4–7, 26 speaks of a variety of life and yet a common good. The myth of a single culture in political life ('Victorian values') has been a long time dying. A Christian vision would affirm the pluralism but want to assert that there could still be a common good. Equally individuality is to be praised as the worth of every person because they are so created by God, without accepting individualism. Finally the hope which is there in worship must seek a dialogue with the secular hope found in entrepreneurial activity, so that the two worlds of economics and Christian faith are neither seen as separate realities nor one identity.

Notes

1 Peter Sedgwick, *The Enterprise Culture* (London: SPCK, 1992).
2 Commission on Social Justice, *Social Justice in a Changing World* (IPPR, 1993), pp. 20–1.
3 Alistair I. McFadyen, *The Call to Personhood: Christian Theory of the Individual in Social Relationships* (CUP, 1990).
4 R. Holloway (ed.), *The Divine Risk* (Darton, Longman and Todd, 1990).

Crime and violence

The UPA as the place of the demons?

ALISTAIR I. McFADYEN

After ten years

What has changed?

Faith in the City identified a number of factors which conspire together to make living humanly in the UPA situation an uphill struggle which too easily traps people in its harshness. The situation in UPAs has worsened in the ten years since that report in relation to all these factors: unemployment, poverty, housing, and arguably health and education too.

That is quite true, yet it offers a misleadingly pessimistic picture of what has happened since *Faith in the City*. The Church (and, indeed, other agencies and UPA people themselves) has been working to address and respond to the factors which the report identified as requiring urgent attention. The Church Urban Fund, for instance, although not without its critics, has done an immense amount which is positive. And whilst there can be few who work with any realistic hope that 'facts of UPA life' like poverty or unemployment are going to be abolished in the near future, there are many signs of small-scale transformation and of hope in relation even to these factors. But there is one factor which the original report identified which has so far remained largely unaddressed by practical action. And it is this factor, more than any other, I suspect, which makes living in UPAs in 1995 a much darker and more apparently hopeless situation than it was even in the gloom of 1985.

That factor is crime. The relative absence of practical measures in the wake of *Faith in the City* is not, I think, a sign that crime is not being taken seriously, or has been forgotten about. Quite the reverse, I suspect. It rather reflects the seriousness of crime, the way that it appears to be absolutely endemic and out of control, beyond any effective measure, which reduces the wise to silence and extreme caution in action – which begins to look like impotence. *Faith in the City* itself noted a three-fold increase in general rates of crime across the country in the thirty years preceding the report and adduced evidence that strongly suggested that the crime rate (and also the rate of increase) in UPAs (particularly for robbery, burglary and thefts of and from vehicles) was significantly higher than the national average.[1]

The situation was bad then, but all the evidence points to an exponential increase in crime and violence in UPAs since the commission took its evidence. There has, indeed, been a general increase in disorder and crime, predominantly amongst young males, across all sectors of society. In addition to the highly visible increase in disorder, there has been a perceived increase in corporate crime, which is significant in its effect of undermining the reliability of structure and order as mediated by key institutions. The deterioration in the situation of law and order is clearly not confined to UPAs. However, because of the general situation in UPAs, the rate of increase tends to be sharper, the fall into disorder less episodic, than elsewhere. As in many other dimensions of life, the economic and social pressures within UPAs mean that the tensions and pathologies of society at large stand out in sharper relief and in need of more urgent action and attention than they appear to do elsewhere. The UPA is the place of the demons, in the sense that it is there that the demonic forces operating in society as a whole are made visible and reveal themselves for what they are. The demons of society represent the inner essence (spirituality or interiority) of material and social institutions, systems, structures – in fact, all the tangible forms which power takes in society – as they turn pathological.[2] The pathological denotes that disorder which occurs where societies organize themselves in ways which are opposed to God's sovereignty and order. So to speak of the UPA as the place of the demons is to speak of it first and foremost as the place possessed by the spiritual forces operating in society at large; the place disordered by those forces; the place where the spiritual resources for opposing and resisting the demonic are at once weak and dissipated and where they are to be marshalled and concentrated. The UPA is the place where we must do battle with the demons of our society which, among other things, order UPA people into places of marginality, poverty and sometimes of criminality.

How has crime changed?

The rate of increase in crime would itself be enough to suggest that the situation is out of control, that there is a breakdown of order, of the effectiveness of law enforcement and of social and moral norms which inhibit criminality and violence. But it is as much the *kinds* of crime being committed and the *ways* in which they are committed which generates the now widely held impression that the situation is out of control, beyond hope.

Perhaps the major tragic ingredient of crime in many UPAs now is drugs. Drugs were certainly there in the early 1980s, but not in such volume and without such intensity of use amongst the young (and, indeed, the very young). In some UPAs a drug habit is the norm. And where use is the norm, the capacity of drugs to suck people into a total environment is very great. And by this I do not only mean the general capacity of drugs to take over people's lives; more particularly, I mean the way in which they may trap people in the grip of criminality by enticing them into involvement in some part of the process of selling drugs, as pushers, runners, couriers (even between cities, offering a widening of horizons in a way which might have been unthinkable otherwise). None of these activities receives the level of opprobrium it would have done not so long ago in working-class areas, at least among the young. The increased extent of drug use is probably largely responsible for the massive increase in robbery, burglary and prostitution (as the only possible way of paying for an expensive habit), and is certainly responsible for the increased use of violence in the prosecution of these more 'traditional' crimes. In the last few years, in one or two UPAs (principally Manchester's Moss Side, but also parts of London and Liverpool), it is clear that the drugs trade has brought with it a small arsenal of firearms to protect the economic interests vested in it. It has also brought for some an increasingly casual willingness to use firearms against competitors in a fairly wild way (Moss Side again and Chapeltown, Leeds are recent examples). Guns are, nonetheless, still rare on the streets of most British UPAs, but other weapons, particularly knives, are now commonplace. But most alarming of all, it is often the very young who are armed to protect the drugs business.

The moral panic of recent years relating to crime has been a response to juvenile criminality, particularly in UPA areas. Joyriding high performance cars and civil disturbance have become symbols for this, but it is much more the attitude and age of those involved which is the cause of concern and of outrage than the offences themselves. On the whole, it is the perceived endemic nature of the criminality, its wantonness and brazenness and the apparently total disregard of possible consequences which has troubled many. Pictures and stories of children and youths committing offences individually or together haunt the pages of daily newspapers (such as taking and driving away cars, then racing them before a crowd). The young people either appear completely uninhibited by the thought of being caught, or repeat offences immediately after being caught. The fearful image is one of being out of control, of a complete disintegration of the ordering effects of culture or any form of authority, of total disaffection from society, of the breakdown of moral standards, coupled with the apparent ineffectual nature of the criminal justice system and law enforcement. Police who have lost (where they ever had it) the confidence and trust of local communities seem themselves now to have lost confidence in their own ability to deal with juvenile offenders who have fear neither of being caught nor of being punished. Often it is the police who have to exercise wariness in pursuing suspects in certain areas, not just because the suspects may themselves produce and use a weapon to evade capture, but because of the danger of being attacked by other young people who happen to be in the vicinity.

The view from outside
'UPAs are dangerous places to go'

There has always been an association made in popular consciousness between high levels of crime and violence and 'bad' areas. Whilst areas which achieve some notoriety as 'bad' do so for the perceived levels of crime and violence, rather than for the evidence of deprivation in them, these areas will usually be among the most deprived economically and socially. Not all UPA areas experience high levels of crime and violence, especially where the population is relatively older. But there is a rough correlation between levels of deprivation and levels of crime and violence, and an even closer correlation between levels of deprivation and the perceived level of threat of crime and violence. So UPAs are often seen and experienced as violent places.

In wider public perception, these are places of danger, where the normal, civilized codes of behaviour do not operate, at least in respect of outsiders: places where the demons lurk. They are dangerous places to visit or pass through, but they also pose the perceived danger of overspill – that the violence and crime, and the breakdown of social order they represent, may invade the rest of society. Making a connection between deprivation and violence or criminality does not always imply seeing the former as the cause of the latter. The reversed explanation, that places are 'bad' because 'bad' people are housed there has a fairly wide currency. UPAs are then seen as something like the U-bend of society: they are violent and experience high levels of crime because 'that kind of person' has been drained off there: people who have no will to work or act as decent members of society, who are to blame for their situation. They are not to be sympathized with; the rest of us are to be protected from the danger which UPAs and UPA people represent. All this supposes, of course, that the demons 'decent people' might encounter in UPAs only live *there*, and only have power because UPA people bow down to them. But what if they are the demons of our whole society, given power through an entire means of social and economic organization which, when they encounter people already ground down by the experience of living in a UPA, overpower them?

The fear of contagion

This strategy of blame accompanied by a sense of danger has, if anything, increased recently in the face of the apparently exponentially increasing rates and seriousness of juvenile criminality – from joyriding and exhibiting high-performance cars to mini-riots, the murder of Jamie Bulger and other prepubescent serious crime. At its worst, such a view implies the increasing ghettoization of UPAs. One is encouraged towards a 'realism' which accepts that UPA crime is endemic and out of any possible control. There is no answer for the UPAs – they are criminal places and cannot now become decent. So the only viable strategy is to isolate UPA criminality and fence it off from the rest of society. For 'decent' society is understood to constitute actual and potential victims of UPA people, who are seen overwhelmingly as criminal perpetrators. Private security patrols, physical barriers and systematic alertness to 'strangers' (neighbourhood watch) partly express this fear of UPA crime overspilling into 'decent' neighbour-hoods.

High levels of crime seem to invite those of us who live outside of UPAs, not just to give up on them, but to demonize them too. To see the suburbs in the role of *victim* and UPAs as *predator* is to connive at a reversal of the relations of power which really pertain in society as a whole, between those living in UPAs and those living in the suburbs. It is so axiomatic that it should hardly bear repeating, that the UPA situation is one in which people have precious little power in their own lives, let alone in society at large. It is a place where people are 'ordered out' of society; they are, in a sense, the victims of 'decent' order.

What is happening when those in a relatively weak position in society are cast in a role that ascribes to them a pretty awesome, predatory power, so potent that it threatens the fabric of ordered decency supposed to pertain in the rest of society? The perceived chaos of UPA life (and therefore of UPA people also), for which crime functions both as its defining characteristic and potent symbol, is extensively regarded as the absolute antithesis of order. It is not, as it might have been seen in the past, a matter of a different order (like East End criminal culture) opposed to decent order; it is simple absence of order.

The fear of UPA criminality represents something more than the fear that one may individually be the victim of a burglary by a UPA resident. This fear relates to the UPA as a whole, as a black hole, threatening to swallow up the rest of us.

The demonology of the UPA is somewhat paradoxical. It invites us to regard UPAs as places of criminal residence – it is where the criminals who prey on individual people and their property come from. We may therefore regard the boundary between UPA and other urban areas as that between victim and perpetrator. But, at the same time, it draws our attention to the UPA as a place of criminality bordering on the chaos of disorder – as a place where crime *takes place*. Yet the demonology prevents us from seeing that this must mean that UPA residents are overwhelmingly the victims of crime, because our concern with crime and violence in UPAs lies not so much with those who live there as with those who pass through: ourselves. We worry that the demons might catch us as we pass through, or might prove powerfully seductive to our children, who might be drawn into its vibrant street life. So even when we recognize the seriousness of the situation *in* the UPAs, we are often possessed by demons of self-concern which prevent us from seeing the humanity and vulnerability of those in UPAs as *victims* of crime and violence, actually living in a situation which we fear as we pass through it in a matter of minutes.

One of the primary questions for an urban (priority) theology is whether it can begin or be done by those who are only passing through, in one way or another. This is as true for the theme of crime and violence as for any other; yet I would like to stay for a little while longer with the perspective from outside, in order to help clarify how things look from inside (insofar as this can be clear to me on the outside).

Order and control

The sort of view I have been presenting sees crime and violence primarily as threats to order. It is certainly possible to have a positive view of order, and interpret crime in this way without any attendant demonization of UPAs, but they are often found together. Order may be viewed as a fundamental good, necessary for any rational and human existence. Concern for order has so often been wedded to support for the forces of reaction and oppression which coerce all disorderly elements, including the criminal, into line that it is almost bound to court accusations of reaction. Many who are concerned with the complexity of human situations such as that in the UPA are often, understandably, profoundly suspicious of talk of order – *whose* order? *whose* good? they are likely to ask. Is it the general good of order as such which is being projected or is it the particular goods and interests represented by this specific social order? I am resolutely challenging the assumption that order is necessarily oppressive – that which the oppressed need liberation from – as well as the assumption that concern for order is the property of the ideological right. Crime in UPAs radically undermines the view that being 'for the poor' makes social order suspect.

Regarding crime as a threat to order does, at least, respond to the seriousness of crime which we are faced with in UPAs today. Any individual criminal act is always more than a transaction between the particular perpetrator and victim. Any crime is an offence against society – social order – and not just against particular victims. For that reason, society has an interest, quite independent of the injured party, in dealing with crime and those responsible for it. But society obviously has an interest in remaining blind to the ways in which its own order may itself create pressures towards criminality, so that crime might be considered to be something for which society as a whole is to be held to account, not just individuals. Non-individual factors are, in any case, hard to take into account in a criminal justice system which can only bring individual perpetrators to book.

All this feeds the common assumption that crime is a matter of 'bad' individuals setting themselves against the fabric of social order. Perhaps the most fundamental affirmation one hears in common views of crime lies in the idea that individuals are free, and therefore choose to behave in the ways that they do. Crime exists because certain 'bad' individuals (more densely populating UPAs than anywhere else) choose to commit it. Response to criminality must therefore, on this view, attend properly both to the seriousness of crime and to the fact that this person has made a decision to act in this way. The response must consequently concentrate primarily on protecting social order from this person, and then on providing punishment and deterrence through punishment – on the assumption that the way to influence future choices is by making it clear that the consequences of crime are unpleasant. The possibility of serious punishment may then forcefully enter into any future calculation concerning the wisdom of further criminal acts. This does not necessarily entail the view that the criminal is reformable, capable of being transformed from 'bad' to 'good', just that he or she is capable of rationally calculating self-interest. Naturally, an assumption is made that people are free to will and act rationally.

The main aim, on this view, is the protection and maintenance of order necessary for the normal functioning of society. Criminality is seen primarily as an offence against the fabric of social order necessary for decent, civilized life. It is as a poison against social order that lends criminality its seriousness.

A major example

Putting these elements together, it is possible to understand why, on this view, analysing or understanding the general or individual causes of crime is not only considered to be unimportant, but also as potentially dangerous, in that it colludes with the criminal in providing an alibi and excusing him or herself from personal responsibility. If the 'bad' is to be dealt with, one requires a clear picture; it does not help to cover the canvas with broad brush strokes of grey. The general attitude underlying this view of crime was pointedly expressed by John Major in commenting on a series of 'disturbances' in Newcastle in 1993. He called for a little less understanding and a little more condemnation, in an attack on those who espouse 'liberal, 1960s' values.

John Habgood, among others, at the time pointed out that crime could not effectively be dealt with unless it was understood in all its complexity. But by 'understanding', Major was probably not thinking so much of intellectual analysis of the causes of crime as of compassionate human fellow-feeling. Presumably, he fears that this is bound once again to excuse the perpetrator by drawing attention away from the crime itself (and so from victims of crime) to the life-situation of the perpetrator. 'Understanding' here stands as a cipher for that interpersonal expression of empathy which imaginatively places oneself in another's situation and comes to understand how the other behaves in this way. It is to be criticized, Major thinks, because it will necessarily blame the circumstances rather than the individual, and so will not give the person a clear moral framework within which to operate, since (as he seems to believe) one cannot simultaneously understand and judge. But exercising good judgement is precisely what real understanding can do: discerning what is really going on here, in terms of whole syndromes and pathologies ('demons'), rather than identifying and rooting out the symptoms (individual criminal children).

It is significant, from a Christian point of view, to note that Major's sentiments effectively place these children outside of the moral community constituted by the rest of us. We are not to exercise care, concern or responsibility to them, beyond removing them and making life unpleasant enough for them to see the error of their ways.

There are many (especially in government) who speak as though it were axiomatic that mentioning social conditions is a ruse to excuse and alleviate from personal responsibility for actions. Yet even hardliners

are prepared to expand their account of juvenile criminality to incorporate cultural (if not societal/economic) conditions because of the age of
the offenders and the endemic nature of offending in some UPAs. What
this amounts to, I think, is another kind of moral blame. A decline or
collapse in moral standards and authority in certain areas of life, such as
the family (always, of course, spheres of life which are not a direct part
of government responsibility), is blamed, sometimes in combination
with 'UB40 culture' or teachers' supposed '1960s liberal values'.

Understanding crime in solidarity with UPAs

Many Christians active, living and working in UPAs react strongly
against strategies of blame such as those I have been outlining so far.
Understandably, they rush to the defence of the people and places
which they know to be much more nuanced and ambiguous in reality
than in prevalent demonologies. But as well as objecting to what they
see as misrepresentation, there are at least three other elements here: (1)
the observation that what is being condemned is often class and
cultural difference (as if no violence or crime is hidden in suburban
respectability); (2) that violence and criminality are related to the social
and economic situation which constitutes the UPAs; (3) that crime is
often the only available way to pursue the values of society as a whole
– acquisition, materialism, self-help, personal enterprise, etc.

Finding possibilities for understanding the human situations of
those who commit crime validates working with people and in situations where crime and violence are part of life. This depends on
interpreting violence and crime in UPAs as symptomatic of the wider
social and economic situation which constitutes the reality of UPA life.
So those who are violent and criminal, particularly the young, are to be
understood and supported as people responding to their situation, not
condemned or given up on. The UPA is a situation in which people
typically have little experience of power and precious few affirmations
of dignity and worth, as well as few material resources which, for
young people in an incredibly materialist culture, are a means to
establish and express worth as much as the means for physical survival.
Crime and violence may offer a route to satisfy or at least palliate this.
It is a situation where people are under many interrelated pressures,
where much of life's strain is close to the surface and where there are
not many avenues open for the skilful management of anger and
frustration.

Towards 'traditional', especially non-violent, forms of criminality
which have, for generations, operated as an alternative economy within
some areas of deprivation, one can find a basically positive attitude

among many who live or work in UPAs. This is particularly striking in UPA areas where there is a core population which has been relatively stable over generations, and which is largely homogeneous (do I mean traditional, working-class whites?), and in which there still remains some sense of community and a unifying culture.[3] Here, criminality is a part of a culture; it operates within certain established rules of social conduct and patterns of respect. One basic rule which is supposed to operate is that one does not prey on one's own community or on the weak. Undoubtedly, there is an element of romanticization in the way the stereotype of the traditional criminal fraternity is portrayed, especially in the supposed benefits of order which the tyrannical violence of people like the Krays brought to some areas. But there is still some truth in the picture of a general acceptance of crime which is targeted against businesses rather than hurting people.

There is a sense in which much crime, as an economic activity of a sort, is enterprise; and a sense, too, in which all enterprise requires the kind of energy which is akin to aggression – it is energy directed in creative ways. Violence which does not relate to other criminal activity might in part represent undirected aggression and energy, or the overspill of the energy needed to survive a situation like a UPA – refusal to cave in to pressures, to be a victim.

Theology beyond the polarities?

The views I have characterized (hopefully not caricatured) as from the outside and in solidarity with the inside present us with two polarized positions. One takes crime very seriously as a threat to established order and insists that people take individual responsibility for their actions. In extreme (but not rare) versions, this view deploys a language of blame and of wickedness which demonizes UPAs and those who live in them.

At the opposite pole stands the view which wants to take the *situation* in which crime takes place with proper gravity, regarding crime more as a *symptom* of social disease than its cause. Some hear such talk as carrying the implication that crime is *caused* by social conditions and is not therefore a matter of individual responsibility at all. In any case, this view often leads to an advocacy on behalf of those who commit crime, especially the young, so that they be helped to find their way forward in the UPA situation. In another variation, the view can lead to a more thoroughgoing advocacy of crime as merely alternative economic activity.

Some adopt such a view as a corrective to the demonization of UPAs and of UPA people which they detect in the other view. But in a strange way this motivation may actually collude in that demonization. If all UPA people are supposed to be defended by understanding or excusing or condoning crime, then that seems to carry the suggestion that all UPA people are simply and unequivocally criminal, or at least do not need protection, support or advocacy against crime. For they are presented here as victims of society which turns them to crime, and not as victims of crime themselves.

A view from inside

One of the most notable markers of just how serious crime and violence in UPAs have become is that one is increasingly likely to find UPA people voicing pleas for firm action against crime and criminals, especially the young. I want to begin thinking this through on the way to a theological assessment because it drives a coach and horses through the assumption that crime and violence can be dealt with adequately by dividing the world up into criminals and victims.

One is more likely at present to encounter a 'reactionary' rather than a 'liberal' point of view in UPAs themselves. That does not necessarily mean that attitudes towards the police or to the prevailing social order have necessarily changed. Neither, I think, does it indicate a shift away from positive or at least neutral attitudes to 'traditional' crime, where that existed before. It is a response to a worsening of the situation in UPAs themselves. It should not be assumed, then, that when firm attitudes towards crime and violence are heard from UPA people that they are invoking a bourgeois moral framework where previously none existed.

Such opinions 'from the inside' speak powerfully of the total helplessness which many now feel in UPAs because of crime and violence, not merely in their particular occurrence, but as a prevailing malevolent atmosphere and reality. In order, I think, to grasp the desperation of the situation, it is necessary to understand the extent to which UPA people now find themselves increasingly driven to adopt frames of reference and patterns of thought about themselves and the places they live which have more in common with the 'reactionary demonologies' from outside than with 'liberal understanding in solidarity', which attempts to maintain a sense of people's dignity and worth. The 'liberal' view seems to fail to take the gravity of the situation seriously enough and offers neither protection in the present nor hope for the future.

Some residents of UPAs do hold the demonology in pretty well all its aspects: 'This is a "bad" place now (even if it was good in many respects before), full of "bad" people who can and will do whatever they like to you, your property, your space ... they just don't care.' Others articulate a more restrained form which nonetheless accepts the basic premiss of the 'reactionary' view without its excessive demonization: there is what threatens to be a total breakdown of order which leaves one at the mercy of whatever powerful or irrational elements one may come up against (since one can't expect much from the police).

The sort of disorder which UPA people are subject to is more like a state of war than anything else – although it may be a war without clear sides and certainly without any purpose. But the sense of being constantly at the mercy of crime, so that one cannot walk to the corner shop and back without the fear of robbery or assault on the way or discovering burglary on return; cannot get taxis to fetch or return you home – that is fear of something which may land on you like a mortar bomb. Like mortars, crime may pick its particular targets without a great deal of reason, but it manages to communicate the general enmity, malevolence or lack of interest which aims at or is careless of the destruction of your being.

Disorder makes rational life impossible, partly because one cannot count on being able to enjoy anything, to make progress, to hang on to the little that one has. Disorder drives people into despair because it offers them no hope that, even little by little, they may improve their situation (one frequent example is that insurance is prohibitively expensive because of the crime rate. If goods are stolen before the credit is paid off, then people turn to buying goods which they know have been stolen). Criminal disorder also breaks the felt bonds of solidarity with other people in this place, which might sustain humanity in the face of adversity. Instead of solidarity, there is war.

Disorder drives out hope and opens the black hole of despair. That is why it is so serious and why it is a theological issue. It encourages people to give up on themselves and on their place. It is the disorder of crime and violence which is now driving out hope for transformation from UPAs, no matter what little anticipations and tastes and glimpses may have been gained over the last ten years. It is crime and violence in UPAs which makes it extraordinarily difficult to see them, from the inside, as related to the promised kingdom. How can one believe or hope in transcendent, transforming possibility when one cannot even retain what one has, let alone move forward? It is only order which holds out the promise of and possibility of a future, which consequently may mediate hope.

That is why we need a theology of order. That will be dangerous, because order can be used to oppress those already at the sharp end of existing order, who have every reason to object to it, since it does not carry or nurture their interests nor sustain their hope in or praise of

God. But order is absolutely necessary to human life; without it, the world becomes entirely unreliable, making intentional activity and the taking of responsibility impossible. Order tends to become problematic and pathological when it is imposed from the outside and when it is so imposed in the form of prescriptive rules – a static rather than a dynamic and local order. If order is to be based upon the creative and transforming activity of the triune God, then its basis lies not in some arbitrary and imposed set of legal and moral standards, but in our being together as community – that is, in the ordering of society as an organic network of reciprocity and mutuality.[4] Order would then be a basis for hope and transformation in community, not an impediment to them. From the perspective of that kind of order, UPA crime and violence would have to be judged pathogens because they inhibit the growth of trust and reliability necessary for community. However, the destruction of the values of community, and so of the very possibility of community order, happens at least as much in the supra-personal causes of crime as it does in criminality itself. So the material institutionalization of a spirituality opposed to community would also have to be named in any act of Christian discernment of the demons of disorder. And it is that which would prevent a theology of order from simply colluding with the forces of reaction in naming and judging crime as disorder only in relation to prevailing social order.

Notes

1 *Faith in the City* (London: Church House Publishing, 1985), pp. 329–32.
2 See the first two books in the trilogy by Walter Wink, *Naming the Powers* (Philadelphia: Fortress Press, 1984) and *Unmasking the Powers* (Philadelphia: Fortress Press, 1986).
3 See, for example, Janet Foster, *Crime and Community in the Inner City* (London: Routledge, 1990).
4 This is, I think, the vision which lay behind Reinhold Niebuhr's contribution to the 1948 WCC consultation: 'God's design and the present disorder of civilisation' in *The Church and the Disorder of Society* (London: SCM Press, 1948), pp. 13–28.

Sanctuary

SUSAN HOPE

It was early morning – the hour of the Eucharist in the UPA church. A man entered breathlessly, his head bleeding from a wound, dishevelled, unkempt. He sank into a pew and remained motionless. About half-way through the service, he left. He returned at the end and asked the curate for a copy of the confession which had been on the overhead projector. He took the copy and went. But was it possible that, during his brief stay in the church, he found sanctuary in its dual form? – an encounter with God which necessitated an encounter with himself, a place of refuge but also a place of reform, a place of security but also a place of challenge.

'Asylum' – shelter and protection from which a refugee is not allowed to be forcibly removed – has always struggled with the two-fold demands of refuge and reform during its long history among the great variety of cultures in the world.

For right of sanctuary is invariably linked with 'the holy place' and in ancient Israel we encounter a double-edged experience of 'the holy'. Although it is not enough to say that the holy place was sacred and everything else profane, for religion penetrated the entire social life of the nation, there was, nevertheless, at the same time, an innate sense of the holiness, the 'otherness', the separatedness of the being who came to be known as Yahweh. This led to the development of the sanctuary as the holy place, a place which became a place of danger, a place associated with the dark symbols of the transcendent – darkness, smoke, fire, fear, blood, thunder, lightnings – a place, be it mountain, or tree, or the Tent of Meeting, approaching which any unauthorized person or any 'unclean' person would be put to death (Num 3.3). A great deal of the teaching of Leviticus is taken up with prohibitions to exclude the 'unclean' from the Tent of Meeting, and with acts of ritual cleansing to enable the sanctuary to be approached. Ethical demands are seen as an essential part of this: 'by giving a child of his to Molech he has defiled my sanctuary and profaned my holy name', declares the

191

Lord in Leviticus 20.20. In addition to not violating the sanctuary by the
sin of humanity, Judaism also felt the need to protect the sanctuary
from ritual impurity. Women were particularly 'unclean' and unable to
approach the sanctuary during menstruation or at the time of childbirth
– an ancient primal horror of menstruation which may inform some of
the debate surrounding the ordination of women to the priesthood
today. The 'separatedness' of the sanctuary did not apply only to the
holy mountain, which was unapproachable (Exod 19.12f.) – awe and
fear were attached to any place where God communicated with human
beings. Those places became 'holy' – such as with Jacob, 'How fearful is
this place: this is none other than the house of God, this is the gate of
heaven!' (Gen 28.17, 18), and Moses, 'the place where you are standing
is holy ground' (Exod 3.5).

Separatedness means boundaries, and the boundaries became even
more important in a cult where no images of God were allowed. The
sacred space, the 'emptiness', the 'darkness' becomes 'the place where
God is'. In this freedom from images Israel of course differed from its
neighbours, as it did in two other essentials of the cult – namely, that
there is only one God, God transcendent, the Holy One, and that this
one God is a personal God who intervenes in history, God-with-us.
These two aspects of God presented themselves in the Israelite understanding of the sanctuary – God transcendent, dangerous and
death-dealing (Num 18.1–7), a stumbling block, a rock to trip up the
house of Israel (Isa 8.14; cf. 1 Pet 2.7, 8), a God of holiness who shows up
sin: 'Woe is me for I am a man of unclean lips . . . for mine eyes have seen
the King, the Lord Almighty!' (Isa 6). Yet the God of the sanctuary is
also God-with-us, the one who the psalmist tells us is our refuge (Pss 11,
18 etc.), who sends us help (Ps 20.2), who inspires us with his glory (Ps
63.2), who is 'Father of orphans, defender of widows, such is God in his
holy dwelling' (Ps 68.5). And just as the concept of 'asylum' juggles
awkwardly with the twin demands of mercy and justice, so 'sanctuary'
struggles with the holding together of the character of God transcendent, and God-with-us, God in our history. For 'sanctuary' in its
developing sense in post-exilic history becomes none other than God
himself. The harrowing experience of the exile became for Israel the
place where God was able to reveal to them: 'I have been a sanctuary for
them in the country to which they have gone' (Ezek 11.16). Exile meant,
for Israel, a deepening of its knowledge of God. And the great vision of
the sanctuary in Ezekiel (47) overflows with an abundance of life-giving
symbols and images of God: the water of life, flowing from the sanctuary, the fruiting trees, the leaves for the healing of the nations (cf. Rev
22.1, 2). The presence of God, while holy and other, is a presence which
brings life to all creation, and healing in the most 'political' of events.

Jesus, in the New Testament, takes hold of this highly developed image of sanctuary as being God himself, and gives it its most vigorous meaning – that he is the new sanctuary. But if he points to himself as the true sanctuary in his incarnation, it is in his crucifixion that 'sanctuary' is most fully realized. For here we are again back with the dark symbols of the transcendent, as holy communion takes place between God and us, the body and blood given as the 'meal of meeting'. Here is 'the meeting place' where the angels ascend and descend upon the Son of man (John 1.51; cf. Gen 28.17) – here is the gate of heaven. Here, too, is the place of refuge, asylum, for 'in Christ Jesus we have been brought near' (Eph 2.13), and all can cry with the hymn writer 'Rock of ages, cleft for me, let me hide myself in thee'. Here is the sanctuary which is the cornerstone, the rock of stumbling (Isa 8.14; cf. 1 Pet 2.6). Here is the place whereby boundaries are both acknowledged and destroyed (Eph 2.14) and in the supreme tension of the cross, here is the place of sanctuary where the symbols of destruction and darkness and symbols of creativity and life meet as 'in him, all things hold together' (Col 1.20).

It is with this tension between the transcendent and God-with-us that we are obliged to grapple as ministers and congregations and as workers in the inner city. For although the crucifixion, 'the work of the sanctuary', makes God fully present to humankind, yet Jesus in his *incarnation* undeniably also confronts us with 'the holy'. 'No one has ever seen God: Jesus Christ, he has made him known', declares John. His incarnate presence conveys 'sanctuary'. Thus Peter can cry 'Depart from me, for I am a sinful man', and discover that confrontation with the holy in Jesus leads to a call to self-consecration: 'Follow me' (Luke 5.8–10), in much the same way that Isaiah, perceiving the glory of the Lord cried out 'Woe is me ...' and received his commission as a prophet. The incarnate Lord demonstrates the unity of the sacred and the secular – in the words of J. G. Davies:

> healing is a secular event – notice the story of the paralytic, 'Which is easier, to say "your sins are forgiven" .... or "Rise up and walk"? But that you may know that the Son of man has authority on earth to forgive sins' – he said to the paralytic – 'I say to you, Rise, take up your pallet and go home'.[1]

Here the integration between the need for forgiveness and the need for physical healing is total, there is no 'separation' between 'spiritual' and 'material'. This tension between the understanding of the integrity of the sacred and secular as clearly displayed through the incarnation, and the reality of 'otherness', of separatedness, which is so much an experience of creatureliness in relation to the Creator, is one of which we in the city are made most acutely aware. Kenneth Leech perhaps sums up the experience of many urban ministers, as he describes life as a curate in Cable Street:

> It was the very ordinary life of this obscure London street which brought home to me the common-ness of grace and the ordinariness of spirituality. I think I went there believing that I was bringing love, bringing intellect, bringing care, possibly bringing Christ, to the deprived Cable Street community. I came to see that it was I who was deprived, that it was I who was in need of their love and care, that Christ was to be found there and did not need to be brought in from outside, and that until that fundamental truth of God's presence and activity in the midst of the oppressed and downtrodden is recognised, all pastoral ministry and all religious life will be unreal.[2]

Those of us who live and work in the inner city recognize, and are humbled by, the presence of the Holy Spirit in the ordinary lives of those among whom we live and work. Yet this is not the only reality of which we are aware. We know, too, how the experiences of alienation and fear and guilt, and the complexities of sin oppress many; many of us in inner-city churches have discovered that sense of travelling *from darkness to light* as we have embraced the faith of the Church, we know and believe that, while the Holy Spirit is not limited to the Church, nevertheless 'Church' in all its weakness and sin is the vehicle which God has chosen as the primary focus for his activity in the world, just as the bread and wine, while not negating the presence of Christ at every feast of friends, yet focus his presence in a specific and particular way. It might be argued that to talk in this way is to juxtapose concepts, rather than to integrate them; nevertheless, it is the raw experience of the Christian that one way to integration, both intellectually and prac-tically, lies somewhere in the experience of being stretched between opposing and conflicting poles. How can we, as Christians, live in this tension? One way might be to stop thinking in terms of boundaries and start thinking in terms of 'relationships'.

Perhaps I can illustrate something of what I mean by thinking in terms of relationships, rather than boundaries, by a story from the city.

Terry was an out-of-work boxer who took to dropping in to our church's open morning in the week. Gradually his story emerged. He was alcoholic, he was terminally ill with cancer and he wanted to see his daughter from whom he had been estranged for fourteen years. Phone calls by him to Sally resulted in her putting the phone down; letters from him were returned unopened. We wrote, on his behalf and at his request, to his daughter, explaining his illness and his longing to see her. She agreed to meet him in a motorway café, somewhere in the

Pennines, on a Sunday. Terry came into church just before the service on the Sunday (the only time he did!) in his best suit, to see if he 'looked all right'. We assured him he did, hugged him and sent him off, and during the course of our service many of our thoughts were turned towards the meeting of that lonely man who was searching for forgiveness and his daughter 'somewhere in that motorway café in the Pennines'. The meeting went well; they met many more times after that and Terry died having been reconciled to his daughter. As far as I know, Terry never made a 'profession of faith'. He never came to a church service. But he was part of us, he 'belonged'. He was 'caught' in a loving network of relationships, he participated in the life of the Body through those relationships. This is not to set up 'relationships' as the way to salvation. But it is to affirm that there are many ways of believing, some of which involve 'participation', not mental assent to credal statements. Frequently, 'belonging' precedes 'believing', is a part of believing, and Pauline theology is full of a happy confusion between what it is to be 'in Christ' and what it is to be 'in the Body'. For a church to define itself in terms of relationships which include and embrace the community, and through which the church may equally be nourished and challenged by the community, rather than thinking in terms of 'boundaries' which exclude, is surely closer to the model of the 'new sanctuary' where on the cross boundaries are destroyed and the veil in the temple is torn in two.

As soon as we start thinking in relational, rather than in doctrinal, terms to describe the dynamic between the church and the community, two things happen. One is that the boundaries between church and community start to disappear, at least in our minds – what we are talking about is people being friends, being 'with' and 'for' each other. The second thing is that we are compelled to pay serious attention to what it is to 'be church' in a way which gives credence and authenticity to the things which we most deeply believe, including credal statements and theological doctrines. In other words, removing the boundaries, thinking in terms of relationships, is not an invitation to 'stop being the church' but rather to discover again what 'authentic church' is – and to start being that. It is in a communal life, committed to the danger of holiness, in which doctrine, apparently long rendered irrelevant through lack of being lived, is taken from its theological closet, shaken out and applied radically to the life of the believing church – it is this life which makes theology *accessible* to the local community. This is incarnational theology, lived out by human beings in human terms which can be recognized, grasped and understood by other human beings. Terry may never have grasped intellectually the doctrine of forgiveness, but he learnt to forgive and receive forgiveness, and he did so in the context of the loving support of the local church. After all, it would be hard to deny that the coming of the Holy Spirit on that small group of Jesus' friends at Pentecost was the beginning, the formation, the creation of a new community, with a new way of living as a sign of liberation and hope in the world. This is the new sanctuary; it is sanctuary capable of containing the whole world, and its only boundaries are set by those who resist and reject it. This new sanctuary is birthed in fire and wind, those dark symbols of the transcendent – it is the temple of the Holy Spirit (1 Cor 3.16, 17), it is the Body of Christ, Spirit-breathed, wherein God dwells (Eph 2.21, 22). It is the agent of the numinous and the transcendent (see the story of Ananias and Sapphira in Acts 5) where 'great fear came upon the whole church' and it is the agent of the incarnation, where 'all who shared their faith owned everything in common, they sold their goods and possessions and distributed the proceeds among themselves according to what each one needed'. The life of the authentic Christian community is one in which transcendence and the numinous, including in all likelihood the pente-costal gifts and charisms, and the incarnate 'ordinariness' of love and relationships and commitment and joy and pain sharing are woven together into one fabric – a tapestry which proclaims in many colours the good news of the gospel.

This life in the Christian community which is 'sanctuary' can never be solely a life of refuge. Yet the temptation to offer refuge without repentance and reform is one to which the inner-city minister, serving as she is among those who are deeply hurting and damaged, will be especially prone. Of course, this community-which-is-sanctuary offers 'asylum', refuge, unconditional love, but true sanctuary will also be the place of judgement, crisis, challenge, risk and change – the place of liberation. We have, in the gospels, an apt illustration of this when 'in the evening of the same day, the first day of the week, the doors were closed in the room where the disciples were, for fear of the Jews' (John 20.19). Here was a place of refuge. Yet it could not remain that. For 'Jesus came and stood among them' and he brought gifts: peace through his word of forgiveness, authority to bind and to loose that same forgiveness on others, and call: 'As the Father has sent me, so am I sending you' (20.20–21). As with Isaiah, and with Peter, the place of sanctuary, the 'meeting place', becomes the place of healing and of being sent. 'Belonging' is one of the most essential features of life in a small urban church, and it is through experience of belonging that the politics of liberation in all its forms – spiritual, sexual, racial, emotional – can be experienced. Mutuality, both in joy and in sorrow, is an immensely powerful aspect of inner-city life and I still remember with awe and gratitude the way in which, after working all night at the

Hillsborough disaster, I was greeted in the morning at church by a congregation who wept with me. Yet Christian community can never be 'club' – it must, through its very identification with the suffering Lord, be in Moltmann's words 'drawn into his self-surrender, into his solidarity with the lost and into his public suffering'.[3] In its more pragmatic style, *Faith in the City* reports: 'Our collective view is that a different approach is needed. We believe that churches in the UPAs have to become local, outward-looking and participatory churches.'[4]

Four comments are perhaps needed in conclusion:

I have said nothing about other forms of sanctuary in the city, because I have been trying to utilize a model of sanctuary which does some justice to the duality of transcendence and immanence, justice and mercy. There are, of course, many places of refuge to be found in the city – the pub, the club, the women's refuge, the Samaritans, the psychiatrist, the hospital, friendships – the list is endless. Some of these, for example the psychiatric hospital, will also offer the opportunity to crisis and for change. Then there are other refuges – escape routes from the city down the long corridors of drug addiction, promiscuity, alcoholism: forms of refuge which take on with increasing speed the menacing aspect of imprisonment.

I have also said little about other 'models of the transcendent' in the city. It would probably pay the Christian minister and our Christian communities to look for them, to try to identify them. That is because symbols of the transcendent are especially valuable to inner-city people, symbolizing as they do the things which people feel are *there*, restlessly, like a caged lion in the subconscious, but lack the language or the confidence to express. A helpful exercise might be to ask 'Where are the images of the transcendent in the parish? In the community? What are they and what is their power?' We can start with the mosque down the road.

An enormous topic related to 'sanctuary' is that of worship and church buildings. Over the last thirty years, since J. G. Davies set up the Institute for the Study of Worship and Religious Architecture, and the Hodge Hill Project was dedicated as a multi-purpose building in 1968, architecture has been moving and shifting in emphasis between expressing the need for the numinous and the need for intimacy. inner-city churches need to juggle with care between these two poles, in their worship and in their liturgical ordering – for city people have a tremendous capacity for, and appreciation of, both. There also needs to be a serious and committed listening to black-led, Pentecostal churches, whose practice of worship conveys both the transcendence and the nearness of God. When will the time come when white, middle-class churches stop laughing nervously or cynically about Pentecostalism, and start to listen?

It is always to be remembered that the Church, and the world, are judged by Jesus, through the eyes of the poor. See Matthew 25.31–46 for our relation to 'the poor', in all their guises, which is our judgement.[5] The Church can never be unrelated to the poor, can never stand apart in self-sufficiency, for her Judge is there within calling her, and the world, to account. The Church's guide, her measure, is in the eyes of the poor. In their eyes is her life reflected back. Their need is her need too. For 'the rich will only be helped when they recognise their own poverty and enter the fellowship of the poor ... the abasement which is meant by humility is not a private virtue but the social entry into solidarity with the humble and the humbled'.[6] The place of sanctuary always reveals to us our poverty, and that place of sanctuary is the poor.

Notes

1 J. G. Davies, *Everyday God* (SCM, 1973).
2 K. Leech, *The Eye of the Storm* (London: Darton, Longman and Todd, 1992).
3 J. Moltmann, *The Church in the Power of the Spirit* (ET; London: SCM Press, 1977).
4 *Faith in the City* (London: Church House Publishing, 1985).
5 J. Moltmann, 'Holiness in poverty', *The Church in the Power of the Spirit*, pp. 352f.
6 J. Moltmann.

Transformation

____

DAVID F. FORD

The transformation that this chapter is about is the sort that we have seen happening, usually in small and fragile ways, in various Urban Priority Areas where there are worshipping communities. We hope for more of it. We want to distil some of the wisdom of such transformation, to discern how God comes together with the world in it. It will be described mainly from the standpoint of those communities, as our group has experienced them through being part of them, visiting them and learning of them in other ways. We have been deeply affected by all this, and as a group have tried to think it through. This chapter is just one 'journey of intensification' and needs filling out with the other material we have gathered and produced. It is not, like some of the other chapters, in the form of stories or social analysis or wrestling with one issue. It aims to begin to do justice to what is affirmed with surprising regularity by those whose home is, or has been, in such communities: that they are places of amazing transformation; but they also challenge many images of what 'good transformation' is.

As I write, the particular communities I am specially bearing in mind are two in which members of our group live and which the whole group has visited: Sue Hope's Church of England parish in Sheffield, from which pp. 191–8 in this book have been written, and Margaret Walsh's Hope Community in Wolverhampton, which has given rise to pp. 27–71. I am also deeply influenced by the inner-city parish in Birmingham where I lived for fifteen years.

At the heart of the Christian understanding of good transformation is Jesus Christ: his life, death and resurrection, his presence in community, and the orientation towards meeting him face to face. The heart of the good news is that in this person transformation has happened already. It has endless aspects but is also very specific – it has this face. This has been the face of a baby and a child; teaching, angry, compassionate; eating, drinking, tired, crying; transfigured and shining like the sun; anointed, agonized in Gethsemane, kissed by Judas; running with blood, silent, crying out in abandonment; a dead face; a face strangely unrecognized yet recognizable in stories of resurrection appearances; breathing the Spirit, giving blessing; and then related to in faith, shining in hearts, desired above all: 'Come, Lord Jesus!' Jesus' ministry was face to face; he gathered disciples and shaped them into a meal-centred community; and the news of him spread by word of mouth. Without this face and the continuing face-to-face community and communication there would be no Christianity.

Christian transformation is therefore essentially face to face.[1] It was for Jesus' disciples. It was for Paul in its glory and fragility:

> And we, who with unveiled faces all reflect the Lord's glory, are being transformed into his likeness with ever-increasing glory, which comes from the Lord, who is the Spirit . . . . For God who said, 'Let light shine out of darkness,' made his light shine in our hearts to give us the light of the knowledge of the glory of God in the face of Christ. But we have this treasure in jars of clay. (2 Cor 3.18; 4.6, 7, NIV)

The dynamic of Christian community in its faith, its hope and its love is face-orientated. Its calling is to be the Body of Christ, facing others as he did.

And who knows what goes on face to face? Our identities are formed here from infancy and through our deepest and our most traumatic relationships. Our interior lives are often dominated by faces in our hearts. Think of those before whom we live our lives – parents (perhaps long dead), brothers and sisters, sons and daughters, friends and enemies, public figures and private obsessions. Our whole lives are performed before the faces of others, present and remembered. Yet we have no overviews here, over our own or others' face-to-face identities; and there are many mysteries. What we do know is that here the questions that matter most are answered: Am I loved? Can I love? Am I respected? Am I rejected? Can I trust anyone? Do I matter?

But even that 'I'-centred way of asking the questions is misleading. We do not start as an isolated self. We always already find ourselves part of face-to-face dynamics, for better or for worse. The more basic question of identity is: What are we a part of? We slowly come to answers to that question about our families and our other communities. Usually the answers tell stories in which there are many other characters. If asked who we are, we are likely, after giving our name, to tell a story that has all sorts of groups, events and relationships. Some stories gather more and more characters, or allow more and more people to identify with them. These hospitable stories have great potential for good and for evil. You can be caught up in a drama of tribal or racial or family hatred, or in one which tells of different and even alien groups living in peace.

If that is how we are formed – face to face, over time, in complicated stories – then that is also how we can be transformed. The whole pattern of Christian faith suggests exactly that, with love at the heart of it. The transformation we are concerned with in UPAs is made up of many stories. The main thing is to listen to the stories. But it is also worth trying to catch some of the wisdom they contain, to think them through with a view to distilling something of value for those engaged else-where and for those who continue to have roles in the stories.

In the New Testament many of the letters are written to small and fragile urban communities of Christians. There are many ways in which they were very different from our UPAs and there can be no simple application of these letters to our situations. But there are extraordi-narily rich resonances between them. I want to draw attention to some of these in order to offer a theology of transformation which has in mind not only the particular urban communities mentioned already but also the letter to the Ephesians. The style will not be systematic or scholarly – I have already done something more in that style for the Corinthian correspondence in relation to *Faith in the City*.[2] It will try to be more like wisdom sayings designed to illuminate experience and practice.

Dignity

Issues of dignity are very near the surface where there are poverty and severe problems with housing, unemployment, crime, violence, family breakup, healthcare, education and lack of amenities. From the stand-point of a local community with little power over the structures and policies that might affect such problems, how can dignity be sustained and enhanced?

Dozens of things help people to know they have worth, and there are examples in most areas of UPA life. It is not just the fact of self-help groups, sports clubs, dramatic productions, credit unions, debt counsel-ling, victim support, latch-key clubs, Estate Action, City Challenge development trusts, housing associations, partnerships between gov-ernment and the private sector, community organizations of many other sorts, or individual helpfulness, but the ways in which they operate, their 'tone' and 'ethos'. What is the Church about here? Obviously involvement in all those and more: there is nothing exclu-sively Christian about the building up of dignity. But the Church is also about news of a dignity that is beyond our wildest dreams. Ephesians chapter 1 is perhaps the most daring statement of human identity and worth conceivable – every spiritual blessing; chosen before the foundation of the world; destined in love to be children of God through Jesus Christ; redemption, forgiveness, riches of grace freely lavished on us; all wisdom and insight into God's purpose; and being part of a process through which 'all things in heaven and on earth' are being united in Christ. In an outer-city council estate in Birmingham, Ephesians 1 has inspired a litany 'celebrating our dignity'.

Revd Stephen Winter, writing from Pool Farm, tells of this in response to an earlier draft of this chapter. His response included the following statements:

> My normal week is an encounter with those forces that seek to deny this dignity. For example:
>
> – the funeral of a man dying of an alcohol-related illness in his early forties leaving two sons aged 11 and 12. In the last year of his life he attended church regularly, encouraged his sons to receive baptism and sought to make preparation for their future. In one respect his death is a terrible denial of his dignity, in another the last year of his life was a wonderful affirmation of it.
> – A family, struggling with the fact that their mother has mental illness, being summoned to a meeting with the psychiatrist, with less than an hour's notice, to discuss her treatment.
> – A couple with five children living in a building due for demolition and redevelopment by a housing association. Because of cuts in government grants to the Housing Corporation the demolition has been delayed indefinitely. Because the building is due for demolition it is being allowed to fall into an advanced state of disrepair. Because this family refused a move into a property in an area of equal deprivation no other offer has been made.
>
> I could continue. These are the experiences of one week. They are not even all the experiences. They are all stories that both tell of a denial of dignity, of community, love, maturity, but also stories that affirm those qualities wonderfully. They are wonderful stories of humanity. They are not a description of hell.

Celebrating dignity could read as a claim to exclusive, superior identity. It is better seen as utter confidence in God's inclusive hospitality, his generosity and welcome beyond anything we expect or deserve, or, in the case of people we tend to condemn or exclude, anything we can imagine. What does it mean to be part of a process uniting a world in which there is such injustice, tragedy, enmity, misery, sin of all sorts?

First of all, it means a dignity that is so firmly rooted in God and God's abundance that, through all that happens, we can be sure that those things do not have the last word and are not the basic reality. Second, we are offered an identity that cannot ignore any of the tragic realities, that sees its own reality bound up with the suffering, violence and death represented by 'through his blood' (Eph 1.7). Third, we are called into community, a dignity that is shared and that embodies the same hospitality and generosity: 'the church, which is his body, the fullness of him who fills all in all' (v. 23). Fourth, as the final chapter of Ephesians makes clear, there is the dignity of confrontation; we can see ourselves in a fight against powerful forces and still standing.

Dignity rooted in the love of God is at the heart of Ephesians, as the prayer in 3.14–21 says: 'that you, being rooted and grounded in love, may have power to comprehend with all the saints what is the breadth and length and height and depth, and to know the love of Christ which surpasses knowledge, that you may be filled with all the fullness of God.' That is the transformed identity which is there to be matured into, through all the ups and downs of events. It is by no means obvious. The good news is contradicted by much experience and by the dominant media images and world views. Nevertheless, this news grips us as we take part in the community of faith. It grips us because it is a faith that is grown into, for the message resonates throughout the Bible, church history and our UPAs as the deepest motivation for living. Baptism and Eucharist are its sacraments, dynamic embodiments of this dignity. Worship and prayer are, as our chapter on 'Praise' discussed, the ultimate realism, and being drawn into them energizes community, ethics and politics.

If even a few people mature into this identity they are a sign of what is possible. I think of the 'ordinary saints' who have grown into this extravagant sense of dignity before God. One school building super-visor says frequently 'Think what we're part of!' – and is more effectively immersed in Ephesians 1 than anyone else I know. Because vulnerability ('clay jars' – 2 Cor 4.7) is part of it, when a lot conspires to threaten dignity the sense is always of fragility. The face to face remains at the heart of the nurture of dignity. The welcome of the face; the little leap of trust; feeling free to pour out one's heart or tell one's story; finding acceptance instead of expected and 'deserved' rejection; being willing to ask for as well as give help; enjoying a meal with others; being encouraged in open or subtle ways; risking speaking the truth directly; expressing gratitude; coping with fear, anger, despair, jealousy and sheer foolishness; being challenged without coercion; all sorts of other exchanges that are the unstable currency of our self-worth. All that can be part of any relationship or group. The church is not in competition with other places where transformation occurs in these ways; it gives thanks to God for signs that things are being united like that. But it also offers a vision of the extravagant dignity before God described above, and an invitation to grow into that.

Of the many features of this dignity before God, I want to remark on just one. A basic form of dignity is to do with speech, articulateness, confident expression, creativity in word and gesture. Families know the thrill of dawning speech in children and the expansion of reality that this makes possible. In Christian community, as fringe or new members learn the language, the stories, the symbols and the forms of expression in prayer and worship, there are comparable developments and joys. How Christian language does become accessible is a critical issue, with all sorts of problems. It is fundamental to Christian identity that it becomes accessible. The testimony from UPAs is of minting language afresh there. We have found, in the groups we have been part of, new improvisations on Christian speech as people learn to tell their story, pray, praise, thank, sing, testify, repent, feel at home in liturgy, teach, argue, lead worship, apply the Bible, and respond to events. The sheer vitality of language and the living world of meaning that it creates and expands are realizations of the 'speech-giving Spirit'. That 'saint' quoted in the previous paragraph has an amazing eloquence in such forms, and it has overflowed in dozens of ways, from confronting authorities on behalf of the local community to beginning a prayer group at home for her extended family.

Christianity has continually found new forms through needing to be worked out afresh in new situations; and the situations have often involved deprivation, suffering, marginalization. The shift from the province of Judaea to urban centres in the rest of the Roman Empire was the first such transition. As the churches founded by Paul matured, their faith was distilled in letters such as Colossians, Ephesians and 1 and 2 Timothy. The question of Christian identity was critical then as now, and in all of them we see distinctive ways of speaking and a massive emphasis on the quality and content of communication. Whatever the hardships, reinforcing the news of the transformation in Christ as the reality in which they lived was the key to a dynamic corporate identity. And this endlessly generated fresh speech. The resultant identity was universal (in Ephesians explicitly cosmic) in scope while affirming that each person is chosen by God for love. In a UPA culture where there is a global horizon (often distorted) through the media and where so much conspires locally to undermine dignity, only something with that scope and depth will do. As in Ephesus, there can be a 'sober intoxication' as an alternative to drink and other addictions and escapisms:

> And do not get drunk with wine, for that is debauchery; but be filled with the Spirit, addressing one another in psalms and hymns and spiritual songs, singing and making melody to the Lord with all your heart, always and for everything giving thanks in the name of the Lord Jesus Christ to God the Father. (Eph 5.18–20)

That is the sort of transformation of speech that, in various ways, is a characteristic of communities which have resisted misery, oppression and disintegration in diverse situations in history and around the world today.[3] Sustaining transformed communication in our UPAs is one of the most striking signs of the movement of the Spirit. Such speech and song is the realization of a confident dignity that puts everything else in perspective 'according to the eternal purpose which he has realized in Christ Jesus our Lord, in whom we have boldness and confidence of access through our faith in him. So I ask you not to lose heart over what I am suffering for you, which is your glory' (Eph 3.11–13).

Community

The transforming dignity described above has already shown how community is essential to it. That is clearest in the final thoughts about speech. Speech is unthinkable without community – we are each spoken to for a long time before we speak. UPAs are notorious for the pressures they exert on community in its various dimensions, and to live in one is to know these pressures as ordinary life. Families are often disintegrated or able to offer little support to members. Poverty, bad housing and all the other 'indices of deprivation' increase the pressure, and there are rarely the means or the opportunities for building up structures and patterns of living that enable stable communities. Often, in church and other forms of community, there are hopeful beginnings, glimpses of the good possibilities, and then disappointments. Yet transformation into community does happen, in church life and else-where.

There is no formula for it. Because of the pressures there is great need for basic reference points, fundamental convictions to sustain persever-ance. The church in UPAs flourishes best when it is clear about its centre and open at its boundaries. Ephesians 2 gives a classic, powerful statement of this sort of identity. The main conviction is that already in Jesus Christ the transformation has happened into 'one new humanity'

(v. 15) and that this transformation is to do with creating community against all the odds. In Ephesians that means between Jews and Gentiles who were divided religiously, racially, culturally, socially and historically. There has been a breaking down of 'the dividing wall of hostility' between those two, and it happened in the crucifixion of Jesus Christ. The death of Jesus is the deepest root of community. In it Jesus has undermined all division. Risen from the dead, he embodies a new humanity. That is where we start from now; the walls down, the actuality of community achieved and open to all.

This is community with a crucified man at its heart, a gathering around one who was poor, rejected, persecuted and executed. It not only affirms community in general, but indicates that there is a special promise from God attached to the creation of community around the weak, marginalized and those not valued by society. For Christians this is the awkward truth of the Beatitudes, of 1 Corinthians 1, of much church history and its saints and, today, of prophets such as Jean Vanier and his L'Arche communities for the severely handicapped. It is not an ideology aiming to exclude from community those who do not fit a particular category. It is Christian wisdom that often seems like foolishness until you see it happening in UPAs or elsewhere. It is not about exclusive boundaries but about getting the centre right: Jesus Christ crucified, and the good news for the poor, the broken-hearted and the oppressed. The open boundaries are created by the sorts of communication that this message generates. The abundant hospitality of God has no limits; the signs of welcoming and enjoying it are often most obvious where the options to attend other feasts are fewest.

There are also other feasts going on in our cities. Christian community is formed and tested not only in situations of inadequate and distorted sociality but also where there are other well-developed communities. Perhaps the most important form of this at present is the encounter with communities of other faiths. It might be that the most instructive school of community is in this sphere where different long-term traditions of worship, ethics, belief and imagination engage in situations that stretch them all. 'Encounter ought to revise our judgement about who we truly are and why.'[4] Kenneth Cragg says this as part of a profound discussion of inter-faith dialogue as it relates to conversion and to the practice of 'compassionate alertness'. Some of us in our group have experienced the transformations that occur when the inter-faith reality becomes part of the ordinary life of a Christian congregation. But this was one of the several significant areas that we decided not to pursue as a group. Suffice it to say now that for myself the theology of Cragg and the theology and practice of Roger and Pat

Hooker in Smethwick, Birmingham, seem to offer some of the best available Christian approaches in this country at present.

Maturity

The long haul – that is the perspective of Ephesians for an urban theology that can sustain dignity and community into the next generation. I was at a conference in 1994 for 300 lay people representing most of the parishes of the Sheffield diocese. It is a diocese with a very high ratio of UPA parishes. Talking to the people I recognized again and again variations on that often unspectacular person, the mature faithful Christian. These were people used to taking responsibilities. They knew there were no quick fixes and had plenty of experience of disappointment. Each parish represented had sent a graphic account of the things they were doing in church and community life and the array was vast, from beer-making and baptism visiting, to prison crèches, housing action and study courses. The question I wondered about was: Where did it come from, this maturity that was evident in so many of the people who were helping to sustain such activities? They were not always like that, so how did it happen? They had grown into something complex. Worship, teaching, all sorts of relationships, learning by doing, responding to particular needs and calls for help, discovery of gifts and abilities, personal prayer, home groups, and so on – all the obvious things that are part of ordinary Christian living were the main ingredients. There were also dozens of problems, tensions, irritations, fears and complaints. The picture was of transformation shot through with ambiguities and qualifications, and of maturity that happens through all those. Above all, there was a sense of long-term perseverance. That is one of the most precious of all qualities in a situation of disintegration and instability; and, as anyone who has tried to sustain a church or other community in a UPA knows, it has to be shared, joint perseverance to have any chance of survival. The letter to the Ephesians has the theme of strength, energy and power running through it; 'the immeasurable greatness of his power in us who believe' (1.19); 'he may grant you to be strengthened with might' (3.16). It concludes in vivid battle imagery, of fighting against what seem like overwhelming odds, 'against the principalities, against the powers, against the world rulers of this present darkness, against the spiritual hosts of wickedness in the heavenly places' (6.12). It is recognized that there are situations in which the aim is simply 'to withstand the evil day, and having done all, to stand' (6.13). All the verbs are plural: it is shared truth, righteousness, gospel, faith, salvation, Spirit, word of God and prayer. And the culmination is 'To that end keep alert with all perseverance, making supplication for all the saints . . . ' (6.18).

Ephesians was written to a church beyond the first generation and into the long haul that has been going on ever since. The letter recognizes how crucial Christian maturity is and how all the gifts available are needed to build it up (4.11–16). It is clear about the destructiveness of a range of verbal and other behaviour but is equally confident that they can be transformed (4.17 – 5.20). The sheer daring of such confidence in the face of the dynamics of lies and deceit, desires run wild, stealing, malice, stupidity and drunkenness is a tribute to what had been glimpsed to be possible. The church is seen to offer a context for ethical discernment and character formation. Beyond the fundamental habits of life with others before God (patience, speaking the truth in love, honest work, kindness, forgiveness, gratitude, praise), the thrust is towards shaping the basic relationships of that society – marriage, family and household (master–slave). Ephesians does not just repeat what the letters of Paul say (I assume, with most scholars, that Ephesians is not by him) but arrives at fresh insights appropriate to its situation. The challenge is, as Andrew Lincoln says in a perceptive chapter on the critical appropriation of Ephesians for today, how 'to do what its writer has done, that is, to bring to bear on the marriage conventions of the day what is held to be the heart of the Christian message'.[5] The same applies to every other area of life.

Encouragement

The wrestle with ordinary living in conditions of stress, and the discovery of resources to 'more than cope': that is at the heart of the urban church life that is seen through Ephesians and also at the heart of the communities we know best. What happens when the two come together as Ephesians is studied in a UPA? Across the centuries and through the complex density of the letter (even in the Good News Bible!) the essential thing is communicated: here are a daring testimony to God, an alternative world of meaning and energy, a new identity and dignity, a community which can stand against the worst that can happen, and Jesus Christ the living embodiment of transformation. This letter can be a springboard to prayer and to politics (Edward Schillebeeckx has written that 'if any book lays the foundation for a political theology in the New Testament, it is Ephesians'[6]). The cosmic scope can encourage global thinking as well as local acting; its stress on the unity of the Church makes sure that ecumenism and co-operation between churches is essential to self-definition. The pervasive concern with the everyday constantly invites us to be transformed in our daily lives.

But the right note to end on is that of the letter itself before its final greeting. Tychicus is sent in person 'that he may encourage your hearts'. It is through such face-to-face meetings that hearts are most deeply encouraged. The line goes back face by face to Jesus and back again, family by family, and meal by meal to Moses and beyond; then forward Eucharist by Eucharist down to today and around the world.

Notes

1 This is not to ignore or downplay other levels of life, such as large-scale economics and politics. But a crucial test of their being good or bad is whether they contribute to our flourishing in friendships, families, localities and face-to-face groups of all sorts.

2 David F. Ford, 'Faith in the cities: Corinth and the modern city' in Colin Gunton and Daniel W. Hardy (eds), *On Being the Church: Essays on the Christian Community* (Edinburgh: T. & T. Clark, 1989), pp. 225–6.

3 There is also, as Revd Alan Hargrave pointed out in response to an earlier version of this chapter, an eloquent and dignified silence, especially in the face of those who use their power in communication to maintain and mask the misery. The ability to refrain from speech, or speak only occasionally, is the other side of freedom in speech.

4 Kenneth Cragg, *Troubled by Truth: Biographies in the Presence of Mystery* (Cleveland, Ohio: Pilgrim Press, 1994), p. 265.

5 Andrew Lincoln, 'The theology of Ephesians' in A. Lincoln and A. J. M. Wedderburn (eds), *The Theology of the Later Pauline Letters* (Cambridge: Cambridge University Press, 1993), p. 162.

6 Edward Schillebeeckx, *Christ: The Christian Experience in the Modern World* (London: SCM Press, 1980), p. 196.

Part Four

━━

Implications

Fear of the city?

PETER SEDGWICK

Fear of the city is one of the oldest themes in Christianity. Chrysostom in the fourth century wrote graphically: 'Thus does the devil stealthily set fire to the city. It is not a matter of running up ladders and using petroleum, pitch or tar; he uses things far more pernicious: lewd sights, base speech, degraded music and songs full of all kinds of wickedness.'[1] By the nineteenth century the brutality of the city was a common motif among intellectuals. Southey, the Anglican poet, said that 'a manufacturing populace is always rife for rioting ... Governments who found their prosperity upon manufactures sleep upon gunpowder.' Even Engels, in 1844, saw Manchester as 'the crowding of the great city ... the very turmoil of the streets has something repulsive, something against which human nature rebels ... And still they crowd by one another ... The brutal indifference ... becomes the more repellent and offensive, the more these individuals are crowded together.'[2]

While there are many examples of Christians affirming the city, the quotes above and the remarks from the atheist Engels show where we begin. Again and again fear of the city returns to haunt Christianity, or to stand beside those intellectuals who have replaced the theologians with secular truth claims. It is as though there is a dark side to the vision of the new Jerusalem, which focuses the pain and dereliction of life into one area.

When the urban reality does indeed become sick, with obvious and manifold deprivation, the task of affirming the presence of God in her city becomes harder. Yet that, in the end of the day, is what we are about. Where is God in Manchester, Leeds or East London? These chapters attempt an answer, tracing the presence of God in sexuality, the sense of place, the hope of transformation and the despair of estrangement. We also wish to celebrate the UPA church as a place of confidence. There is confidence in the proclamation of faith, in worship, in organization and in the creation of partnerships. Here then is one place where the Spirit of God might be said to live and move, quickening life from death and sustaining hope.

But what else? The presence of God is found in the life and the relationships which make up the city, far beyond the Christian Church or indeed beyond any faith perspective at all. Fear is one response to the way in which life has become tough and hard in such places, but it is not the only response. How then might such a proper response be made to the love of God and the relationships of the city?

Relationships

The recent report on poor families, *Hard Times?*, shows their deep commitment to children and the future.[3] In all the bleak statistics, it is highly impressive how families are utterly certain that the children come first, and that if their future can be different, anything can be sacrificed to that. The sense of hope beyond hope, hope when it is no longer sensible to hope in a practical sense, drives families on to find almost any solution. Equally, the integrity of those who are not responsible for their plight, those who are vulnerable and need to be maintained, remains central for families who look after children, or the elderly. Of course there are countless examples of brutality and the loss of innocence among children. Nevertheless, this pattern of relationships survives in many complex forms of single-parent families, cohabitation and marriage. The energy that is present in such relationships can be seen as the gift of the Spirit, where the basic possibility of relationships given by the Father is quickened and affirmed. The Board for Social Responsibility's report for the Church of England in 1995 argues that family relationships have changed greatly over the centuries, and continue to change.

The complexity of relationships around the family remains great. The importance of complexity must be recognized. As the life of the city changes, so the responses made to it will vary. One of the implications is that social relationships will no longer be stable, unified and delimited. Yet this must not be read as the breakdown of social relationships in the city.

There is a Christian moralism which presumes that the only pattern of relationships is the nuclear family, and that the economic or physical (in the sense of buildings decaying) sickness of the city will penetrate all forms of life. This is again a variant on the theme that the city is to be feared. Rather, human life is shown in these chapters to be immensely rich, life-giving and full of diversity. Given the resources to do so, human life again and again can remake itself.

The life of God is not a rule-bound moralism, but instead is marked by changeability and pluralism. The statement in Matthew 28.18 that all authority is Christ's is not a restatement of an ultimate, tyrannical purpose. For the authority which is from Christ (Col 1.17–18) holds everything together, and binds it in perfect harmony (Col 1.14). It is not an imposed authority, for it can be rejected.

This authority is mediated through new, and evolving, structures and relationships which respond to our needs of love, hope, peace and creativity. Just as children grow physically and in personality, and often go beyond their parents, so we grow into Christ's authority – without surpassing it. Perhaps the ultimate Christian claim is that Christ shares his authority with us, so that relationships can exist in this world to build others up by the authority of God.

The Church in the city

The task of the Church is to share the 'fullness of God' (Eph 1.23), and Spirit of Christ (1 Cor 2.12) in a manner that is non-coercive. Fundamentally, this turns on whether the city is seen as fearful. Henri Nouwen has written perceptively on the need for Christians to turn the loneliness of the modern city, and urban relationships, into the gift of solitude, which affirms others without being driven either by the need which the fear of loneliness brings or by the fear of the city itself. Solitude as the quiet centre in the complex, and often lonely, reality of urban life is not an individualist ethic, for it can be held by a community which celebrates its common life (in ways well articulated by Gill Moody's chapter) and yet knows that its centre is in God.

What we have discovered again and again in writing these essays and living in the city is the enormous variety of ways in which the Church is changing in the city. The change often involves those who in the past were least allowed to share any authority in Christianity: women, lay people, black people, gay as well as straight Christians. A common theme is that of spirituality: naming the Lord in one's own language, one's own culture. A second theme is that despite the collapse in working-class culture referred to in both my earlier chapter ('Mapping an urban theology') and Laurie Green's chapter on the urban church, nevertheless the cords of death do not entangle in the end (Ps 116.2): there is the possibility of trust despite all appearances (Ps 116.9). A third theme is found in the deeply moving new book by Hannah Ward and Jennifer Wild, *Guard the Chaos*, which describes how tentative, painful and fragile the emergence of new forms of church life, especially for women, can be in urban life.[4] Nevertheless the new reality of church life which is often lay-led, open to non-Christians, and aware of the pain of urban life, speaks powerfully of the transforming grace of God and Christian maturity. These chapters seek to catch a glimpse of this reality and share the experience of transformation and newness.

'The Church' is a community of women and men who follow the way of Christ in different ways and styles, but it always follows the path from Galilee to Jerusalem. Galilee is where the ordinary reality of human life is set, while Jerusalem is where the powers of the world have their seat. The Church, like Christ, lives in Galilee, but it confronts Jerusalem. It seeks to share the authority of Christ with those who feel trapped and powerless by the fear which so often dominates the lives of people. Against that, hope, dignity, the need to love and the urge to create out of one's life must be set as the ultimate realities. In this sense the catholicity of the Church points to the whole, the universal, the gathered, and it looks to the unity of the healed, reconciled world we long for. The gospel message is then about the transformation of society and the relationships within it. As Bishop David Jenkins puts it, the message of Jesus is 'not a matter of handing over packages of information with instruction about their application. Unless doctrines changed the responses of heart, soul and mind there is no point in speaking about them.'[5]

The presence of the risen Christ is one which encompasses the whole of creation, and is not to be seen as an ideal form of society which perhaps existed centuries ago and does so no longer. Nor is the presence of Christ a utopian ideal in the never realized future. Christ is present in and through the complexity, pluralism and changeability of society. As society becomes more unpredictable and random, this is no threat to the presence of Christ, for Christ can be envisaged in a dynamic, energetic relationship to the world.

Implications

This leads to two implications in an Urban Priority Area. Again, before spelling out these implications, the central theme must be restated. The problem with urban mission is not a matter of will but of imagination. It is often unthinkable to see how complex human relationships are, and yet how they are bound together. The assumption is that human beings are always the same, and that God has made them in the same way. But Christ nourishes us through his Body, the Church, and through the Spirit, in ordinary relationships. Christ is at the heart of the complex, rich, goodness of urban life. Imagination and love must challenge fear, moralism and the presumption of uniformity.

So the two implications for urban mission are the re-imagining of the Church, and the re-creation of community. The task for every Christian body is where to find the presence of Christ, and how to serve him there. Combining for the common good is a statement about the day of deliverance offered by Christ. The message of reconciliation in 2 Corinthians 5 ('we come therefore as Christ's ambassadors . . . not counting humanity's misdeeds against them') is a powerful testimony for urban life. Urban life is not to be feared. There can be communities of reconciliation, from tenants associations which bring together Muslim and Christian, to co-operative agencies, and women's aid centres. And there can be equally diverse forms of Christian discipleship. What the Church needs now, and what urban policy needs even more, is to let the imagination run free. The great message of City Challenge, for all its difficulties, was that new forms of creative partnership are possible. There can be equally stimulating expressions of Christian community. The common good is not a simple reality, but a dynamic, non-linear process of change.

Where in all this is the ordinary Christian? In the victim support network, in the affirmation of sexuality, in the urban saints gathered for worship, in the mother struggling to bring up her child and in the elderly person with memories of a different city life. But Christ is found beyond the Christian, in a creative energy which challenges fear and builds new patterns of life. Whatever else, these chapters are not afraid. However much there may be economic sickness or violence, still there is celebration and hope, life and laughter. What is most important to say about the city is that its name should be 'The Lord is here'. That is the central reality which these essays affirm. As the city changes in the next century, all that matters is that the Church should have the courage to look for the presence of Christ in the complex relationships which we celebrate in this book. Celebration, then, is the note on which these chapters conclude: the laughter, joy and creativity of urban life.

How do we hope that the response will be? Primarily it must be an affirmation of others to continue what is occurring in many countless ways. These chapters prescribe no pattern and offer no presumption for successful urban ministry. Instead they describe, affirm and celebrate the Spirit of God, and ask that such transformation should continue. Equally that transformation will be articulated in new and different theologies of urban life. The ceaseless praise of all creation to the Father, through the Son, in the power of the Spirit cannot be foreclosed. All these chapters have done is to speak of some aspects of urban mission in the decade since *Faith in the City*, and how we have tried to articulate the life of Christ in the city. Others in the next decade will sing the Lord's song in their own way, but without fear.

It is in that confidence and with that invitation that these chapters end, open to the new promptings of the Spirit in urban life.

Notes

1 John Chrysostom, *De Poenitentia* VI: trans. in *Homilies on the Statutes to the City of Antioch* (Oxford: J. Parker, 1842).

2 Frederick Engels, *The Condition of the Working Classes in England in 1844*; cited in David Lee and Howard Newby, *The Problem of Sociology* (London: Hutchinson, 1983), pp. 33–4.

3 *Hard Times? How Poor Families Make Ends Meet* (York: Joseph Rowntree Foundation, 1994).

4 Hannah Ward and Jennifer Wild, *Guard the Chaos: Finding Meanings in Change* (London: Darton, Longman & Todd, 1995).

5 David Jenkins, unpublished talk, diocese of Durham (1 December 1984); quoted in P. H. Sedgwick, *It's Your Choice* (Cleveland: Respond, 1986), p. 9.